Strange Attractors

strange
attractors

Lives Changed by Chance

Edie Meidav & Emmalie Dropkin, eds.

University of Massachusetts *Amherst and Boston*

Printed in the United States of America
ISBN 978-1-62534-424-3 (paper); 423-6 (hardcover)
Designed by Kristina Kachele Design, llc
Set in The Serif with Steelfish display
Printed and bound by Integrated Books International, Inc.
Cover design by Kristina Kachele Design, llc
Cover art © Danica Novgorodoff.
Library of Congress Cataloging-in-Publication Data
Names: Meidav, Edie, 1967– editor. | Dropkin, Emmalie, editor.
Title: Strange attractors : lives changed by chance /
Edie Meidav and Emmalie Dropkin, eds.
Description: Amherst : University of Massachusetts, [2019] |
Identifiers: LCCN 2018051827 (print) | LCCN 2018059196 (ebook) |
ISBN 9781613766729 (ebook) | ISBN 9781613766736 (ebook) | ISBN 9781625344236
(hardcover) | ISBN 9781625344243 (pbk.)
Subjects: LCSH: Women authors, American—Biography. | Authors American—
21st Century—Biography. | Creation (Literary, Artistic, etc.)
Classification: LCC PS151 (ebook) | LCC PS151 .S77 2019 (print) |
DDC 813/.0099287—dc23
LC record available at https://lccn.loc.gov/2018051827
British Library Cataloguing-in-Publication Data
A catalog record for this book is available from the British Library.

Contents

CREATIVE SPARK

POLARIZING FORCES

EPIPHANY

SURVIVAL

Strange Attractors

On Strange Attraction

Edie Meidav

A writer friend of mine—nonbinary, midlife—recently said that for every hour of relationship-related drama in which this friend participates, two hours of writing are then required, ending on this triumphant note: *so you can imagine, I've been getting lots of writing done!*

If part of what helps us step forward in life is our belief that around the bend lies greater meaning and ease, how often do we meet some disaster which then cracks into our desired destiny, and, if not disaster, the chance occurrence or puzzling magnet, a moment of being lost in the woods, which then turns into the exact path called the rest of our life?

Often, it seems.

This book you now encounter—whether you hold it in a store or by a bed, whether people or children or animals nose about nearby or if you are alone, reading or listening as you happen to tumble through some desert of your imagination or present reality, whether you drive past a strip mall in traffic or are on a curving country road up through the mountains toward a waterfall—this entire project containing these vital voices seemed necessary to me in the cool of eastern woods when I grasped that so many I respected, artists, mothers, others, all dreamers, tended to tell the story of their lives in this way: I was wandering in the woods of my life and then felt the strongest pull to *this* which so clearly led to *that* which then led me so obviously *there* and all of it so spun me I speak now from some wholly startling and also inevitable landscape.

Out of surprise burst a new and yet fated person. Without that linchpin minute, the speaker would still be back in those woods and almost another person altogether, barely recognizable in lineament and gesture.

You might say fine, okay, aren't all stories like that? Someone scents coffee and springs toward journey, a stranger comes to town offering cherry cake half-price, and because of the way quest is hardwired into our marrow, we swap our past selves for a fantasia of the future.

Yet certain moments of happenstance bear greater urgency. Sometimes we cannot help but heed these. You don't have to believe in predestination to find a moment in your life when accident helped you find your truest self. Whether you came by this particular book honestly, by chance, gift, or sacrifice, collected here you will find a few blazing writers of our time answering this question: how did the unpredictable pattern become their own strange attractor?

Young and older, mostly centered in the United States but also international in scope, origin, environ, these voices know that paradox, the urgency of serendipity. Each writer, a person whom the world called woman at some point in their path, took on this idea of how future bloomed out of chance if not utter chaos.

The tune of the strange attractor goes a little something like this, and here I apologize to both the scientists in my family and those beyond, hoping this particular voicing serves as temporary guide for those willing to wander the woods a bit. Try it out:

Strange attractor: A set of numerical values toward which a system tends to evolve, for a wide variety of starting conditions of the system. . . . A trajectory of the dynamical system in the attractor does not have to satisfy any special constraints except for remaining on the attractor, forward in time. The trajectory may be periodic or chaotic.*

Perhaps another way to consider it might be this: we each bear highly particular starting conditions, born with our own warp in the weave, some gene or circumstance which sets us on whatever course we embrace, reject, recombine. Call this course karma, biology, or socioculture, how often in life have you asked whether—had one variable or another been altered, had you just been born left of center, right of north, in some other household with a parent creating a wholly different set of attachments, injuries, repairs—you might have ended up in a different sphere?

And yet here you are, inevitable you, your flaw or wound become the burden of your gift. To use this volume's parlance, somewhere a strange attractor granted you momentum, and perhaps you've been lucky enough to be led to the exact vista from which you see the gifts along your path.

In one story, redeemed in every sequel to a particular long-running sci-fi blockbuster movie, we meet a straight-necked hero who hears a call and sets out to slay the dragon who ends up being a reminder of his own shadow side. In contrast, the writers collected here tell how they danced with a dragon they ended up transforming.

Some knew change was necessary and then it arrived all too soon. An Eros toward life stirred, their recognition altered. Often the strange attractor became a new set of values toward which they evolved. Some recognized new prowess, traveled beyond prior self-definition; others found themselves newly recognized. Lives jerry-rigged by drastic measure or the banal commonplace soared. Either daily existence had become untenable or all too tenable, a raft for the mutely drowning. Whatever the case, on x day, a quality of y burnt through and z flickered: now the writer found, invented, or recalled an entirely different alphabet.

Who sets out with a plan to be surprised? You would then have the snake of desire swallowing itself. Rather, these writers share an openness. Call it a congenital readiness to leap from failure to failure or to be astonished. Consider it a recipe for wonder: such a quality alone can torque destiny.

Virginia Woolf in *A Room of One's Own* considers the woman "crazed with the torture that her gift had put her to" and ventures the guess that "Anon, who wrote so many poems without signing them, was often a woman." These contributors found a way to sign their wild guesses. Hardly all surprise is happy, nor all art, but the renewed and aware life, contributors say, seems to have made all the difference.

Some voices you will find here are lyric, compressed, experimental, singing from the margins of the received and the boundary of nonfiction; others are more straightforward even as their worlds contain the extraordinary. Some croon to the concept of the strange attractor while others let the idea join overtly or underneath the sheets. All use words as pictures, yet one trio lets pictures ride the words. One commonality you will discover is that these writers wandered in a field of assumption that might have kept them numb or asleep had it not been, by grace or misfortune, that they were found, grace so amazing, their eyes finally opened to some previously crushed shard of experience. Recognition changed a life, and respect for it still spreads, an insight like ripples in a summer pond.

2

During high school, an artistic girlfriend asked me to forego painting, believing in that particular scarcity economy that can draw tight the lives of girls not taught otherwise. In love, I heeded her.

The dictate meant that, soon as I left her for college, with great thirst I began to paint. In one classroom I encountered a pompous gesticulator of a professor who took the thrill of some twenty students, at least one of them now a king of the art world, and chose to insert it into a gulag of brown.

What did this mean? For a year we were to abstain from the rainbow and instead paint solely a massive still life made up of discarded brown cardboard we'd thrown into a pile, a potlatch he made impeccable if starved of any sunrise joy.

After we swallowed our shock at this hell, perhaps a week later, our teacher told us that at night he came and listened to our paintings. Only the most gullible may have believed. Your work *talks* to me, he said.

Does it? I thought: was his truly the artist's way?

Disingenuous, this puffed-up monologuist whom I had hoped would lead me into the promised land cannibalized cleverness, his own past success and that of others. Nothing in how he presented art or its corresponding world dovetailed with the dream figures stalking my own canvases, satyrs and strange women running after hoops in apocalyptic landscapes with Lascaux bulls pressed against masking-tape grids. When, at points, I disobeyed the brown-gulag assignment, my *narrative art failed to allow for the metaphysical,* as one of the professor's assistants said, and, further, what galleries wanted, in that cultural millisecond, was abstraction! Such a great finite set everyone presented to us: the myopic commercialism of the New York gallery scene would affront anyone's idealism.

Back then I bore the deluded belief that what you pursued as a career should stretch beyond what you found meaningful, pleasurable, easiest, and even then, the art this teacher professed felt at once too materialistic and disembodied. Surely it stayed inauthentic.

For twenty minutes, I considered entering neuroscience.

And then came the flare: my tight little painting teacher was

5

an emissary bearing an olive branch. By slamming shut the door to visual art, he reminded me another had always been open and how story itself had played mother to me.

From all those books read in the loneliness of girlhood I had found one of our last technologies of empathy: from those books' dreams had arisen all that imagery, the bulls, hoops, satyrs, apocalypse.

Happily, the solipsist's cardboard catapulted me back toward love.

3

When, years ago, I first saw the possibility of a story of mine opening up meaning for another, a small elderly woman with bright jewel eyes gripping my wrist after a reading, I felt happy to have found my way into this forest of books, and continue to feel it as this volume comes into the light.

Daily we receive gifts of quantum awareness, though these can come mutely and are always built on the incremental. My hope is that a book which contains myriad voices might help its reader fix and set some deeper and richer cause or direction. The lures in these writers' lives, as may be true in yours, act as both offerings and calamities. In this forest you will find a few divisions for you to use as crossroads to use as moments of pause. *Cusp, guides, partners, creative spark, polarizing forces, epiphany, and survival:* these categories arose after contributors answered particular questions. When in life did the unexpected lead you to the inevitable? When did you find Eros in Serendib?

Warmest thanks go to all who acted as strange attractors on this project, including Chelsea Hogue and Shastri Akella, who offered early and inspired help to this project's birth. Indelible, tattooed thanks go to the fearless clarity and organization of collaborator Emmalie Dropkin: without her lucidity, brilliance, and closing energies this book would not be in this form in your hands. Contributors and editors both are deeply grateful for the great prospect-view vitality of Mary Dougherty, Sally Nichols, Rachael DeShano, Dawn Potter, Courtney Andree, and the entire University of Massachusetts Press team, as well as for the support of Julie Hayes, the UMass Amherst MFA faculty and students, and Jeff Parker and Annie Liontas. We also bow to the originators of the concept of the strange attractor: David Ruelle and Floris Takens.

Thanks go to all first and later families who have opened so many pathways toward love and inquiry. Bouquets land on these doorsteps: Dalia for brilliant depth, Eliana for engagement with surprise, Stan for all supportive energy, and Mae Ziglin Meidav for a sparkling lifelong practice of strange attraction.

Our greatest appreciation surrounds collaborators who knew the risk of chance, people alive and patient in equal parts, thirty-five writers who delved deep and ended up speaking, with nuanced timbre, to one another, creating a true community of voices.

We are especially grateful to you reading this book, to those of you allowing turbulence to bring you toward the beauty of inevitability. Have faith in those woods! It is our hope that you who stumble across this volume might find at least one of these tales acting as your own strange attractor. Who knows to what dream you might wake? Only you.

Amherst, 2018

* Joseph Cambray and Leslie Sawin, eds., *Research in Analytical Psychology: Applications from Scientific, Historical, and Cross-Cultural Research* (New York: Routledge, 2018).

cusp

A Certain Devotion

Pamela Thompson

So many good reasons to stop at one. So many examples: John and Yoko's, your paternal grandfather, your maternal grandmother.

Our souls were stretched to snapping. One night I crawled across the floor to the toilet. I did not remember before. I thought, How? How on *earth*?

Sure, what's the big deal? We had a kid.

So you joined the world, my mother said. What did you expect? A diploma? An operating manual? Imagine *three*.

I folded, to keep or give away, which I didn't know, your tiniest sweaters and creamy cotton ramekins.

That isn't the word?

Well, those, over there, that stack of little suits with feet and arms.

When I was a girl, I read that Catherine the Great's appetite was so mammoth that it could be satisfied only by a horse. The horse was lowered down onto her with some kind of pulley system. I fixated on those pulleys, their wheels and ropes—that someone had built the contraption. That someone had to operate it. Someone strapped the horse into it. How did private and unfathomable desire bear such planning? If I'd heard that the entire world was rigged—held in place by gravity and centripetal force and fire—I couldn't have been more surprised.

But who does not love a wild horse? The thunder of hooves our own beating hearts.

Outside, sleet was sticking and then skidding off the metal roof. Mist rose from the tired snow, snaking up the gray bars of the trees. You held onto the windowsill and looked out at the rectangular world.

Out, you insisted, foot punctuating. Out!

So I tied the purple hood under your fat neck and lifted you onto my shoulders. Yes, we could go out. You were all. Your soft baby thighs squeezed my neck. You wiggled. You tugged my hair to steady yourself.

No, I told you. *That hurts.* No, not another.

On accident, Mama, you apologized sweetly, for an instant your body curling into mine, pressing me gently, a pause of acknowledgment, of unspoken peace: you are mine and I am yours. Then again urgent, wiggling, your small heels pattering my heart.

I reached back and up and put my hand flat against your spine.

How? I asked again. How? I would have to be in *and* out. Here *and* there. If yes, then only one who would follow, with no opinions of his own.

Up past the barn and toward the woods we walked slowly, a top-heavy, two-headed, two-hearted creature. Papa saw us coming, came to the door of the studio, wiping clay across his apron, calling to you.

Then we saw him.

Shh.

Did *he* see *us?*

The horse was weaving his way through the silent vertical trees behind the studio.

As if—

drunken?

Was he alone?

Maybe.

Yes.

No wool-shirted stranger or neighbor. No person holding a rein. The snow's melt suspended in mist. The sun neither in nor out. The trees impassive witnesses as he emerged from them, an ancient creature making of our woods a forest primeval and the April mist time's own.

He paused, stood regal, enormous, considering. Then moved slowly our way.

A hitch in his gait made a kind of bony roll to his movement and his four-legged path toward us was more deliberate than direct. We could see his ribs and long leg bones and where they fit into their sockets and so the spectrum of choice contained in each step our way. To move at all, he made circles inside circles. Inside, a twinge, a flip, a uterine tightening and turning.

Because he was too big. Too big to be a horse.

The bulge of his bones too awkward. His coming unheralded.

Were we afraid?

Not exactly.

Papa moved quietly toward us, like a hunter losing his steps to the earth.

It's a moose, he hissed, his *S* too loud.

We had never seen a moose.

Yet here we four were, as though called to an assignation on the west side of the barn, just down from the berry brambles. We all headed to that spot at that hour on that day, during the last spring melt of the millennium.

Was it your idea, Rosa? You asked to go out.

Wordlessly, Papa lifted you from me and we stood, shoulder to shoulder, transfixed. Mama, father, child. A wall of human family not much, if the moose decided.

Transfix: from the Latin *transfigure,* to be *pierced through* (from *trans,* across, and *figere,* to fix or fasten). Usually, to *be* transfixed. The piercing done to you, like April weather.

You ask, did you really not know?

In fact, I did not. I often did not know where I was—whether I had already taken the left turn, or driven straight past it. I did not know that knots were the places branches had grown. I did not remember to water plants. I had no idea that the males of the species lose their antlers each winter and, in the wildest, most extravagant multiplication of cells in all the animal kingdom, regrow them every spring—seventy-five-inch racks of protein-dense fuzzy antler in mere months. I did not then understand the range of quadrupeds with whom one might become intimate: moose, mules, miniature donkeys, Romeldales and Jacobs, draft horses, wild stallions, Guernseys and Galloways, fainting goats, Belgians and Morgans and Icelandics, zebras and moonbeams, dappleds and grays. I did not know. I am happy to catalog my ignorance. I had made a drunken horse of a moose.

We went back to reading books on the sheepskin by the fire and making doughy messes in the kitchen, and the moose went back, we supposed, to eating his high-fiber vegan diet in our woods. Life was—immense. Reminded that the miracles of the world outpace my meager imagination, I was overcome by a strangely complete happiness. I packed up the creamy cotton ramekins and gave them away, to some other mother's baby.

You were more than enough.

He's a freaking idiot, one student says.

A dumb ass. She pauses to make sure everyone's listening. It's a *guy* thing.

The whole class laughs.

But what about his *mother,* asks the first, who is fond of men, has dallied with a number of them, we've heard; the latest is going to buy her a car. I mean, throwing him out in the woods? That's nasty.

What would you have done if you were Jocasta?

Watched him like a hawk, she answers with no hesitation whatsoever.

I listen to them the same way I read: for enlightenment.

Never look away, confirms someone else.

Don't give someone else your dirty work.

Not bad as principles to live by.

And don't chuck your baby in the woods, adds the one with the big round belly. Duh!

But can you believe, I ask as we stop laughing, that Oedipus meets his fate exactly as he runs from it? Doing exactly what he thinks he should be doing. That doesn't make you wonder?

We looked for the moose that summer, but found only traces. There were cloven tracks larger than any others we'd ever seen near the marsh. Giant patties, where no cow had been. Might this path have been his? Had he rubbed off the velvet of his antlers on this tree? Our doting neighbors gave you a moose puppet nearly as big as you were, so that you could practice imagining someone else.

We imagined, since our deciding minds had been proven so wrong. Someone was growing inside me. Secretly, we tried out names: Mose, Amos, Vera.

Why did you name him *Amos?* you wanted to know, as you sucked your first lollipop and peered at the bundle in my arms.

Because his name has three of the same letters as yours, I realized only as I told you, dopily loving the round open *O*. And also the word *os.* A magical word: the opening that he came through, that you came through. And also *bone* in Latin. Can you believe that tiny word means both? I asked.

15

A moose, a mouse, you answered, crunching through the sugar rock of your pop.

A moose, a mouse, timak, a mos. You lullabied him thus, peering, brow creased, between the bars at the strange creature asleep in your crib. *And all the pretty little horsies.*

Did this event make me a connoisseur of not-knowing? Just last week at a nearby college, a woman showed a movie about when she was young and part of a movement for the liberation of all people, starting with her neighbors, and their hungry children. First, they cleared the trash from the streets. Next, they occupied the brick church on the corner, for serving food and other social services.

A student wanted to know more about how things had gone wrong, when the movement fell apart. We had all heard, many times before, about the informants. We knew about the FBI. Some people thought that in retrospect they'd made a strategic error, trying to be two places at once, the island and the city. The problem of overreach.

The older woman nodded as the young man outlined possible answers for his own question. Finally, she said, Maybe we don't ever understand what story we're living inside. How history is moving. She smiled sweetly, blinking a little at the lights and the crowd.

My father asked my mother if this was it.

How should I know? she answered. I have never done this before.

By *it* he meant dying and by *this* she meant *lived my final days.*

Everything that matters we do not know, I wake in the night, wanting to tell you both, my bones. It is something like an apology—for the piles of books, for my questions and worries and lists and plans. But everyone is asleep, and an ocean floats between us.

When Amos finally learned to talk, which took a full two years—
he didn't seem, particularly, to need words, with you nearby—he
woke up one morning and asked to go see a moose.

You can't just decide to see a moose, Papa said.

Yes, a moose, he insisted.

How about we go to the hardware store?

Delay, humor, distract.

Narrative suggests. Makes too obvious what in life was somewhere far south of possible. Not at all on the day's map. Papa goes
back upstairs to look for his wallet; he stamps into his mud boots;
he bends to button the baby's corduroy coat; he writes *90-degree
this* and *3/8-inch that* and *diesel* with a tiny stub of a carpenter's
pencil; he glances at the thermometer, though he already knows
it's above freezing. He buckles Amos into his car seat and cranks
the music from the birth of rock and roll. *I'm gonna tell you how it's
gonna be.*

Why did the bullmoose cross the road?

Because the boy said so.

Because *a moose, a mouse, timak, a mos.*

Because he was born, if you count back, exactly ten moons from
the appearance of the moose.

What do you want to know about rural sorcery? Everything.
"Whom do you want to ask and who is supposed to teach you a certain devotion, natural rhythm, and free-flowing time?" asks the
Czech geologist Václav Cílek, in an essay collection that includes a
story of a masked moose and a trench-digger and two surrealists
who "lived in order to live." They made up questionnaires inves-
tigating how our psyches are shaped by the landscapes we live in
and the objects we touch. A slope of land, a nook, a crooked tree as
important as anything else.

"And if we are to play the game of where we belong, what do we answer?" Cílek asks.

You drive for two hours across the state, and you know you are near when there are only trees. Past the turn in the east branch of the Westfield River and the lookout over the WPA dam, the road is lined with pines and maples and ash and cherries and spruce and hemlock.

The bullmoose, his antlers grown into full mating display, and the boy and the father came to a stop in the middle of this road.

Because the woods, the pottery studio with the boarded-up cupola, the side-missing barn with the bats swooping out at night, the bear caves of Archina, the hidden well, the cobbled beadboard hallway trod by abolitionists and preachers, the black circles thrown up on the plaster from the flames of candles, the doors without knobs, the frames without doors, the feral garden, the hoot owls and the peepers, the split-trunk peach trees and ancient hydrangeas, the tipsy stone walls and the path in the woods where we affixed a *No Hunting* sign across from the old sugar maple with the trunk that grows in two: one half standing tall and the other half bending home.

Double Exposure

Rebecca Bell-Gurwitz

A slight exhale in the room where dust meanders, the film on screen, a sigh of our heroine, the woman who cannot be alone. Her face fills each corner of the projection closing in on the desert color of her lips, a newish concept, Technicolored saturation as if the wavelengths themselves were aged. Gena Rowlands has a face lonely enough to be considered classic. When other trends fall out of favor, search the theaters, art house or block-busted and yellowed with butter dust, for this familiar scene. In every film, there is a heroine boasting the wide-eyed stance of a woman who, sequestered in her agoraphobia, looks out onto the busy black-and-white or color or cyber-generated street with a measured longing. On my lap is a pad of paper and array of pens; I am supposed to be taking notes. Gena Rowlands lounges on the chaise, painting her toenails, behaving as if no one else is present.

It is fall. It is my final year of high school, and everything is about leaving. My mother is dying in our living room. This makes everyone afraid; I should mourn however I want; I should mourn by not mourning. Where I am began the year before, when my English teacher, Mrs. L., urged me to write without fear. This year, my last living at home, it feels like my gravitational pull is faulty. My mother was once my North and South, each pole converging in her embrace, but I don't want to write about her, I want to write my own stories without horizon. I take film class with Mrs. L. because I think I am in love with her, and this is the complication. She won't let me write without horizon, and I have nothing to watch without her. So, Mrs. L. becomes North and South, the air and horizon, with her elongated, out-of-fashion denim skirts and high-heeled leather pumps the boys in class call her fuck-me boots. She wears night-blue eyeliner stenciled around and overemphasizing; she would be easy to judge but she's the smartest person I've met. She is brave enough to remind me I'm mourning.

In film class, Mrs. L. introduces me to my favorite director, Cassavetes, with his vast close-ups and his fuzzy, budget cameras, his family and friends borrowed as actors. There was no one better suited for these films than Cassavetes's intimates themselves, their private intricacies already exposed and ripe for his plucking. I can't take my eyes from Cassavetes's wife, Gena Rowlands, who is less blonde and more expressive than Marilyn Monroe. Mrs. L. brings Gena Rowlands to screen, both of their smiles upturned, downturned, lipsticked, chapped, fading. I double-expose myself over them, Gena Rowlands with her desert lips, Mrs. L. lined by night eyes. I want to give something in return. All I have is bad posture.

Gena Rowlands has the wonderful, high-pitched but sultry, grounded voice of the late sixties and early seventies. In Cassavetes's 1974 film, *A Woman Under the Influence*, Rowlands answers to "Mabel" and Peter Falk is a rough and tumble "Nick." On screen, Mabel's kids scamper around the backyard, stuffing birthday cake in each other's faces and letting go of balloons the colors of fruit. Peter Falk yells a lot; desert rose accentuates the licked-over lips of women at the party. The film's coloring is saturated in tempered orange and yellows; the hues of old photographs are forsaken in favor of modern preference for desiccated cyber-colors like purple and the darkest blue. Think *The Matrix*, think an actor conversing in practiced precision to a green screen. At this moment, at the helm of the cyber-revolution, we want everything fast and furious, virtual reality, pumped to the brim with stimulus but without the pitfalls of a skinned knee. We revel in Mrs. L.'s tales of her past, riveting retellings of Technicolor and black and white and cyber-regenerated memories like her encounters with prostitutes and pimps playing nice downtown, like almost getting kidnapped but jumping out of her assailant's van in the nick of time, like watching a loved one get sick and die. She has a reputation for teaching kids with adult respect, appraising sex in movies the same way she would a simple dialogue between two actors. "Everybody does it," she says with her arms bowed, hands on her hips. She stands at the front of the classroom beneath a frozen frame of two actors making out. "You just want them to do it realistically. None of this Disney stuff." For comparison's sake, she describes in great detail a scene from the 1995 drama *Kids,* the camera fixated on two adolescents literally swapping saliva, their braces clashing, lips chapped in confusion, "It's more like this," she says, grinning, "at least at first."

But when Gena Rowlands and Peter Falk kiss, they overturn each other's boundaries; they cannibalize one other and straighten their mouths after the fact. Their enmeshing is neither attractive nor repulsive, faces together and struggling to separate. Mrs. L. pauses the scene and says little in response, waiting for our input. Mrs. L. sits at a grade-school desk in the dark of the film class, one of the last rooms in the building without windows. The darkness here is purposeful, as it is in the photography lab, as it isn't in the janitor's closet. Mrs. L. pauses the film again. She asks a question, then, satisfied with the answer, sets the story back to motion. Off screen, I watch Mrs. L. because there's no one else. On screen, Gena pushes her hair out of her face, walks about the kitchen, sits, ties her hair up, and lets it loose once more.

I still don't know if Mrs. L. hoped to be a filmmaker before becoming a teacher, but she's always had a knack for creating visuals in her speech and for engaging without condescending to her audience. For this reason, many of us love her and seek to know her beyond these pesky student-teacher boundaries. One student raises his hand in the middle of class, trying to analyze Mrs. L.'s handwriting, claiming that the swoop of her Rs holds special significance. Mrs. L. shakes her head, visibly uncomfortable. "I don't like to be psychoanalyzed," she says, which only makes her students more determined. Mrs. L. receives proposals from young men in Converse sneakers; girls three years removed from their braces try desperately to be like her. Before we leave for an overnight field trip she says with a wink, "Don't do anything I wouldn't." She's a teacher well loved because she's suburban like Mabel, equal parts ordinary and brilliant, an easily consumed cliché. But then I see more strength in her than Mabel; she wouldn't tolerate someone like Nick with his low-to-the-ground anger, his working-class grimace overwhelming all.

The walk home from film class is exhausting because it requires thought. A hill slopes upward, past the mansions, with its rocks frozen in place mid-tumble, almost breaking the bounds of yard, creating the impression of a cliff over water, except here there is only street. For fun, I run my hand along these rocks, first my palm callused and conditioned for texture, then turned over to expose my knuckles, the skin thinner and less resistant to the neighborhood's jagged landscaping. After two minutes, the land flattens, and the houses recall vast plantations more than Byronic manses, their columns tall and front yards prairied. I miss the shadow of the cliffs. Before my mother went away to the hospital, I used to sit on my living room floor and do homework with my mother a few feet away. She liked knowing I was there. I shorten my pace to extend the emptiness before I fill it with math problems and AP exams.

As I walk, I imagine Gena Rowlands explaining to me the filmic reasoning behind this street's emptiness. I wish there were a passing school bus so I could run after it as she does in the movie. I wonder if Mrs. L. runs after her kids' bus in the mornings but remember there probably isn't one because her family lives so close by, and they need only walk two blocks. I know this because I once drove to her house to pick up some films difficult to find online or at any dying video store. I dialed the radio loud enough so she might hear and pulled up to her house with my car windows down, psyching myself up before stumbling from the front seat, remembering how I once told her I couldn't parallel park or tell time properly, and she scoffed at me, but kindly. It was the teaching impulse she attempted to repress. Her house was average suburban, with a two-door garage and white front door.

When I rang the doorbell, she immediately answered, her son bounding down the stairs in his baseball uniform, his excitement tempered when he saw it was only a girl he didn't know, probably one of his mother's students. Mrs. L. introduced us, hands braced on the tops of her son's shoulders, pushing him tentatively forward as if he were an offering she might also have to protect. We spoke for a minute about baseball, him practicing his batting in the air with considerable might and me regaling him with stories of my short career as a high-school softball player, neglecting to mention the sting of having been reassigned to outfield after an unsuccessful stint as first baseman. The problem was I didn't perform well under pressure. But I didn't say this aloud and commented instead on his seeming prowess at the sport, considering how committed he was to his invisible batting. Growing bored, he bounded back up the stairs, and Mrs. L. made a casual comment about how I should babysit for her and her husband some night once I graduated. I thought of asking her how long she believed I would stay in town, but didn't want to jinx my chances of seeing her again in the coming year. Resting on the piano in the living room where we spoke were an array of photographs I could barely distinguish, impressionist depictions of family and friends, leaving only blurs for my consumption. A cat stretched out on the porch through the window. Mrs. L. asked me about my mother, who was dying.

I shrugged and said that I had been doing okay, that I spent most of my available thought on applying to college, which was better currency than mourning anyway. She appeared concerned. In her hand, I saw Gena Rowlands's face, the pile of DVDs gathered and tied into place by the careful strain of a rubber band. "You're going to burn yourself out," she told me. I watched her cat on the back porch while she held the bouquet of films in offering. After the exchange, there was little reason to stay.

"Thanks," I told her. Under the piano, there were two metal barbells, about five pounds in weight and pigeon-toed in position toward one another. Mrs. L. went on to let me know I was welcome in her office anytime. "Sure," I said, already aware I wouldn't be seeing her there unless I needed to turn in an assignment or ask a question about the length of a paper, anything technical, nothing personal. I left the house with the cat and the weights and the baseball-playing son and drove home to my own two-door garage, preferring to park my mother's car atop the square patch of gravel running between our garden and the play structure my brother didn't concede to our cousins even though we were too old and never used it anymore, except occasionally as a safe space to smoke weed, always one of us hovering over the swing's misshapen smile before an exhalation.

It's fall when the time comes for my mother to die. She has come home from the hospital specifically for this reason. I return from a college tour, one I'd attended with the full knowledge she would soon be gone. For days while I was at Tufts discussing dormitory placements, I made myself believe there was no one dying in my living room, that the white sheets with my mother beneath were draped over a sculpture as yet unveiled. It's hard to continue with this version of the narrative when I arrive home and see my aunt and uncle's car parked in the driveway, still and waiting.

My family gathers in the living room under the painting of Venice my uncle made for my mother to remember her honeymoon. The blues in the painting catch the sparkle of the Venetian canals as well as the dirt. My mother is not bedded under the painting, as she would have been if I had set the mise-en-scène. Gena Rowlands's pale colors are my mother's lips chapped from dehydration. Gena Rowlands's mania is my uncle pacing the room and kissing my mother's forehead over and over.

When she dies, her brother-in-law, my uncle, is the only one with her. It's the small hour of morning when streets glean rain, absorbing around the scars where the asphalt splits, and the traffic lights reflect red-green-yellow against slicked tarmac for the sake of a few early risers. I fall into the car with my father and brother after the moment of her death, my aunt and uncle left with the body. I want to tell my father to drive us to Mrs. L.'s house, her brick sanctuary. I want her to meet me between North and South with an embrace; I want to wake her up in the night to tell me again how afraid she is for me. No one else has ever said such a thing aloud. Since my mother's illness, only Mrs. L. chases me as a mother would, running after the school bus like Gena Rowlands in the movie.

But in the end, we do not go to Mrs. L.'s house. We drive aimlessly and no one stops us.

Two weeks after my mother's death, I get stoned with a friend before film class and listen to Outkast's *Hey Ya* on headphones split between my ear and hers. We wait for Mrs. L. to walk in and admonish us. I want someone to see me, shake me by the shoulders, and make me ashamed. *Hey Ya* is supposed to be fast. My friend tries to make me laugh by slowing the tempo. The film screen is pulled down but blank. Students filter into class, settling their backpacks and tucking pens behind their ears. Gena Rowlands as Mabel's mind is a vast desert rose of longing and loneliness. I project her face over the screen, willing her to show herself, to watch and see me slow, slow enough for Mrs. L. to chase me.

On screen, Gena Rowlands is alone, alternating faces, laughing and crying, frowning and grinning like an overworked mimic. I want to make faces just the same, for all to see. My friend turns to me, pulling the headphone from my ear. There in class, I cry, the screen still. Mrs. L., late. I compose myself. When she finally arrives, I impersonate the girl who studies, who is quiet and without passion. I wait to reveal myself to her but she doesn't see.

As suburban boredom infiltrates, pan to me, young and avoiding the camera, zoom out, and watch for the pixels on my laptop as they come together and grin. Gena Rowlands delivers monologues in the kitchen. As I watch, I remember her. The intensity I once felt for Mrs. L. is a distant star. I will have difficulty locating this intensity again, my need to know so much of Mrs. L. I fade into her. After my mother died, I wanted to be recognized, acknowledged, and I wanted to disappear completely. In my late twenties, I kiss women and men and I maintain the separation. In my late twenties I become a therapist and out of necessity, I inhabit the separation between self and other. When my mother left so unwillingly, I returned to that newborn state of resenting the separation, but the hard work of living is the knowledge we will not have someone following behind in the small spaces of the day, whispering, over and over:

It will be okay. You will be held.

Chain of Tools

Kris Brandenburger

I wiped my bike down, the frame voluptuous in my hands as I fingered the delicate lugwork clean. The transition from straight line to curve pleasing as I worked my way down the frame, around each rim, gently poking the cloth between, then along the spokes; pushing, polishing, rubbing up to the hubs.

Careful not to drive the link pin all the way out, I removed the *Sedis Oro,* the golden chain, admiring its elegance, the beautiful butterfly that caterpillars over the chain ring and cassette transforming the vertical motion of legs into the forward motion of the wheels. As it separated, I lifted the chain off the sprockets and sat with it across my lap, counting the individual links and feeling for unwanted stiffness.

Part of the chain's beauty for me lay in its function of measurement. Since working at an electrical repair shop, I had a whole new appreciation of measurement. More than a fixed answer to someone else's question, measure now meant tool, it meant relationship, something to calculate with; something on which to rely. I could now literally count on my bicycle; all the relationships of the bicycle both to itself and to its rider correspond to some measure of

27

the chain. The number of links in relation to the number of teeth on the gear sprockets in relation to the size of the wheel determine how much effort it takes to turn the wheels. I dropped the chain into a pan of solvent to soak.

Chain-link fence, chain letter, chain reaction, chain of life. I considered these links, boundaries, and ties. The chain of my own life had, early on, been linked to machines and tools, my attraction both magnetic and magical. Rather than being someone who effortlessly saw *how* things worked, I was someone who saw *that* they worked and wondered how. I nested into the language of their descriptions and made up my own mechanics, unburdened by measured understanding.

I still remember my father's fly-tying vise rising like a great heron out of the piles of feathers and pelts that swamped his desk. The entire green-black steel body was etched with a crosshatched net of iridescent lines that pulled my child's eyes in and held them, suspended in wonder. I loved to open and close its mouth, to feather my hands down its body, wondering how something so graceful was *made*. How to go from intent and vision to the physical fact of many intricate and fine parts to a precise and working whole?

That same splendid sense of purposely measured beauty was present in my bicycle. The hand-cut lugs would have been beautiful for their lines in any setting, but their magic lay in the coupling of the beauty with their perfection of purpose. Someone had loved measuring, cutting, fitting, and welding these lugs onto this bicycle. And it showed. Not only showed, but felt; the frame came alive on a ride; the greater the effort demanded, the surer the response. The bicycle positively quickened in your hands as you pushed up a long grade, giving rather than taking energy. This quickening was a direct result of the architecture of this particular bike, the material, length and geometry of the frame tubes, the tubes, which were connected by the lugs. The lugs, which someone had to understand the measure of to be able to cut, hone, and fit so perfectly.

I fished around in the solvent, found the chain, and scrubbed off the remaining crud with a toothbrush before dropping it into a pan of oil. I slipped the rag over my index finger and worked on the bottom bracket. Hidden in the frame between the pedals, the secret passage linking them, this muscular heart of ball bearings was not part of the obvious beauty of the bike; you had to get past appearances to know the bottom bracket. It was for me a kind of recognized rather than known beauty, the promised magic that I had always imagined to be possible with certain kinds of mechanics. An ecology of function allowed as much appreciation as curiosity and understanding could bring. In many ways, the bicycle was my own mind-map to problem-solving, the vehicle for my ever-increasing sense of engaged self.

As I thought about it, I realized that bicycles were my first guides into the worlds of self I still recognize. My first bike had training wheels intended to protect my five-year-old self. We lived in Portland, Oregon, on the Alameda, just above Dead Man's Hill. My dad was still home a lot. Summer evenings he would walk me riding. He trotted alongside me on the sidewalk until finally I could leave him in my dust, me as proud as I could be and him shouting encouragement.

One day after school, I just *knew* that I didn't need the training wheels anymore: they were holding me back. My bike was kept out in the garage next to my dad's workbench. That particular afternoon I sat looking at those training wheels, trying to figure out how they were attached and how to unattach them. I had no trouble *describing* what I wanted to see—the trainers off the bike—but the seeing itself came in a tardy second place.

My dad had what I now know to be a complete set of householder tools rather than mechanical tools. Tools he used doing home repairs and landscaping. It was my dad who designed our yards and defined our spaces. Hung on pegboard above the work-bench, none of the tools looked so new as known. I easily found the adjustable wrench that fit my hands and leaned over the rear wheels to take my chances.

I still remember my mother's look of shock as she came out of the back door to see me cruising out of the garage that was lit-tered with the castoff training wheels. That was one of the best moments of my entire life, one I'd forgotten until now, until work-ing on my first real adult bike, the only bike I'd ever bought for myself.

Refitting the crank bolt I wondered at this memory. I'd forgotten how proud I'd been at figuring out my problem with those wheels. How much it had meant to me to *see* the solution, to know that I'd made the links in my chain of problem solving. It was very similar to the morning that I finally *got* the lathe, and with it the ability to make a tool of my own process, myself as a tool.

Early, it was not yet light, and I was alone in the shop after riding down in the damp pre-dawn. I was struggling with turning an arma-ture, my frustration more numbing than the cold. I was determined to learn this, to be able to do what I could describe.

I kept gouging the copper of the commutator. I knew it was a ques-tion of being able to sharpen the leading edge of the tool, the cutting bit, to a nearly concave V; knew it but couldn't quite shape it. I took the bit back and back and back again to the grinding wheel to put just the right face on it. As I adjusted the angle of the tool for another cut, it struck me that a functional cutting face was about more than the shape and angle of the tool; it was also about the vertical tilt of the tool. Just like in my father's fly-tying vise, the face of the cutting tool was a measured relationship, a made relationship, one in which I had to understand my intent so thoroughly as to make it work. Angle, tilt, and edge: all links in the chain of that work. I made a test cut before turning on the automatic feeder. My fingertips lightly rode the feeder lever, feeling for any deadening or thickening if the cut went wrong. I turned it off to check the commutator for ridges or grooves, riding the chuck to a stop with my left hand. Nothing. I turned it back on to finish. Copper shavings roostered off, flecking my hair, stinging my cheeks like granular sleet. I could hear my perfect cut—it made the same high-pitched hum as water slinging off my bike tires at speed.

I looked out the west-facing window at the gauzy mixture of moisture and light, a scrim beading each shape into distinction. I had it and I knew it. I knew that from now on I would be able to count on my capacity to sharpen the cutting tool any time it was needed. I could rely on myself. And somehow it was the gift of my bicycle, of the lugly beauty that I had so recently come to know.

Taking the chain out of the oil I smiled. I liked the precision of going through the bike piece by piece, knowing when things felt right, when something was done, or what was needed to finish it. I hung the chain over a nail to dry and started on the brake calipers. A drop of oil on the pivot bolt, a mental note to change the pads next week. I removed and checked the rear wheel. It spun true, the bearings felt fine. The rim looked a little rough in one spot so I smoothed it with a file before cleaning the rear cluster. I got between the cogs with a toothbrush and sprayed degreaser on the outer surfaces. Good. I would put it all back together before my ride home this evening.

My bicycle was a thing of beauty. Like anything else I'd ever take apart, there was an internal set of relationships, a pattern informed by measured intent. And it was for me to become informed, to become a part.

The Unclimbable

Danica Novgorodoff

'***ve always felt at home on the road, which is to say, I don't quite
feel at home anywhere. When someone asks me, "Where are
you from?" I say I live in New York, because that's where I pay
rent right now. If I'm in New York, I say I'm from Kentucky, because
that's where my family lives. If I'm in Kentucky, I say that I was
born in Chicago, or that I spent my childhood riding horses in
Michigan. But it was at the foot of a volcano in Ecuador that I first
learned about silence, and longed for stillness—so maybe that's
where I really grew up.

Once, I fell in love with a volcano.

In 1802, scientist and explorer Alexander von Humboldt declared
Cotopaxi volcano unclimbable. He also said it was one of the most
majestic sights he'd ever seen—its massive white peak gleaming
against the blue "vault of heaven."

*Perhaps if I go somewhere that is definitively unfamiliar, I thought, I
will learn what home is.*

When I was twenty-two, I traveled to Ecuador with a large-format wooden camera, a pocket thesaurus, and a pair of hiking boots. I found a hacienda called Tierra del Volcán in the shadow of Cotopaxi volcano. I volunteered to teach the farm's tour guides English, to translate this and that, to oil their saddles with butter. A young man named Klever worked in the kitchen, guided tourists, fixed fences, and wrangled horses. I asked him the names of plants, and how to use a lasso. I wanted to ride the horses. I wanted to know about the volcano.

I shall try to find out how the forces of nature interact upon one another and how the geographic environment influences plant and animal life. In other words, I must find out about the unity of nature.
—Alexander von Humboldt

Original artwork by Danica Novgorodoff, provided courtesy of the author.

When I began working at Tierra del Volcán, I was given a scrappy horse to ride. He was named Diabluco because of his crackling personality and his ugliness—a head too large for its skinny neck, his roman nose and beetling cranium, the sway back and spindly short legs, craggy withers and his color—which was no single color but a mottled grey with white whiskers and irregular splotches of tea-stain brown. I had asked for a fast horse, and they had given me this. "He's got no brakes," Klever said. Diabluco was, in fact, very fast.

I rode him to the local grade school on weekdays and tied him to a goalpost in the yard as I taught English lessons to wind-burned children in a one-room schoolhouse. I rode him up into the *páramo*,

a landscape wind-blasted and rain-spackled, strewn with volcanic ejecta and low, leathery plants. In his *Personal Narrative*, Humboldt refers to the *malpaís*, or badlands: "This term, in use in Mexico, Peru and all places where there are volcanoes, refers to regions stripped of vegetation and covered in lava fragments." I've heard *páramo* translated as highlands, moorlands, or wasteland—the Andean terrain above the continuous treeline, but below the perpetual snowline. *Wasteland*, I think, is ungenerous toward a land so astonishingly—if forbiddingly—beautiful.

Whenever I had the chance, I rode Diabluco up into the *páramo* just to get a better view of the volcano. Klever told me that Cotopaxi meant *Neck of the Moon* in Kichwa or some lost language, and so I watched the volcano craning toward the sky, its lunar face lolling, and sometimes it breathed smoke, and sometimes it wore a scarf of woolen, coiled cloud. At night, I sat alone in the drafty house next to the milking barn where I was now staying, drawing comics and making collages out of old bus tickets and newspaper clippings. After boiling water for tea, I held my hands over the burner to absorb some lingering warmth. The house was so silent the air vibrated. Unless the wind was blowing—then the night sang like a wolf. *Could this be home?*

It is exhausting to be at home on the road. Over and over, you must decide, *Where will I sleep tonight? How will I eat? What am I doing here? What am I doing anywhere?*

Sell your lands, your houses, your garments and your jewelry; burn up your books. Buy stout shoes, climb the mountains, search the valleys, the deserts, the sea shores, and the deep recesses of the Earth.—Severinus, Danish professor of literature, meteorology, and medicine, 1571

In the first days of the wet season, Klever and I led a group of tourists into the national park on horseback. I was on Diabluco. The tourists wanted to trot, wanted to canter, and within seconds Klever's horse and mine were flat out racing. Our stirrups touched with a clink. We were racing across the lava field, and Diabluco, small as he was, pulled out ahead. I could no longer discern

individual hoof beats, heartbeats. I was alone. *If he trips, I fall.* A divot, a rolling stone, a knoll of feather reed could do it. *If he trips, I fall. If I fall, I lose.*

We were far out ahead of everyone else. I felt nothing but lungs and muscle and wind freezing my eyeballs. Then Diabluco was veering left, a slow curve away from our path, away from return. I forgot that we were racing—we were flying. What would it be like to be on top of the volcano? What would it be like to be inside it—solitary, silent? Or roaring, searing? I lost Klever, the people, myself. The white torch of Cotopaxi's snowcap burned before me. How can a woman, a wanderer, a mortal in love with an unclimbable mountain, ever settle for stillness? I couldn't stop Diabluco; he had no brakes. The voices behind us called for me to stop, stop, but I saw the volcano and let him run. I would never be as at home as I was then, hurtling toward my volcano, my beloved, always approaching, never arriving.

Children and All That Jazz

Liesl Schillinger

Mama was lying on the loveseat, holding a glass of Chablis, tears slinking out of her eyes, which were already mascara-streaky, her mink-dark hair falling in sleek, long strands down the arm of the couch, almost to the floor. It was a hot August Saturday, and I was sitting stiffly beside her in the TV room, with its brown, cracking, leather-look couches, the walls of books, the oriental carpet a little blurry in the spots where Scooter, our dog, had gone to the bathroom on it and Dad had scrubbed it with Scotchgard. I was exasperated that Mama was crying, and hoped my showing up would make her stop. There was an old wooden stereo console on legs in the TV room, with built-in rattan-covered speakers. When our parents were at work, or gone, or upstairs, my brother Chad and I would play *Magical Mystery Tour* and *Sgt. Pepper* and *West Side Story,* sing along, and turn up the volume. We scratched the records sometimes, by accident, but Dad never complained.

The Nilsson kids from across the street came over a lot that summer and crowded in beside my brothers and me on the couch and loveseat, listening to the Beatles with us, eating bowls of our Trix, and watching *The Carol Burnett Show* or *Match Game*, or whatever was on TV. I used to think they came mostly for the cereal (their mother used powdered milk, which tasted disgusting, and she only bought bargain, unsweetened cereal), but later I found out it was because their dad, who was an English professor, wouldn't let them watch TV in their own house. This afternoon, though, it was just me and Mama in the TV room. She was listening to Joan Baez's *Diamonds & Rust* album over and over in the sun-streaked room, sobbing steadily and quietly. She hadn't wanted to be overheard. She hadn't wanted company. She had wanted, I could tell, to revel in a solitary sulk, as if my brothers and I didn't exist, or Dad, and she occupied her own private house. And I was not going to let her. She'd played *Diamonds & Rust* so many times that year that I knew all the songs by heart. I looked at Mama uncomfortably—I was ten, she was thirty-four, lovely and tragic, and I wanted to cheer her up, but wasn't sure how. "Why are you crying?" I asked, even though I basically knew why.

"She *loved* him," Mama said, between sobs. "Bobby," she said. "He was so cruel to her . . ." and the crying resumed. I understood "she" was Joan Baez, and "Bobby" was Bob Dylan. Mama had told me about them before, on days when she was in one of her defiant, world-conquering moods—about how mean Bob Dylan had been to Joan Baez, when the two of them were together, and how unfair it was. Both of them were a little older than Mama; and the way she talked about them, you would have thought she'd hung out with them at college or something, but she hadn't. Still, her voice took on a sword-edged quality when she talked about them, as if she personally intended to avenge this wrong. Bobby had left Joan for someone else, even though Joan was famous and lovely and young; even though she had a voice of molten gold and he sounded like a crow with catarrh. He had even mocked her on *film*, Mama had told me—in a movie I hadn't seen, called *Don't Look Back*. I held this deeply against him. How arrogant! How callous! He had mocked the singer who loved him, and then left her. Who did he think he was? But I also knew that all of this had gone down a long time ago, and that Mama wasn't crying for Joan and Bobby, she was crying for herself.

I assumed she was pining for some Bobby of her own that muggy day—some heel or heartbreaker from high school or college who had disappointed her when she was as young and beautiful as Joan was when Bobby let her down (though, frankly, I thought Mama was more striking and, besides, Joan was older): before she was a wife, before she was a mother; back when her future was all unfixed fantasy. I'd read enough novels to have expected Mama to have dated before she got married; I'd watched *Happy Days*. It stood to reason that she had gone to sock hops and proms before she met Dad, that she could have ended up being someone else's mother; and that, every now and then, she might want to mull her might-have-beens—like opening up a box of time-crisped corsages from dances past: dried-up roses and carnations shedding their clovey scent, trailing faded ribbons. But that didn't mean I wanted to know about it.

Still, I believed in Mama's right to be sad as strongly as I believed in her right to be happy. When she laughed, she made all of us laugh; and when she cried, it tended to be over things anyone would have cried over, things that would have made me cry, too, if they had happened to me. She cried when the politics at the advertising office where she worked were unfair, and when the hours were too long but she still had to make supper. She cried when Granny told her she wasn't a good mother because she worked outside the house and Dad did the laundry. And she cried when she remembered John F. Kennedy. Kennedy had been killed, I knew, and Mama had worked for his campaign before she met Dad. Later the two of them campaigned for McGovern. They liked to tell me how Kennedy had appealed to people's higher instincts, not their baser ones, and how exciting it had been to believe in something bigger than yourself, in the sixties. When I was five, I sent my tooth-fairy money to George McGovern, trying to follow their example. So I understood when Mama cried about work, or Granny; and I was moved when she cried about Kennedy, the sixties, and lost noble ideals. But I didn't like hearing her cry about lost love. I didn't want to feel implicated.

I recalled vaguely, in shadow memory, grad-student friends of my parents, when I was three and Chad was just born, and Dad was working on his dissertation. "Ghosts of my history," Joan Baez might have called them. Tall male shapes with moustaches and glasses, flared slacks and belted jackets with pockets. Smaller, rounded woman shapes, with skirts and Indian-print muslin blouses, or jeans and turtlenecks. Murky-eyed child shapes in Oshkosh overalls, their fingers sticky from gluing glitter on construction paper. An afternoon flickered like a newsreel through my mind, a day when a family with kids came over, and I sliced off the tip of my finger on a fan when everybody was distracted, and nobody saw me testing the protective barrier of the fan's safety grille over and over, until I went too far. Had one of those shapes been worth crying over? I didn't know, but I didn't like it when Mama cried as Joan sang:

> As I remember your eyes were bluer than robin's eggs,
> My poetry was lousy you said. Where are you calling from?
> A booth in the midwest . . .

Did someone call Mama from booths in the Midwest? We lived in Ohio. It was not impossible. Was that why she was crying today? I doubted it. More likely she was crying because nobody had called. "Mother always told me I was so young, I had so much time," she said, sobbing. "And it *wasn't true*. Look at me, I'm thirty-four, trapped in the Midwest with three kids. It's too late, it's too late." Her crying became a soft, cyclical siren, and I looked up at the paisley curtains she had sewn, the gold and ivory opulent fabric, with cunning ivory pull-tassels, and imagined my mother as someone's foolable daughter.

As a teenager, Mama had been a debutante, in a modest, small-town way, but it sounded very grand to me. In black and white photos, her hair neatly bouffant, her dresses smooth and tailored, she stood next to clean-cut young men in tuxedos, in albums Granny had made, albums that only I ever looked at (Mama wasn't sentimental). I thought she looked like Jackie Kennedy at the White House, and marveled at her glamour. I privately thought she was far too exceptional to have to live with us in our little Cape Cod that she'd decorated so grandly. Once, I made the mistake of telling her I was sorry she'd had me so early, at twenty-three, because my birth had kept her from having the life she ought to have had. I was confused when she was insulted instead of flattered. "What?" she said. "You couldn't have *stopped* me from having you when I did!" Then she got angry because it was such a heartless indictment that I could have thought for one second that she hadn't passionately wanted me; and that I hadn't realized that her melancholy moods weren't something I or anyone was to blame for, they were simply part of the human condition—grief at the space between who you'd wanted to be, and who you actually became— something you shouldn't have to conceal from the people you lived among. I liked to brag about Mama to the other kids in the sixth grade. "My mother had a dress made by Worth," I would tell them impressively, "She's a graphic designer, and a good cook, and she plays violin and piano." And though they seemed not to care, I imagined they secretly did, and that they envied me for having such a rare and multifaceted mother. I would never be a debutante myself, Mama explained, because Mama was not a "club woman" and didn't want to be. I accepted her judgment, though I wasn't sure what a club woman was. My grandmother was a club woman, so I assumed it had to do with going to the Methodist church, carpeting your house in light blue, growing daffodils, and having ladies over for coffeecake.

Mama wasn't like that. She'd been a hippie—as much as anyone who married young, had kids, and cared about polished silver and matching china (even in student housing) could be a hippie. My father was a handsome and earnest young professor, and played guitar and wore tinted glasses. The two of them were so politically engaged that once, when my grandparents drove two hundred miles to babysit for a weekend so Mama and Dad could go house-hunting without a stroller and a toddler, they drove to the Chicago riots instead. That impressed me, though I wasn't sure what the Chicago riots were. Mama was an idealist, and Dad was an idealist, and idealists cared about democracy in action, not about the Junior League, clean closets, and garden clubs. They also cared a lot about dinner parties and bridge, it seemed. My parents had parties all the time, which I loved to spy on. The men were sexy—some of them distinguished, like lords out of an English novel; others rough, outrageous, and all-American. The women were sexy, too: some of them brainy, some not, all of them good talkers, all of them with children. It seemed natural that everyone had children, and it did not occur to me then that there were adults who did not have them.

Mama and Dad's friends had many sons—I was one of two girls in the whole group—and I liked to mother the little boys and flirt with the ones closer to my age. At ten, flirting mostly came down to being beaten at tennis. I had a crush on the Blairs' son Andrew, who was in my class at school (but was older than me, because I'd skipped a grade). He was skinny and quick, with dark brown hair and an impish way about him. There was going to be a dinner party that night at our house, and Andrew would be there with his parents. I wanted the party to be a success, so I needed Mama to snap out of her faunch. The Elliotts were coming over, and the Courtenays, as well as the Blairs, and I reminded Mama that I'd promised to help, hoping that would mobilize her. For a minute the room was quiet; then the automatic turntable kicked in, and the record began again.

I looked at the window. Mama had sewn the curtains and made the valance, and edged the blinds with fabric tape, sewing on the ivory crocheted pull-rings that dropped from the center of each blind from a silken cord. Mama could sew well, and knit, and embroider, but I didn't have the patience for any of it. The one time I tried to sew on her Singer, I'd been trying to make a bean-bag shaped like a turtle, which I'd already filled with beans when I pushed the cloth under the foot. The beans broke the needle and destroyed the machine, and then I didn't have to sew anymore. Through a windowpane, I stared past a lace of maple leaves to the house next door, as Joan sang and Mama cried, and tried to think of a way to console Mama. A mean old woman lived in that house, Mrs. Reinhold—she had put dog-doo in our mailbox four years earlier, right after we moved in, because Scooter had pooed on her lawn, she said. Mama baked cookies and took them to Mrs. Reinhold, as a peace offering. "If someone does something vicious to you, shame them with an act of sickening kindness," she had explained to me, in the same score-settling tone she used when she talked about Bobby and Joan.

But Mama had no real taste for revenge, other than saying fierce things when she got angry. I exulted over a rude remark she'd made that week to two eighth-graders Andrew and I hated, bullies who'd harassed Mama and another lady as they were playing tennis in their white piqué dresses on our school's court. The boys jeered and catcalled until Mama and her friend quit playing, but as they left, Mama turned to the boys and said, "So long, cocksuckers." The boys were so shocked that they didn't even tell anyone. Mrs. Kimball (the lady she was playing tennis with) was shocked, too, Mama told me triumphantly. But really, Mama lionized and loved people, and knocked herself out for everyone: never lazy, never passive, always working to deepen bonds. The smallest act of unkindness never failed to lay her low.

I turned my head around to check if Mama was still crying (she was, a little) and said gruffly, "Everything's all right, it's not that bad, you're overreacting," and she looked at me sullenly. I turned on the TV; it was *Paint Along with Nancy Kominsky*, and I sat down at the end of the loveseat so Mama had to back up and scrunch up her long legs under the light-blue blanket Granny had knitted to make room for me. I turned to watch the show, leaning back on her calves. In the background, Joan Baez was singing a song so excruciatingly tender and sad, rejecting a second chance at love, that tears came to my eyes—I, who had no history of lost loves, no passions but reading and my family.

"This is depressing," I said, and got up and turned the music off. I went back to my end of the couch, reached over and turned up the volume on Nancy Kominsky. I thought to myself, illogically, if Mama hadn't had children, who would have comforted her that day? Blink, one of our cats, bounded up onto the desk where the TV was, and began to watch intently. As Nancy's hand darted with her oil knife, scraping away excess colors, the cat's paw lunged onto the screen, trying to stop her fluttering hand. Mama began to laugh, a little ruefully, and we watched the show to the end, as the paw ran interference. Then I went and got Mama a bowl of Trix. "Oh, why don't you go to Milo's and get me some cigarettes?" she said, taking the cereal and sniffling. "OK," I said, and she wrote me a note: "Please permit my daughter to buy two packs of Vantage," and signed it. Milo's was completely used to this; it was normal, in the seventies, for parents to send their kids out with a note to get cigarettes. Unimaginable now, of course. And the butchers would give us free bones to take home for our dogs. "Hurry back," Mama said, "It's already one o'clock, and the company gets here at seven."

As I shut the French door to the TV room behind me, Mama was getting up to close the stereo. I went upstairs to my baby brother Jamie's room (which Mama had designed; she'd had Dad build a bunk bed into one of the wide closets, with a desk underneath). Jamie was playing Chad's *Destroyer* album on his Fisher-Price record player, strumming "God of Thunder" on a broken ukulele. He had painted his face with zinc oxide to look like Starchild from Kiss, and was wearing a silk robe he'd gotten for Christmas, part of a Sugar Ray Leonard costume. Jamie was only five, and I thought he was hilarious. Chad was eight, and I wasn't always as nice to him as I was to Jamie, even though I loved him and was proud of him for being handsome and good at sports. But Chad was popular, which I wasn't, and he didn't need me as much as Jamie did. He was always out with the other popular eight-year-olds. Today, for example, he was at a birthday party at the swimming pool with his friends. He belonged to the Columbia Record club (Dad had signed him up, because he'd joined as a kid) and he played bands I was suspicious of because the cool kids liked them—Styx, Billy Joel, Chicago, and, later, Blondie and Supertramp. Now, of course, I love those bands, because they remind me of Chad and me when we were kids. "Do you want to go to Milo's with me to get cigarettes for Mama?" I asked Jamie. "Sure," he said, so I turned off "God of Thunder," and he followed me downstairs, his ukulele banging behind him on each step. When Jamie was two, the summer Mama went back to work full time, he would slip away from the babysitter, take off all his clothes, and start running, naked, toward Milo's. Milo's was around the corner from our house, and up two blocks. Once he made it all the way there wearing nothing but cowboy boots and a red plastic fireman's hat.

In our neighborhood, nearly every house had a family and children. As Jamie and I left the house, letting the screen door to the mudroom clatter shut behind us, we saw kids on every lawn and on our quiet street, floating in the grassy, humid haze of that Ohio afternoon. They were playing kickball, and smear-the-queer, and the ball kept smacking the asphalt, making that tinny, echoey sound. The Murrays, who lived across the street from us, had eleven kids. (I was best friends with Emily, one of the middle daughters, and her brother Dave was in my class.) If you counted all the kids in our neighborhood, there were easily thirty of us. The lawns were dark green, the pavement was hot, and my Dr. Scholl's clicked as I walked.

We probably looked pretty stupid that day, Jamie in his cape and face paint, me in Chad's Incredible Hulk shirt and my own pale green shorts (I cared about matching, like Mama) and my Dr.

Scholl's. I was conscious that I wasn't exotic like Mama. I had freckles and light-brown hair, and ordinary legs that weren't long, and it bothered me because I thought Mama would have liked it better if I looked more like her, as Chad did—olive-skinned with dark hair. But I took more after Dad, and so did Jamie. Jamie was an eccentric kid. He sang Tom Lehrer songs that he'd found somewhere, and when he wasn't dressed as Starchild, he wore other costumes. For two years, when he was a toddler, he'd insisted on wearing an old man's fedora and horn-rimmed glasses with no lenses, and my parents humored him, even though the sight of a tiny kid with pacifier, hat, and glasses was absurd, not to say pathetic. Once, when my father dropped him off at nursery school, he heard one of the mothers say, "Oh, that poor child," seeing Jamie looking like a midget old man, and thinking he had a terrible illness.

At Milo's, Jamie and I got Styrofoam cups of weak coffee with lots of creamer and sugar from the big urn that they kept filled for customers, and then we stood in line to get a free bone from the butcher for Scooter. At the register, Jamie stole a grape Big Daddy chewing-gum stick while I was buying Mama's cigarettes, but I didn't find out until we were halfway home, and then I just scolded him and took half. When we got back home, Dad had finally come up from his study in the basement and was vacuuming, and Mama was in the kitchen, pounding chicken breasts to make into chicken Kiev. She'd set one place at the long mahogany table, with the fancy china, silver, and crystal, so I set the other seven places in the same way, and ironed the napkins, as I knew I was supposed to do. When I finished, Mama had already made the chicken Kievs, which were perched round and plump in a roasting pan, soaking up breadcrumbs, and she asked me to de-stem the spinach for the spinach and pine nut salad while she made everything else—vegetable terrines, a pilaf, and dessert oranges whose peels she cut into basket shapes, filling them with orange wedges and Bavarian cream. Dad put on Linda Ronstadt, so much cheerier than the Baez, and Mama looked contented, absorbed in her menu.

She sent Dad and me into the garden in the backyard to pick zinnias for the centerpieces, and cherry tomatoes for the hors d'oeuvres. The damp, cushioning grass underfoot, the fresh-black-earth scent of the fertile soil, the buzz of neighboring lawnmowers, the plasticky shower of water from the sprinkler reassured me that what I had told her was true: everything was all right.

I cut an armful of zinnias while Dad plucked tomatoes from the vines, gently dropping them into a basket. I felt proud to be useful. Then Chad walked out of the garage door into the backyard, back from the pool, and asked Dad to play a game of H-O-R-S-E. "In a second, Chaddo," Dad said, and Chad waited while Dad moved down the row. "I'll finish the tomatoes," I told Dad, feeling noble, and he thanked me, and the two of them went off to play basketball. I carried in everything through the porch, through the dining room into the kitchen, and Mama praised me as the sounds of the basketball slapping on the drive came in through the window. "I can't believe it," she said aggrievedly. "It's six o'clock, the guests will be here before you know it, and he's playing basketball. Pete!" she called out through the kitchen window, and Dad guiltily came in and went to work, cleaning something for Mama.

The Blairs got there first—Mr. Blair was as big as Paul Bunyan, and rowdy, Mrs. Blair skinny and little like the mother hen who dotes on Junior in the cartoons. She brought celery sticks and cheese, something I thought Mama would find aggravating, since the menu was French; and then Andrew and his brother Paul came in and asked if I would play H-O-R-S-E with them and Chad in the driveway. The Elliotts came next with whiny Isaac and his older brother Luke, who was eight. Isaac went upstairs to play with Jamie, and Luke joined us by the backboard. Mrs. Elliott reminded me a little of the picture of Joan Baez on the cover of the *Diamonds & Rust* album—slender and angelic-looking, a peasant blouse and no makeup, long, rustling hair. Except that she smoked a lot, and had a Great Lakes accent. Mr. Elliott was Evel-Knievely. At the last party, I'd seen him throw his wineglass at the wall, I don't know why he did that. And then the Courtenays arrived, suave and tall, with their sons, who were close to Jamie's age, and the Webers, with their daughter Valerie, who was a year younger than me, and really creative; she liked to cut pictures out of *Vogue* and *Mademoiselle* and make collages. We practiced doing the hand jive from *Grease* together. Once her dad found us together laughing hysterically, and drinking Sprite on ice with lime wedges, and she convinced him we were drinking gin and tonics (we weren't). But I really didn't know her, because we lived in different neighborhoods, so were in different schools. I assumed she was popular, because my brother Chad had a crush on her, and he was popular.

As for me, I was not popular, but I was not a nerd, because the popular girls asked me to give them Bubble Yum, which meant they knew I existed. That spring, in gym class, a popular cheerleader, Mandy Callahan, had borrowed my backup gym outfit—green Adidas-type shorts with a white stripe, and matching green-and-yellow shirt. I was thrilled. And Paige Colker, a sporty cheerleader in my class who looked like Kristy McNichol and lived a few blocks away, had been coaching me all summer, trying to teach me a cheer routine so I could make the squad. She said I looked like a cheerleader, and that if I could just make the team, I would be popular. She coached me endlessly while we listened to a Meatloaf album over and over, *Bat Out of Hell*. Every time I tried to follow her instructions and do a round-off, I'd come out of the spin and land with a floor-shaking thud on my knees. It was so depressing. But I did think that, if I made cheerleader, Andrew might "go" with me. So I kept at it.

And then it was dinnertime. We kids sat in the kitchen with only the second-best china, but with the adult food, minus the wine, while the adults laughed and talked loudly in the dining room. When we'd finished, the adults were still eating. The little kids followed Jamie upstairs to his room to listen to Kiss and take turns on his ukulele, while we big kids went into the TV room and started watching *Happy Days*, only we ignored it and passed around Chad's electronic football game until we got mad because we couldn't all play it at once, so Andrew stuck it high on a shelf. I thought that was very mature of him. ("Ma-TOOR," Granny always pronounced that word, which cracked Mama up.) Andrew suggested we play Murder in the Dark, and everyone got into that immediately, and I called Emily Murray from across the street, and the Nilsson kids, so we would have a big-enough group. I got Andrew a notepad, and he ripped up the little slips of paper and scrawled ciphers on them—BJ for Big Judge, LJ for Little Judge, C for all the "Citizens," and X for the Murderer—and folded them, and then we all trooped out to the indigo-dark front yard, gathering under the hovering oaks, under the night-song of the cicadas. I just got a "C," and so we milled around cautiously, clustering together to avoid being singled out by the Murderer, bumping into each other amid the forsythia, the bushes, the oaks, the maples. Only, when Andrew drew near me, privately, by the mulberry tree that edged the Reinholds' yard, I didn't try to back away, I thought maybe he was going to kiss me, but then he killed me which was so predictable.

I looked back toward the house, as I waited for Andrew to kill everyone else and for the trial to begin. Through the picture window, I saw the grown-ups like silhouettes on a screen, dancing, smoking, laughing, wine goblets raised like torches in their hands. I wondered if Mr. Elliott would throw another one. They were dancing loosely together, not partnered off, just kind of mingled, I'd see one take another's hand, then let the hand fall, and soon the hand would clasp another's. They'd opened the front door, probably for air, to let in the cool of the night, and a song leaked out, lulling, hopeful: *"Don't let the past remind us of what we are not now."* Mr. Elliott said something that made Mrs. Blair and Mr. Courtenay double over laughing. Little Isaac Elliott padded into the room in his pajamas, crying, and Mrs. Elliott led him away, but she came right back and draped her arm around Mama, and Dad poured them both more wine, and the three of them danced in a ring.

At school that fall, I didn't make cheerleader, and Andrew asked Mandy Callahan, not me, to sit by him on the class hayride, and from then on they were going together. I sat instead between my friends Kate and Sophie, inconsolable. Another boy *had* asked me to sit by him on the hayride—our class pariah, a ballet dancer who did pliés and breathing exercises in the corridors, and was constantly being given swirlies by the jocks. I was kind to him in homeroom; but it was one thing to be humane and another to be humiliated, so I said no. Luckily, a non-disastrous, cute nerd asked me to the fall mixer, so I didn't feel like a total social failure in eighth grade. Even if I didn't have a Bobby.

I never found out who Mama was crying over that summer, if there even was anyone in particular, when she listened to Joan Baez. But I did find a Bobby of my own one day. An unkeepable man, whose existence felt preordained to me. I rushed to accept the disappointment his eyes promised, to redeem the riches of a loss I could hoard for the rest of my life, and burnish. For years, then decades, with him, then without him, I avoided the men who might have remade with me the families, households, gardens of our childhoods. After all, I'd known a house like that, filled with friends and children, on a green-lawned street; and I'd seen that, for my mother, it was a trap for regret. I did not want to build a trap like that for my grown-up self. Too late, I saw that love doesn't need a picket fence to catch and climb and entangle the heart. Today, I live in an apartment, in a city without lawns. But any time I close my eyes, I can re-enter that Cape Cod house in Ohio, left behind so long ago. It's still alive with voices and shadows, laughter and tears, still peopled with the ghosts of my history. My own Bobby haunts the TV room now, hovering amid the gold and ivory curtains, above the old wooden stereo, summoned by Joan's lament.

He still calls me on the phone, from time to time, and whenever he does, I crumple.

I don't play *Diamonds & Rust* anymore; it makes my throat clutch, my eyes dampen. But when I do hear it, by accident, I don't turn it off. Listening to those familiar, plangent strains, I fall back into the arms of Mama and Joan and my seventies childhood. A strange pride steals over me as the music plays. I had shared in its heartbreak before I knew what heartbreak was; now I recognized that the sorrows of the woman who sang and the woman who wept were trophies: relics of the battles of their undefended, undefeated hopes. To have consoled them would have been a theft—from them, from me. In that questing, tender, keening music, I seem to hear the voice of all women: loving, striving; needing to give; needing to be taken from.

guides

Cake

Jenni Quilter

n the fifth century B.C., in southern Italy, there lived a philosopher called Parmenides, who believed that ontological pluralism—the notion that our existence is made up of many moments—was a misapprehension. Parmenides thought that our existence was a single unchanging reality, in which the passing of time, space, and motion was an illusion. According to him, milk might sour, and loved ones might die, but the world was actually continuous, indivisible. We live in a world in which we are all simultaneously unborn, alive, and dead. Parmenides is with us, and we are and were with him.

It's easier to understand Parmenides' sense of indivisibility if you imagine Italy in summer. There, the senses are sympathetic to an unchanging reality; the days have a rhythm, the pulse of a sleeping heart. Olive trees, sunshine, water; the sound of the wind in the leaves. Insects cry out, clinging to the bark. We live within a oneness of comprehension, where everything—even the things we have not yet experienced—is still inside our horizon line of understanding. We may not be able to see this, but that doesn't mean it doesn't exist.

All of this is nonsense on some level, but, these days, I am starting to sense a sphericity in me. Right now it is very slight. I feel it on the days I write in cafés in New York City. There will be three, ten, fifteen people there. A few have laptops. Others sit in twos, talking. Sunny dialectic; they're telling stories to each other. One is dressed in nurse's scrubs, and a second's father has just died. A third wears very large hoop earrings shaped into hearts. A woman sitting at the bar has a flock of starlings tattooed on her back, which are mostly hidden by her shirt. The fan is turning and the Smiths are playing—that moaning voice, Cassandra in the body of a man. Out on the street, people walk by in the soft light, inspecting their phones. When you become hyperaware, your sense of predestination rises like sap. These people belong to me. I am newly compassionate; this is my sphere, for better or worse. It takes an infinity to walk to the bathroom.

You could call it a slowing. You could also call it an adult thing, Parmenides' sphere, when you start to sense an inevitability to the shape of your existence. Olives, water, wine. A girl sits down and tells a boy that nobody likes a man-child. I could go to a different café, could come back here on another day and though the details—the food, customers, weather, and song—would be different, the feeling wouldn't have changed. I am sensing a thickening tradition in my own life, a kind of hardening. The plates of my experience are fusing together. I am living within my own horizon line, and I have not departed from it for some time.

On March 8, 2014, Flight MH370 took off from Kuala Lumpur airport. It was supposed to land in Beijing, but less than an hour after takeoff, the communication transponder was manually turned off. Just before that, Malaysian radar tracked the plane turning abruptly left, deviating from its northerly flight path and heading out over the Gulf of Thailand.

It took less than seven hours for the media to pick up the story. Everyone assumed the plane had been hijacked, but as the hours passed, no terrorist group came forward to claim responsibility. One morning stretched into one day. None of the neighboring countries had spotted the plane on their radar systems. There were no cell-phone calls from passengers. That first night stretched into two, then three, then more.

In that first week, MH370's disappearance was *the* story to follow; experts in aviation, satellite, terrorism, and Southeast Asian geopolitical ambition speculated endlessly on TV about why and how. This talk was all anyone had, because the plane refused to materialize. It must have landed (its fuel would have lasted only until midday of the first day), but without any contrary information, the plane kept on flying in people's minds. The television show *Lost* didn't help. Neither did the sense that the world seemed too small to lose a giant plane. Satellite tracking is ubiquitous, our digital handshakes instinctive and incessant (I must register on a satellite hundreds of times of day), but still—227 passengers and 15 crewmembers had vanished into the blue, along with all of that steel and fabric and plastic, suitcases and food carts and pillows and blankets and toys and clothes. Matter vanished into thin, high, blue air.

At the time, I was using a gym to train; it was too cold outside to run. I grew up in New Zealand, and have never owned a television, so this was the first time I'd really encountered the phenomenon of an American twenty-four-hour news cycle. As each day passed, even with the sound off, I found it harder and harder to watch the monitors suspended from the ceiling. The media couldn't bear to look away. They reported on their not reporting.

There was an abstract force to the extremity of this feeling, a kind of pure aversion. On waking, my first thought was whether they had found out what had happened during the night, but I was always reluctant to turn on the radio; I knew that finding out would not be as painful as being told that, yet again, no one knew. My gait felt off. I kept on tripping on the treadmill. It wasn't a paradox, but it felt like one: the crunching sensation of the mind as it persists in a belief that can no longer be true.

Parmenides' lover was (reputedly) Zeno of Elea, another philosopher. You might recognize his name because Zeno's paradoxes are one of the few pieces of Greek philosophy that persist in popular culture today. People remember the gist of them: a space—a football field, an arrow and target—and talk about moving from one end to the other in steps, each time dividing in half the remaining distance. You can move half of the way there, they say, and then half of that, and so on and so forth. Yet because you can halve the distance an infinite number of times, it takes an infinite amount of time to reach the target. We should never get there.

Such thought experiments survive as a kind of stoner's delight, as a story told by one college student to another as they amble along St. Mark's Place. We're so confident in our empiricism that the scenario seems a pseudo-intellectual amusement rather than a real proposition. But Zeno was serious. That an arrow *did* hit its target suggested that those who thought the world was divisible were just plain wrong. Parmenides' thought that all was indivisible might seem difficult to swallow, but, to Zeno, so was the idea that all of our actions were truly divisible. His paradoxes were thought experiments designed to defend Parmenides. What we perceive as multiplicity was really a singularity wearing the mask of many. The thought dogs humanity. It is also the basis of spiritual belief.

What seems more surprising is that we remember Zeno's name. There is something about his thought experiments that is singular enough to name, a quality in his stories of division and non-attainment that we still find distinct. They are analogies for a thought process we seem to have a hard time explaining any other way.

In some kind of asymptotic echo of his paradox, most people trail off before they get to the end of their retelling; they're confident of the bit about division, hazy about the conclusion. Our fuzziness about the paradox is part of the paradox now. His is the line of a song that everybody in a bar somehow knows to chant, in unison, even if they don't know the singer's name. *"Oh! We're half-way there. Oh-oh!"* It may be that Zeno's paradox persists because, beyond his name, there is no single word that can accommodate that delicate sense of the finite and the infinite. Like oil and vinegar, if left alone long enough, they'll insist on separating. The paradox whisks them together.

Eight days after Flight MH370 disappeared, I flew to Los Angeles with my boyfriend and drove to Joshua Tree National Park. I had booked a cabin in the desert for five days; I wanted to write, and run outside.

One night, as we lay in bed together, looking out through a large window onto the desert, which stretched away for miles, the rocks and yucca lit by the moon, the highway lights flickering in the far distance, my boyfriend asked me to marry him. I felt something snap or spring tight in me, as real as a pulled tendon: guilt and love.

We spent the next few days talking about what marriage meant. I had no interest in being joined to another person for legal or religious reasons, but there was that romance of extremity, of settling down, of never being technically lonely again. There was the hunger for being loved so much that someone would do such a thing. Our paths had crossed rather randomly, and now there he was, whistling as he made the coffee, or standing on the porch, stretching, looking out at the mountains. I choose you. I declare something is permanent, even though I know nothing really is. The distance between yes and no seemed a chasm a foot wide and thousands of feet deep.

So we began to divide the distance up. Talk of a ring. Talk of children. Half the distance, then half again. Summoning our nerve. *I do.* Impossibility and inevitability go so well together. Walking across a room used to feel like the easiest thing, but now when I moved across the cabin, bringing him wine, taking dishes to the sink, the air seemed to crackle.

Zeno wrote approximately forty paradoxes featuring Achilles, chariot races, and tortoises (among other objects), but I'm surprised he didn't use the trembling distance between lovers.

At Joshua Tree, I followed the news on MH370, and registered the fact that two of my countrymen were on the flight. The *New Zealand Herald* published a profile of one of them, Pauly Weeks, an engineer who had been on his way to a new job in Mongolia. Just before boarding, he had texted his wife, Danica Weeks, to tell her that she and the kids were the most important things to him in the world. Since then, Danica said, she had woken every morning expecting to find Pauly lying in bed next to her. She could not shake the certainty of his weight, and so every day she had to unlearn. All of her senses told her something that could not be true. She had started writing poetry about him, rhyming couplets, which the *Herald* published.

The interview was brief, but it stuck with me. I would think about her most days when I went running along the dusty roads. It felt good to run into the desert holding nothing but my iPod. There was no track, no one else about. I kept an eye on my odometer watch, on distinctive rock piles. Cacti, sand, blue sky. I felt like a different woman: an American, who drove a car, who lived nearby, who was married. For the first time I felt like I was in my mid-thirties. Here was another future, knitting itself now, spooling itself out ahead of me: a red thread out or in. My skin was drier. My weight bounced off and onto my joints differently each time my foot hit the sand. There would be a time in which I would come to expect this man's weight in my bed too, when my sense memory might grow stronger than reason.

Ironically, neither Parmenides nor Zeno wanted us to develop a taste for such speed, such transformation. Zeno wanted to divide and divide simply in order to show the absurdity of the motion. But what seems to have lasted is not just the impossibility but also the pleasure that comes from division. How exponential the function of dividing by two is! How quickly we seem to move away from our beginning! There is a charm and terror to the sheer rate of change, to the ever-diminishing room in which we have to move, and how we can continue to move in it. One step, two steps, three—and the sky is suddenly darker, the cliff a different kind of stone. I could return to New York with a rock on my hand.

Regardless of what Zeno intended, this is part of the pleasure of the paradox now; it leans both ways, toward completion, toward dissolution. The closer you get, the more aware you are of the edges between things. That awareness is a pleasure, an acquired taste. It sets you on your tiptoes, gives you balance in any high-wire act of fatalism.

I can't remember when the disappearance of MH370 became bearable. I flew back to New York and continued teaching. The first day it was warm enough to run outside, I pulled my left piriformis, which is a small muscle deep within your ass, partially veiled by your glutes. It attaches to multiple muscle groups, including the ilia-sacral nerve. The injury turned out to be very painful. For weeks I couldn't balance my body weight on my left leg, which meant that every second step down, every time the femur pushed up into the hip socket, I felt a jolt of pain.

Online, I watched many dissection videos of left back legs, part of a flourishing sub-genre of online medical dissections. I was always looking out for the piriformis. Faceless men narrated the names of the muscles and tendons, pushing them this way and that with a silver pointer. Whenever they reached the piriformis, I felt a rush of feeling. There it was! It was like the face of a relative who doesn't recognize you on the street. Sitting at the computer, I'd raise my left cheek up off the seat and prod at the glutes, trying to part them, my fingers digging. That's what it looked like inside I'd tell myself: redder, twitchier, but just as blind, just as instinctive.

Through spring and summer, I sat in bars facing my boyfriend, drinking wine, talking through the early evening. I so wished him to know how I felt, swaying with happiness; how it felt to sweat, or exhale, to feel my tongue at the roof of my mouth, how the ring he gave me felt on my finger: gold, with a diamond that had a smear of orange at the center. I wanted him to know what the pain felt like in my ass, and how it slowly ebbed. But how could I? The impossibility of knowing another, from the inside out, from the blood and gastric juices and neural pathways, is the despair of love and the excitement of the world.

On a mathematical level, Zeno's paradoxes have been solved, and rather easily. Zeno didn't understand that we could move through an infinite set of points in a finite amount of time. He failed to separate the finite number of real things a runner has to accomplish from the infinite series of numbers we can use to describe what the runner does. Zeno was dealing with what looks infinite rather than the actual mathematical infinite.

I barely know how to treat infinity; the word mostly lingers as a trace of my eight-year-old self, discovering swearing brinkmanship. *You're infinitely worse. You're infinitely worse plus one.* But as Bertrand Russell has pointed out, we can't understand the infinite if we have "habits of mind derived from the consideration of finite numbers." Nothing is gained if "we pass its [the infinite's] terms in review one by one."

One fall day, when I read this sentence, I stopped, and took a big breath. A thought came to me, and I could not unthink it. Zeno's arrow, its clumsy impossibility, was also an analogy for a finite love that is trying to be infinite.

When knowledge arrives whole, it has a singular flash to it. For an instant, a scene is illuminated. The English philosopher Alfred C. Whitehead argued that Zeno's paradox was an attempt to isolate precisely this experience. Wesley C. Salmon summarized his point this way:

> Whitehead maintained that the physical world is an extended spatiotemporal continuum, but he believed that it came into

existence in chunks; these pieces came into being as whole entities or not at all. In retrospect they can be conceptually subdivided into parts—even infinitely many parts—but the parts do not represent entities that can come to be by themselves. An act of becoming is an indivisible unit; if you subdivide in any way the resulting parts are not smaller acts of becoming.

What I suddenly understood was that my love for this man *was* a divisible unit. In my relationship, there was no mathematical infinite. No manner how many steps I took, I still wouldn't reach him; even if I said, "I do," the arrow of my heart would keep on flying.

A future spooled back, retracted like the cord on a salad spinner. I returned the ring. I felt sick about it. I still feel sick. But the thought had the inevitability of a cake; I had made this thing, and here it was, rising in me.

The filmmaker Andrei Tarkovsky thought art was a way to comprehend the infinite, writing, "An artistic discovery occurs each time as . . . a hieroglyphic of absolute truth. It appears as a revelation, as a momentary, passionate wish to grasp intuitively and at a stroke *all* the laws of this world—its beauty and ugliness, its compassion and cruelty, its infinity and its limitations." His emphasis on the instant is in line with Whitehead's. It is an insight that cuts through rather than points at. To me, poetry does this particularly well. It crystallizes emergent thought, aims at that sensation of endless becoming. There is nothing—and then there is suddenly something, a thought, like a piece of space rock. It is no surprise to me that Danica Weeks began to write poetry as she began to mourn her lost husband. She was mourning an absoluteness.

Rather than thinking of the infinite in terms of addition, we might understand an infinite set of numbers by its characteristics; how that set of numbers operates rather than how big it is. One way to imagine this multiplicity might be to think about uncountable forms in nature like a flight of birds, a beach's worth of sand: groups of which it makes no sense to think about what happens when you add one more of that thing. The salient feature is how that group of infinity moves: how they tumble, how they separate. My problem was that I could not think or imagine how my love for this man moved.

More than a year later, I read this out loud for the first time to a group of people. It was in the evening, and we had just finished dinner. Olives, water, wine. The light was soft and warm, and I could hear my voice in their ears. As I read, I realized that all of this had become a thought experiment, a paradox to tell other people, an analogy for something else they might feel altogether. The reality of what had actually happened had begun to drift away from me. The thought had completed itself; the cake had stopped rising. Someone had found a piece of MH370 washed up on a beach on Réunion in the Indian Ocean. The details of the crash were still fuzzy, but the end was absolute. The arrow had hit the target.

The next morning, over breakfast, one of these people who had listened asked me if I thought all love was finite. "No," I said. "I don't think so. Even if I never thought about it this way before, I can imagine my feelings for others as infinite sets."

She nodded, and disagreed. "I think all love is finite," she said. But I did not ask her if she sensed Parmenides' sphericity in her own life, if there was a quality to her consciousness that persisted, which could not be divided. I suspect there is. She has that quality to her; like a statue that may have eroded over time, the acuity of her lines still springs forth: that brow, that eye. She said she was looking for a paradigm shift. She had given up her apartment, was going to stay in a different place every two months or so for the next year. She had seen a bird in her dream that she had never seen before, and, having looked it up on Google, she knew which country to visit. She was departing, moving, swiftly traveling into the dusk.

64

Right now I can imagine her waking in the morning, and watching the world, seeing the way people swarm and separate, rise and fall. She will notice how she isn't surprised, even when she ought to be. The shift may come, but it was already part of her. It is silly that I see the infinite in someone who believes in the finite, and the finite in someone who so badly wants the infinite: as silly as a racing tortoise, or a chariot that never arrives. The clumsiness turns out to be vestigial, a tail I cannot shake. The sphericity, a hidden muscle, a hidden intuition, hardens and grows.

Mr. Rochester and Mr. Matthiessen: On Mentors (and Romantic Confusion)

Sharon Guskin

My model of love when I was a young woman came from *Jane Eyre*; I was looking for Mr. Rochester, that figure, craggy and charismatic, who could see into Jane and appreciate her when no one else could. I held onto this notion for years, despite the fact that the world seemed disinclined to hand over any Rochesters. High school and college boys, trembling and sardonic, yes, a few; but no larger-than-life romantic figures on which to attach my passionate feelings.

Then came Mr. Matthiessen.

I was twenty-two by then, finishing my senior year at college after a year spent teaching at a refugee camp in Thailand, from which I had returned disoriented and adrift. My parents were splitting up. My class had graduated while I was away, and the friends I still had on campus were moving through their last year with alarming drive and ambition. I had loved teaching the Lao and Cambodian children at the camp, but it had not clarified anything for me regarding my own future. And I was unnerved by the contrast between my two locales: that unmoored city of dust and earth, where my classrooms were made of bamboo and blue tarp, versus the university's gothic grandeur and solid, stone-cold belief in itself.

Distractedly, I picked my courses. I'd always liked writing, had wished to be a writer as a child, so I applied for a well-known visiting writer's fiction and nonfiction classes, sending off a few pages describing a visit to Bangkok's red-light district. Perhaps something of my confusion and loneliness bled through strongly enough to summon the teacher's interest; in any case, I got into the fiction class, so that's the way I went.

Peter Matthiessen was in his sixties then, and his face was weathered, but his handsomeness was intact. He was lean, high-cheekboned, erect of carriage, altogether remarkable-looking; you couldn't separate his looks from his presence, or at least I couldn't. His vitality was amazing and manifested as much in stillness as in motion. He came into the class and nodded formally at me, blue eyes bright, a faint smile on his face. It is possible that he nodded at everyone. Probably he did. But I can't tell you for sure, because when he nodded at me I saw a spark of recognition leap from his eyes, and my breath caught in my chest. For the duration of the semester I didn't breathe again.

To this day I have little recollection of the other courses I must have taken or anything else I might have done during those months. I lived for his nod. When I wasn't in class with him or doing my work, I read his books, marveling at the wild, solitary joy of the isolated main character at the end of one of his novels, or the way, "laid naked to the sun and sky, he felt himself open like a flower." I read his most famous book of nonfiction, *The Snow Leopard*, and though I didn't understand much of its eastern mysticism, its feeling resonated through me like the sound of a bell.

I wasn't foolish enough to think that anything might actually happen between us. Peter was married and my teacher and at least forty years older and a Zen Buddhist priest besides. In our interactions in class there was no tinge of inappropriate interest on his part; he seemed to regard me with fondness and mild amusement. Nor was I his favorite; there was another writer in the class, now one of my closest friends, whose brilliant prose style met his high standards for boldness, and she was the one he recommended for an award. I loved him anyway: fiercely, hopelessly, the way I loved then.

Even though he came into town only on the day he taught, the air seemed always imbued with his presence, as if he were watching me. I spent hours wondering if the connection was imagined and deciding against it; for surely there was something there, surely he felt something, too? I walked around cupping this spark in my hands like a precious flame that might go out at any moment. I may have been obsessed but I felt awake.

And I wrote. I was on fire. I began a novel about a girl working at a refugee camp who fell in love (impossibly) with a handsome Cambodian monk who just happened to have very high cheek-bones and an erect carriage. I wrote pages and pages. I called the novel *Samsara,* which I vaguely understood as the Buddhist wheel of life and death; it had a pretty sound. What did Peter think of my novel? I can't imagine that my ardor escaped his notice, or the similarities between my Zen teacher and the monk in the plot. But he merely looked at me with that half-smile of his and wrote at the bottom of my pages in pencil: "I like the feel of it. Keep going!"

I visited him during office hours; he sat behind an empty desk, its only occupant the bottom half of a peeled orange.

"So. I was wondering if you had any more suggestions for my novel," I said.

"No." He looked at me calmly.

A moment of silence ensued that he apparently wasn't interested in breaking.

There was nothing else to say, so I told him the truth.

"I want to be a writer. But I'm . . . insecure." I mumbled the last word, wincing.

He laughed. "All writers are insecure." He leaned across the desk. "I'm insecure."

I sat there, stunned. I'd been fishing, of course; I'd wanted him to say something about my work or me that would put an end to my insecurity forever. Instead, I got a challenge. Of course you're insecure. Now what are you going to do?

I kept going. The girl and the monk ran off together and began a doomed, *Jane Eyre*–infused romance. The class finished. On the last day, walking out of the building toward the pizza place where Peter was taking us all as an end-of-semester treat, he mentioned that I could send him my novel when I had made it the best it could be, and that if he liked it he'd recommend it but he'd be honest in his response, I had to be ready for that. "I am," I said vehemently. Some knowledge passed across his face. "Yes, I see that about you." I looked up at him, utterly dazzled, and he spontaneously leaned over and kissed me on the cheek. "I'll kiss all the girls," he said afterward, and probably he did.

In the Matthiessen-less days and months that followed, a flame persisted, a sense of possibility onto which I affixed his name. I traveled to Spain and France with my sister and felt his presence as if he were watching me among the Pyrenees. I wrote about him in my diary: "Peter's like a bright place inside."

I never sent him my work. Nothing ever seemed good enough to share with him. I kept writing, though, for more than twenty years. I finished that novel and wrote another one, though I didn't find a publisher for either. As I kept going, trying to get better despite my insecurity, I sometimes thought of his belief in making the effort to get it right. When recently I began practicing Buddhism myself, at first a little, and then a bit more, and finally with whole-hearted feeling, an inner brightness, I realized something about my love for Peter and that wave of emotion I had assumed was both hopeless and romantic. It was neither.

Imagine you are a twenty-two-year-old woman experiencing a

powerful sense of possibility, and the conduit for all this feeling is a handsome, renowned, extraordinary man: how could one not mistake this feeling for romantic love, which our society tells us is the most powerful emotion there is? Yet the difference matters.

Of course, there are teachers who might have taken advantage of this situation. And had Peter been one of them, this story might have been sordid, or it might have been more exciting and heartbreaking. But in either case it would have been less important. By Mr. Rochestering Peter Matthiessen I had perceived the link between us as fleeting, romantic, and disappointing, when in reality the influence of this brief connection turned out to be as lasting and as encouraging as I could imagine. This man was a high priest of literature and the first spiritually present person I'd ever met. He committed fully to both paths in his own life, and in the darkness of mine he lit both sparks.

A couple of years ago I visited him with that friend from the class. He showed us the Zendo he'd built on his property; I told him I'd started to meditate, though I hadn't yet found my teacher, and he laughed a little at what he called the "softness" of my approach. By then I knew that my third crack at writing a novel was going to be published, but still it didn't seem ready to share with him. Besides, he was sick. He'd been traveling in Mongolia to research wildlife, staying in a yurt, and had realized with surprise that he felt tired. When he returned he went to the doctor and discovered he had leukemia. He was eighty-five. He was still writing, finishing his last novel.

A year later, he died and soon after appeared to me in a dream, showing up abruptly, with a questioning look. "I didn't send you anything because nothing seemed good enough," I said to him. He nodded impatiently. "And I became a writer in your class," I added. He laughed. "I'm not surprised," he said. And he was gone.

The search may begin with a restless feeling, as if one were being watched. One turns in all directions and sees nothing. Yet one senses that there is a source for this deep restlessness; and the path that leads there is not a path to a strange place, but the path home. ("But you are home," cries the Witch of the North. "All you have to do is wake up!") . . . The holy grail is what Zen Buddhists call our own "true nature": Each man is his own savior after all.

—Peter Matthiessen, *The Snow Leopard*

In a Woman's Kingdom

Sheila Kohler

That summer, on my arrival at the train station in Florence, Madame, as we call her, is waiting eagerly for me, smiling broadly on the quay, waving gaily. *"Eccola!"* she calls out triumphantly. She is obviously delighted to see me, though I am soon to discover not entirely for the reasons I expect. Short and rotund, her white hair fanned back from her broad shiny face, she wears tight-fitting dark clothes over her corsets and totters forward daintily on narrow ankles and high heels.

Beside her, I am happy to see, is my older sister. I have not seen her pink cheeks or blond curls since she left home in December, and I have missed her. She gives me a glad hug. "You made it!" she says exultantly, referring to my long solo voyage from Johannesburg.

Madame interrupts our effusions to introduce me to the girl beside my sister, who stands there mysteriously, looking bored. She wears dark clothes and a sort of superior smirk on her long pale face as she offers me her cold hand. She looks to be about my sister's age, seventeen, and is English, I gather from the accent. "This is Penelope, she's going to spend the summer with us too," Madame informs me proudly, as though Penelope were some sort of royalty.

Then Madame grandly hails a porter and a *carozza*, a carriage, which to my amazement is to take us to her apartment on Via Guicciardini. We are to arrive in style. Though I have ridden in a rickshaw in South Africa on holiday in Durban, I have never been in a horse-drawn carriage. It seems extremely grand to me, almost part of a fairy tale.

The horse trots smartly, carrying us all, with my luggage piled behind us, down the narrow street to a palazzo which is not far from the Pitti. My sister sits beside me pointing out the places of interest. She has already matriculated from our boarding school and has been attending Madame C.'s finishing school in Florence since the beginning of the year, which is 1956.

"Finishing schools," I understand, are supposed to be places where foreign languages, deportment, flower arranging, and a smattering of history of art and music are taught to young girls so that they can find wealthy husbands who will support them in the style they are accustomed to, though, of course, they are not advertised as such. What I will learn there is quite different.

My sister seems already to have learned a thing or two. She seems altered, other, removed from me, now part of this strange new world and able to describe its beauties in Italian, which seems almost as if she were singing in an opera, magical: *Ecco! Il Duomo, Santa Maria del Fiore*—Brunelleschi's dome, she sings out as we go by. She shows me the Ponte Vecchio, Cellini's statue, the Arno, the great dark river running through the city. She points out the passage the Medici used to go from one palace to the next in order to avoid the populace.

I gaze, stunned into silence, hardly able to answer her eager questions about Mother, our home, the old Zulu servant, John, whom we both love.

I have never been to Italy before. Indeed, I have only once left South Africa to travel to England by boat with my sister and my mother, after my father died when I was seven years old. It rained most of the time and I found it cold and damp, and Buckingham

Palace was not the palace I had imagined from picture books, perched with its turrets and flags on a hill.

Here, in this hot, bustling, brilliantly lit place, in the middle of our winter, I feel I am dreaming. After my long, solitary voyage, and now riding like a princess sitting close beside my sister and facing Madame and this strange reserved girl, I feel distanced from myself, a stranger in a strange place, a girl in someone else's life.

As in a film or a book, I see myself from afar, as I am to do so often in my life, a voice in my head, a secret sharer recording my own existence: a young girl in a rumpled navy linen suit, a straw hat, dark rings beneath her slanting eyes.

The shadow of Penelope's hovering presence increases the strangeness of the situation. She scowls rudely at Madame, who is making grand efforts to promote some sort of conversation between the three of us.

Penelope comes from a wonderful old house in Sussex. She knows all the English aristocracy, Madame says with breathless admiration, inviting us, too, to admire or so it seems to me.

Why is this girl—obviously our reluctant companion—here? In contrast to my gaze of wonder, she looks infinitely bored by the spectacle and somewhat skeptical of my sister's comments and chatter about the scene. Her haughty stare seems to say, "Just you wait, you fools. Obviously you understand nothing at all," as though she knows something we do not, a shameful, disreputable secret which lies behind the ancient bustling cobblestone streets, the narrow pavements, the sliver of bright moon already in the still blue sky, Madame's smooth, broadly smiling face.

On our arrival in the dark hall of the apartment, with its heavy furniture and ornate round mirror on the wall, Penelope leans against the lintel of the door and watches us with her sarcastic, know-it-all half-smile. I stand there surrounded by my bags on the slippery dark-red marble floor. The ancient floor slopes and makes me feel I might slip. Perhaps because of the long plane voyage, I am giddy, afraid of losing my footing. I feel as if I am on the swaying deck of a ship, as Madame asks me, "*Cherie*, did you bring Mother's travelers' checks with you as she promised me?"

I have been told to tell the truth and answer a question when asked. I nod my weary head and remember how Madame would accost our mother to tell her how lovely she looked when she came, dressed in her pearls, her organdy dresses, leghorn hats and kid gloves, to chapel at the school on Sundays. Madame, who taught us French at our boarding school in those days, would ask Mother to contribute to one or the other of her "charities," which I think Mother must have done as Madame always gave me good marks in French, which I did not deserve.

Now she sighs and explains, as though her protection were urgent, thieves hovering nearby, "Sign the travelers' checks over to me will you, dearest? It would be better for me to put them away in my safe immediately." Before I can gather my wandering wits, or think of a polite reason to refuse, she has had me sign and hand over the considerable number of travelers' checks I have brought with me. Then she smiles and tells me to have a quick shower, and to dress fast, for we are going to a concert held in the courtyard of the nearby Pitti Palace that very evening.

Alone in our room my sister remonstrates, "Why on earth did you give her all our money?" but I shrug and ask what else I could have done, and she looks at me with sympathy and sighs. "You must be exhausted," she says.

As my sister helps me unpack—I have brought heaps of fancy frocks which I will not wear—I ask her who this Penelope is and why she is here. My sister shrugs and says she is just some snobbish English girl whose mother is close friends with Madame. "I think the mother's Madame's girlfriend," she whispers mysteriously.

"What do you mean?" I ask, but before she can explain we are both called forth for the concert.

So there I sit, in the courtyard of the Pitti Palace, that first evening in Florence, listening to Vivaldi's *Four Seasons* and the sound of the fountain playing, which come to me in my jet-lagged state like a dream. The voyage from Johannesburg, an endless one in those days, made alone, with several stops on the African continent and Europe, makes me feel I have left myself behind with Mother and John and that this surely is someone else, a stranger sitting here gazing up at the sliver of moon in the still blue sky.

Giddily, I stare up at the stars and a silver moon, my heavy head falling forward onto my chest from time to time, as if I am half-dead with fatigue, and then jolting back upward in awe and amazement at the strangeness of it all: the ancient walls, the musicians in black tie, Vivaldi's *Four Seasons*, the elegant Italians in their jewels around me, the moonlit sky above me, all the beauty of the scene. I keep glancing at my sister's smooth, oval face for reassurance but even she looks altered, other, years older than I. And where, I wonder, is Penelope, who has not deigned to accompany us on this outing?

Our days slip by fast in an almost continuous daze. We rise late, as adolescents do, and are left to our own devices, lounging lazily in our pajamas in the bright mornings in the rented rooms of the old palazzo. We lie around reading our books and sipping great cups of coffee latte in our pajamas, or slipping out into the street for coffee and a brioche, trying to avoid the stares and calls of Italian men.

My sister and I share a room, and Penny's is down the corridor next to Madame's. The walls are white and decorated with gold filigree, a little chipped in places, the ceilings and the windows high. Many of the rooms are empty as most of the girls have gone home during the summer months. Madame at this point does not have many charges on her hands to "finish."

She does not appear until lunch, when we are served great heapings of pasta or something called Florentine soup, which consists mainly of bread in broth, all of this accompanied by large glasses of wine which Madame herself pours from vast, round, straw-covered vats. For some reason—I have never seen this done before or again—she mixes the red and the white together in our glasses, a toxic brew. "Drink up!" Madame exhorts us, though we are not accustomed to drinking wine at meals and certainly not at lunch. My sister and I do as we are told, my sister's cheeks flushing bright red, her blue eyes shining and glazed.

"No inhibitions!" Madame C. orders us at these long, heavy luncheons, as though we could control the unconscious. "I don't want any inhibitions here!" she says, imperiously waving an arm around, as though inhibitions might lurk in the corners of the room, like goblins, ready to pounce. Perhaps Madame has read Freud or one of his disciples. In any case she maintains that repression is not good for us and that we should speak freely and frankly of our most hidden feelings.

We gaze at one another blankly or giggle a little, half-drunk on this strange mixture of wine, not knowing exactly what we are supposed to say. What is it that we are repressing?

I think of the stories Madame herself told us at school, how she would put a finger to her lips, open her dark eyes wide, and say, "Pull down the shutters, girls, close the windows," so that none of the teachers in the staff room could hear the "lesson" she was giving.

She would then ask which ones of us had our period, which she called the "curse." There would be a few moments of shocked silence while we stared wide-eyed at one another; then a few hands would timorously wave in the air. She would commiserate, telling us that she would have such terrible cramps as a girl that she would pass out.

She told us of the punishments meted out by the nuns in her convent school in Brussels, where her fingers were rapped with a ruler or she was made to kneel for hours in the corner of the room for some minor misdemeanor, or she might go on to tell us, even more thrillingly, how she had been tortured during the war. Where or why this had happened was not made clear.

Are we supposed to come up with a story of this sort? She described how they had removed her fingernails, plunged her into freezing and then boiling water. "The women were much braver than the men," she maintained stoutly, but confessed more credibly, perhaps, that she would have told them anything she knew if she had known anything to tell them, which she apparently did not.

Is this the sort of thing that is repressed? How could one know? We are vaguely afraid what she suggests might be something sexual. I think of how I have let eager boys kiss me in the dark of hot, tangled gardens and felt vague longings for them. But I also, once, let my best friend hold me in the dark of the dormitory and fondle my new breasts. What do I prefer: the hard, thrusting bodies of young boys or the soft, yielding gentleness of a girl?

At luncheon, am I supposed to speak of certain furtive desires I have felt in the warm nights, moments of solitary pleasure in the dark?

Only Penny dares rebel, turning down the drink, the food, and any sharing of furtive feelings. She says the wine makes her too sleepy and the pasta fat. Sometimes she even refuses to attend the long, hot meal. Instead she eats fruit—blood-red oranges which she peels in great quantities directly into the wastepaper basket in her room, the odor of oranges lingering in the corridor.

I am increasingly intrigued and awed by her independence, her ability to argue with a grownup, her blatant rudeness, though my sister is not as impressed. Staring at me askance, she maintains Penny is simply "full of herself and stuck up. I can't understand what you see in her."

Or perhaps Madame, with her imperatives, has other more devious aims.

"Come here, Sheila," she calls me one afternoon and ushers me into her shuttered study with its daybed, striped cashmere shawl, and wide Louis XVI leather-topped desk before the creeper-covered window. She tells me she often spends her sleepless nights in this room, doing her accounts or writing letters. "I hardly sleep at all," she maintains, putting her plump fingers to her brow, though as far as we can see she never rises before noon. Then she stares at me with her piercing gaze and says, "I have something for you," turns her back on me, and runs those fingers over the books in her bookcase. What does she want to give me?

I stare at her barrel-like shape and wonder what brought this middle-aged woman all the way out to our isolated boarding school in the middle of the veldt where I have been a boarder since I was ten years old.

Was she perhaps, like many of the foreign staff, avoiding a troubled past in that isolated place? As far as I can gather, her main claim to fame is that she married a member of a princely Italian family, and she therefore maintains she is a princess. Probably, though, she has no right to the title, having married the younger son.

Was she fired from our boarding school by our headmistress, who had perhaps discovered some of her many indiscretions, despite the closed windows?

And why has our mother entrusted both her daughters, aged fifteen and seventeen, as well as our entire travel allowance for the year, to Madame's care?

Madame says, "I think you might find this interesting," before taking a thick book with a dark cover out of the bookcase that lines one of the walls. I thank her, wondering what dull tome she is obliging me to read, and take the volume back to my room.

I turn the pages fast, with amazement, titillated, enthralled, and shocked. The book is a famous lesbian novel—surely an odd choice to give a fifteen-year-old pupil in one's charge—called *The Well of Loneliness*, by Radclyffe Hall, first published in 1928.

As I read I wonder why Madame has chosen this book. Is Madame a lesbian? I remember how she would go on walks with us across the veldt around our boarding school. We would visit Sir George Farrar's grave, which lay at some distance from the white gabled buildings. Madame would pant and struggle along beside us on her narrow ankles. "Just put one finger on my back, to help me up the hill, just one finger," she would tell us.

And more importantly, I think as I read, is it possible that Madame has understood that I must really be a lesbian too?

After all, I am not sure if I am really in love with any of the eager, sweaty boys who held me so fiercely in their arms and kissed me in the tangled back gardens of Johannesburg. Might I rather be in love with a girl, perhaps even this mysterious, disdainful Penny with her pale white skin who seems so superior, who ignores all of us, or, if she deigns to speak with us, coaxed by Madame, corrects our South African English?

"You don't say *lounge* but *drawing room*," or "It's not called a *takkie* but a *sandshoe*," she tells us in her beautiful, clear English accent, her gaze distant, distracted, and haughty.

Perhaps I find the reason for Madame's choice, and indeed the reason for our presence there that summer, while wandering around her study one morning. Up earlier than anyone else, I dare to wander into Madame's *sanctum sanctorum*. There I find a half-written letter lying lit up by the early morning sun through the open window. I am already a budding writer. I keep an imaginary diary about meeting boys on the beach and swimming naked in the surf, which my mother discovers and takes for reality. Ever curious, looking for intrigue and answers to my many questions, I am irresistibly drawn to peep at the page to see who Madame could be writing to in her solitary life.

The letter is addressed in English to "My dearest, dearest beloved." Of course I read on with interest. Is it possible that this stout middle-aged teacher with her white hair and oily skin could have a beloved? The letter, not really to my surprise, is a passionate appeal to another woman. "I long for you in my wild nights," she writes to someone who I gradually understand from the context can only be Penny's mother. All of this adds to the bored and recalcitrant Penny's charms. I decide I want to whisper to her, "I long for you in my wild nights."

After lunch, rather than taking us to see any of the famous churches or the museums with their Madonnas by Raphael or Andrea del Sarto, or Michelangelo's sculpture of David or even the Tuscan towns around Florence, Madame takes us to her elegant club, which lies in a large oak-shaded garden with blue and white agapanthus growing under the trees and a long blue pool. In our demi-inebriated state, none of us, not even the proud Penelope, protests. Instead we sprawl sleepily in our bikinis on the grass in the sun beside the pool, whispering to one another as we might just as easily do in South Africa. I stare at Penny's smooth white skin. "She's such a pretty girl, isn't she?" Madame says encouragingly to me.

Madame stretches out near us in the shade in a deck chair, in a striped dress, her plump, short legs apart, her feet dangling. She keeps us entertained and enthralled by a running commentary on the young men who pass us by, pointing out the mysterious and interesting parts of their anatomies—"Look at the way he is staring at you and swelling in his bathing suit," she says as some strapping Italian youth lingers nearby, caressing us with his dark regard. Madame explains how men's parts expand like flowers in the sun in the proximity of our feminine charms. We listen, appalled and fascinated and half-drunk with wine, warm air, and one another's company.

Later, Madame takes the three of us on a voyage. Penny's expenses for the voyage, indeed, for the entire summer, I believe, as well as Madame's, of course, are paid for by our travelers' checks. I am happy to have Penny accompany us, even to pay for her, though I can see she comes along reluctantly and also that she increasingly gets on my sister's nerves. I feel sorry for her. Penny speaks occasionally of her own family and confides that she misses them—there is a little brother, I believe, or perhaps a sister, and her mother, of course, though she never explains why she has been banished for the summer. Is it simply an economic decision on her mother's part? A free summer in Italy? Or perhaps she has other lovers. No one mentions Penny's father.

By train we go to Venice and then take a taxi from the station. When the taxi comes to a stop, unable to venture any further because of the canals, Madame tells the driver to continue. When he says he cannot, she shouts, "Avanti! Io sono la Principessa C!"

The man tells her in no uncertain terms that he doesn't give a fig who she is, that he can go no further, and we are obliged to get out and get a gondola to take us and our luggage to our hotel. I have a photo of us in a gondola which is probably sent to Penny's mother as well as our own, with Madame reclining next to Penny and smiling benevolently, my sister and me opposite them.

After Venice we go to the island of Giglio, which means "lily" in Italian. The place is quite wild and primitive, and we spend much of our time on the white beach. It is, surely, an odd destination for young girls who have never been to Italy and who have come to study the language and the culture. Why are we not taken to Rome or Milan or even Assisi? Perhaps because Giglio and particularly our hotel is inexpensive, and Madame is continuing with our "education," or rather the furthering of her plans.

Most of the day she leaves us on the beach, where local boys try to approach us. The superior Penny, to our surprise, is friendly or anyway willing to flirt, and even to let the boys buy us *gelati* or pizzas which she enjoys and which we cannot get at our hotel.

At the hotel, the food is poor. Over some sort of seaweed soup, Madame mainly addresses the conversation to my sister and Penny. She speaks of their "coming out" in London during the season and their presentation to the queen. She is planning a grand party they could give on that occasion.

"You two could do it together. It would be so much more fun that way, and, of course, Penny knows so many interesting people," she says encouragingly. "Who knows whom you might meet, my dear. Perhaps a handsome lord!" she says to my sister, opening her dark-brown eyes.

Though I encourage my sister in this endeavor, probably because I imagine it might enable me to see Penny again, I realize even then that what Madame has in mind is Mother paying for the coming-out party for Penny, whose family, though they have the necessary aristocratic connections, is apparently without any funds.

Or perhaps it is later that I become aware. At the time I am entirely fascinated by this pale girl who seems to belong in some rare, remote region. She speaks so beautifully and can quote from the English poets at length. She knows the famous lines from *Romeo and Juliet* that still give me a shiver down the spine:

> And when I shall die,
> Take him and cut him out in little stars,
> And he will make the face of heaven so fine
> That all the world will be in love with night
> And pay no worship to the garish sun.

But she is not the one to die young. I will never see her again after that summer, and I have no idea what becomes of her or if she ever has a coming-out party. My sister is not particularly interested by her or such an event, and our mother, I presume, balks at this considerable expense.

So my sister does not "come out" with Penny, though she is presented to the queen, as my mother is friendly with Ruth A., the wife of the South African ambassador to England at the time. Ruth and Harry are a couple with an only child, a girl who dared to marry an Indian. Consequently they refuse to speak to her or ever see her again.

My sister goes alone to drop her curtsey in a pale mauve, pleated dress with a décolleté that shows off her smooth young skin and a little mauve pill-box hat perched on the back of her blond curls. I have a photograph of her in her presentation dress and I remember she told me that Prince Philip, who, poor man, looked very bored, peered down the front of her décolleté with interest.

Later she will graduate from Wits with a degree in anthropology but by then she is married. Apparently, despite her fluent Italian and French, her good deportment, and her gift with flowers, she has not learned what she should have at Madame's "finishing school," for her husband is not wealthy but an impoverished young student, someone who despite his surgeon's degree will never support her in the style she was accustomed to, but will rather kill her on a deserted road in Johannesburg in a jealous rage at the age of thirty-nine.

As for me, I do not find out who I am in Italy; our summer there only adds to my confusion. I will marry young at nineteen, to an equally young boy of Russian origin. I will not recall this strange interlude in Florence for many years until Madame C., or parts of her, resurface from the sea of my unconscious, resurrected and transformed in a novel I write. It is a story of thirteen girls on a swimming team and their swimming teacher Miss G., who also closes the windows and pulls down the shutters and says, "No inhibitions, girls. I will have no inhibitions!" One of the girls on the team, an Italian girl called Fiamma, is missing. Like the missing girl on the team, this story is one of the missing parts, the gaps, the cracks, the silences of my life. How sad that we could not have found the words which might have helped us all: my sister, Madame, and Penny, to know one another's hearts and to have helped with one another's lives.

Stanley Adelman:
Magician of Typewriters

Thaisa Frank

One hot summer's day I brought my broken typewriter to Osner's Typewriter Repair on Amsterdam Avenue and 79th Street. I was in a state of panic because my boyfriend had walked out a week ago. I was a student, earning a pittance as a copyeditor, and the landlady had already asked how I'd pay for more than half the rent. My mind skittered with random thoughts. Sleep, when it came, had dreams about the breakup that scraped my heart. But during the day my grief was buried under terror about survival.

New York was in its eternal process of reconstruction and demolition. A third of the sidewalks were torn up, cranes were devouring buildings, and drilling rattled the sidewalks. The heat was so intense that even the subway shimmered. I carried my typewriter up to the street like a stolen offering from Hades.

Osner's Typewriter Repair was pungent with ink. As if the walls had given birth to them, typewriters were everywhere. The owner, Stanley Adelman, was a wiry man with a hawklike face. He took a moment to look at the typewriter and began to tell me the problem in great detail. He showed me gears, wheels, lock-release levers, and lift-frame springs: a mysterious world of silver metal and black spools.

On that particular day I couldn't have followed a recipe. But since I never bothered to understand anything mechanical, I'd long made pretending to understand into an art. While my mind continued to race, I nodded in a display of intelligent comprehension. This never failed, because the expert who happened to be explaining never stopped talking.

But Stanley Adelman saw that I didn't understand. His intense blue eyes telegraphed the urgent message that he wouldn't settle for anything less than my knowing as much about my typewriter as he did. He repeated himself and I nodded.

He repeated himself again.

The more I nodded, the more he repeated himself. I began to feel the way I felt in high school detention when I only wanted to leave. But it was impossible to leave—or even space out: Stanley Adelman never took his eyes off me. I sensed he knew I couldn't listen because I was in a state of panic. Yet he kept addressing the rational being that lived somewhere inside it.

After the fourth or fifth explanation something unprecedented happened: my chaotic thoughts disappeared. Each gear, wheel, and lock spring became lucid. I understood.

I didn't say anything to let him know—the interaction was between our eyes. I met them and felt a startling clarity, an arc of light. When he saw I understood what he was saying, he told me the typewriter would be ready in three days.

Stanley Adelman had powerful arms. His shirtsleeves were rolled up and, from the periphery of my vision, I saw blue numbers on his arm. I'd seen photographs of these numbers in articles about the Holocaust, but confronting them on a survivor made them seem defiant, even triumphant. For a moment I imagined clandestine meetings over fences in the camps, in ghettoes before curfew, or in underground sewers. People met in such places to give and receive messages that were crucial to their survival. Many of them were flooded with terror and in no condition to understand. Yet it was in just these circumstances that one needed absolute and mutual comprehension.

By the time I left Osner's Typewriter Repair I felt as though I'd emerged from a dark passage into light. I still didn't know how I'd pay the rent. But the random thoughts disappeared and I no longer felt the cacophony of New York inside of me. As I walked back to the subway I was cradled by a tangible sense of peace.

Over time, in the way New Yorkers grow intimate by sharing fragments of their lives, Stanley Adelman and I became friends. At first I visited only when my typewriter needed fixing. Eventually I'd stop by the store. There were often other people there—all of them older, all of them male. Stanley always introduced me by saying, "This is the writer, Thaisa Frank." He said it matter-of-factly, not opening it to question. Then he'd turn his attention to me.

"What have you been working on?"

"A story."

"But *what* story?"

I was always vague about my work. He teased me by telling me he'd seen some good movies but couldn't remember their names. Our conversations always focused on details: the pristine velvet couch that had been on the corner of 78th Street for weeks, the five perfectly matched terriers that walked by every day on a leash. I felt I had a fellow traveler in the way I saw the world.

Twenty years later I was living in California and had published a few books. One day, in the *New York Times*, I read "Stanley Adelman, Repairer of Literary World's Typewriters, Dies." He'd never told me that David Mamet, Alfred Kazin, Erich Maria Remarque, Isaac Bashevis Singer, and Philip Roth brought him their machines. Nor did he tell me that David Handler wrote him into a novel, using his real name and casting him as a magician of typewriters.

According to the *Times*, Stanley Adelman spoke Polish, German, Russian, and Yiddish, and could figure out typewriters in languages he didn't understand—Arabic, for instance—solely from keyboard diagrams.

Howard Fast told the *Times* that Stanley Adelman kept his Underwood alive for more than forty years. When the typewriter was so old he couldn't find parts, he suggested an Olympia. Howard Fast, who was Jewish, said he couldn't write on a German typewriter.

"I was in a concentration camp," said Stanley Adelman. "If I can sell that typewriter, you can write on it."

Howard Fast bought the Olympia.

The six blue numbers on Stanley's arm telegraphed parameters that had defined his life in his early twenties. He had been to four other camps by the time he arrived in Auschwitz late in the war. This was when Auschwitz began to tattoo prisoners' arms instead of stamping their clothes.

I imagined his conversation with Howard Fast being like our conversation that summer's day: Howard Fast not listening. Stanley Adelman talking until he got through. I wasn't the first impenetrable wall.

Before I read the obituary I'd had a vague idea for a novel about World War II. It included a title and two indistinct characters. As soon as I read the obituary, I realized one of the characters had always been Stanley Adelman.

Turning away from terror is as instinctual as turning away from a wound or jumping back from fire. But Stanley Adelman turned toward it and met my fear. I don't know if this came from his particular experiences in World War II, but I do know that the long moment when he held me with his eyes changed my ability to cope with panic forever. Not being alone with terror left me with a sense of courage about facing suffering and terror in other people. It taught me not to turn away.

When I read the obituary I remembered the meeting between our eyes—the sense of shock and clarity. This became a lens when I began to read about the Second World War. I could hold the atrocities against a backdrop of lucidity, and this allowed me to create a narrative.

Given the writers who trusted him, I'm sure Stanley Adelman listened to many voices with patience and compassion. I imagine he used these same qualities when he worked on typewriters, asking gears to mesh, lock springs to spring, and obstinate keys to unstick. He spoke to them patiently, the way he spoke to me that hot summer's day. He settled for nothing less than compassion and lucid understanding.

What Do You Want from Me, Life?

Debbie DeFord-Minerva

I rang the bell at the heavy wooden door that needed some paint, and a skinny old man named Herman eventually opened it. Hunched and bony, but with a spark in his watery blue eyes, his hair a thin fluff of white, he said in an accent I couldn't yet identify, Come in.

His first-floor apartment was dark and spare. I could see from his home that he kept only a few nonessential items in his immediate living space. A trinket that had belonged to his wife. A photo of his middle-aged children as kids. Some dark metal pieces he'd bent long ago, his art. His unbearably thin clothing seemed older than me, and I was turning thirty-five.

He showed me the second floor. I loved the light; I loved the surprise closet off the living room, deep and unfinished, with shelves. After I had a baby a few years later, that room was stuffed to the ceiling with outgrown kid gear stored in case we had another, and we did—we'd saved the walker, the swing, the bouncer, the sled. Everything teetering in a colorful, sentimental stack.

The vibe from the quiet bedrooms at the back of the house was good. One would be an office until the babies came. The outdated pink bathtub and ancient drain plug outside it on the floor were charming. The kitchen, too, was unrenovated, and there was no chance for a dishwasher. But it all seemed right. I thought we could make a home there. And if something needed fixing, our landlord was just downstairs.

Herman was eighty-eight then, and ninety-five when we moved out. You met me when I was a young man! he said the day we left. His poignant humor.

Decades before, at eighteen, I'd left Michigan for New York after dozens of childhood moves. Divorced parents and their strained family relationships, a brother in trouble, a sister with a wedge between us from parental circumstance. As a young adult I became my family's mediator. It felt important to keep people talking to each other. Later I saw it had been crucial for me to leave home when I did, but still, buried deep was a need for all of us to somehow be together.

My relationship with the new landlord was bumpy. He was always in our business—I couldn't take the garbage to the curb without him exclaiming about my bare feet outside. It wasn't his way, so it was wrong.

Everything about living in that house came with instructions. Herman wanted total control, forgetting we weren't family living upstairs; we were paying tenants who deserved space and privacy. And repairs. I would often ignore the doorbell when I knew it was him because with the visit would come more aggravation. What would he not get fixed professionally now? What was he going to tinker with endlessly when I just wanted to be left alone, tired after work?

We argued. This man, with his old-world view about women, infuriated me at times. I'd have to stop nursing my baby to open the door, and he'd ask for my husband. He's not here, I'd say. Can I help? But Herman preferred to deal with "the man."

It's unusual for a second-floor apartment in Queens to come with a backyard, especially with no direct access from upstairs—we had to go out the front and walk around. Our yard was an unused, overgrown space where my husband spent many backbreaking hours digging up tires and plastic jugs and glass and putting beautiful plants into the earth instead. Herman saw the digging and lamented, My beautiful nature! We wondered which part of his beautiful nature he missed—the garbage under the grass, or the mass of pesky poison ivy.

His hearing ability was unpredictable—sometimes he heard perfectly, yet when I wanted to talk about apartment concerns, he'd squint at me. And even if I'd just told him I was on my way out, he'd say, One second, and leave me standing in his doorway. He'd return with a letter he didn't understand from the power company, or ask me to follow him into his kitchen, where I helped him locate a misplaced phone number. We needed our landlord, but it became clear that our landlord also needed us.

Herman was a year younger than my grandpa. When he died, I told Herman, and saw a softness in his eyes. He liked to hear stories about my grandpa—his meager beginnings, his service in World War II, his gardens. And I listened to Herman's stories, always the same ones. He'd tell jokes that made me wince, usually in the "men are superior" vein. He sometimes mentioned his wife, who'd died three years before we came. I wondered about her, whether she'd been an assertive woman, or gentle and patient. He talked about his children, grown and older than me. There was pain in his voice, and a stubborn exasperation that they'd made choices he wouldn't have. I sometimes heard their arguments through the floor when they visited, and they told me, with pain in their own voices, that their hands were tied about repairs. The mold in the walls from a roof leak? No expert was coming to look at it. The bugs he wouldn't call an exterminator for? We had to continue our own efforts and hope for the best.

To our frustration, he kept trying to fix things himself—toilet, light fixtures, doorbell. Then one day he finally gave in. Fine, he said. Call a plum-ber. (He pronounced the b.) He gave us a piece of paper with three names and their phone numbers. One was Chaim, who, when he showed up with a tray of tools, was so old I thought it was Herman in a hat, trying to trick us with a disguise. Are ninety-year-olds compelled to hire plumbers who are eighty-five? Poor Chaim. Herman yelled at him down on the porch for not "making the job" and insisted he owed him nothing, not even for his time. Another was Draino, last name—he, interestingly, was the one to finally "make" that job.

But Herman had survived the Nazis. His parents had not. He'd fled Poland and survived. Metalworking was his trade. One day in the basement he showed me his tools, spread out on an old table. They were worn, like everything else, and I leaned closer when I realized there were words carefully printed on the handles. He had written "I love you" in tiny letters on the handle of each tool. When he turned away to reach for something, tears burst out of me, my heart squeezing. He made me crazy—yet, this. "I love you" on each tool? I asked him why, and he said he needed them to do good work, and they would do that only if he loved them.

This man, skinny as a branch, treated himself to a beloved ham-and-cheese sandwich only once a year, on his birthday. This man, who swung a pendulum over his food for guidance in whether he should eat it, moved his hand toward yes when we shared with him something delectable. This man, who loved my two boys, kept their photos on his mirrored dresser next to pictures of his grandchildren. This man, one hundred years old when I last saw him, held me and hugged me like family.

It was what we had become.

By the time Herman died, I no longer had parents, and three of my grandparents were gone. Even when things were tense between us, Herman helped fill that void. Even when the last straws broke: the mold still in the wall, and the ants crawling on my toddler's neck while he slept, the crib with the baby only a couple of feet away. We had to leave the apartment. But that was a technicality.

I loved this complicated old man. His hearing trouble and heavy accent, our huge generation gap, my gender, his eccentricity. He would tell me, Don't be a hero. He meant, Don't take chances. Keep it safe and easy. But this old man had survived, fled, moved, lived. He'd found his way to New York and raised a family. Nothing was safe and easy back when he was a young man, even at a strapping 250 pounds, as he'd tell me, a thump to his chest with a pale, veiny fist.

Whenever I returned to visit, Herman looked at me first with surprise, then delight. It was just like when he was briefly in a nursing home years before, recovering from a bike injury. Herman was pleased I'd come. It had been strange seeing him there, active and independent amid the sedentary old. He told us once that he could never live in one of those places, and if he did, he would die.

In Herman's last two years of life, there was no answer when I stopped by the house and rang the bell—on sunny days or rainy, or as snow fell to the sidewalk where my bare feet had been. Hesitant check-ins with his relatives confirmed that he was still with us. But he was winding down.

Once Herman and I were arguing again about a cranky ceiling fan in the dining room. The light fixture in it kept shorting out, and we couldn't determine what was wrong. Neither could he. This had gone on and on—his scrawny legs shaking up the ladder so he could poke around, then creep back down. We needed light. We needed an electrician. Herman was standing on the stairway landing just outside our open apartment door, and I was yelling in frustration, tired of having to deal with this hardheaded man. As I made a point, I moved toward him, and he suddenly backed away, which threw him off-balance—at the top of the steep staircase. He teetered, and my husband, who was closer, lunged forward and grabbed him. I felt sick that my anger could have caused him to fall down the stairs. Then Herman clutched at his head, moaning, thrashing, hitting his torso with tight fists. He looked up at the ceiling and, with his crooked fingers framing his face, asked in anguish, *What do you want from me, life?*

What did life want from Herman? In the end, did he know? For a man who'd had his own mind, his own way, he seemed restless and regretful. He felt his children had let him down . . . and maybe he'd let them down, too. For someone who seemed to prefer solitude, he was lonely. Yet he pulled me into conversation only to disagree with a good portion of what I said. Was our conflict as stressful on him as it was on me? Would I have preferred an easy grandfatherly relationship with this man, my landlord? Would he? Or were our challenges the glue that sealed us, two strong-willed people with their own minds, their own ways? Perhaps conflict was our driver. Was this what life wanted from us?

There are people who live the deepest in our hearts, the ones we hope will never leave us, the people who know the marrow of us, the ones who can hurt us the most. And kindred spirits, happy connections, permanent friends, or the ones just passing through— these we gather like lovely moss. They fill the empty spaces, especially when families are small, fragmented.

I suppose in my life I've grown accustomed to conflict. Maybe in my connections, in my chance encounters, I magnet toward difficulty in order to mediate internally, to resolve within myself, to bring opposing forces together. Maybe through this I've found my way.

A couple of months before Herman died, I saw an old man in the park near my house. He stood near a city employee who was digging a hole. The old man wore a hat with World War II pins on it. I saw his faded cuffed pants and carefully polished shoes. Hands in the pockets of his frayed coat. He watched the shovel go into the dirt and come out with a mound. Dig, toss. He reminded me of Herman as he watched the digger with curiosity and a vague sense of authority. Herman had watched us like that. We always got the feeling he was about to tell us how to do it better, but we also felt a childlike interest, pure and without experience. Somewhere in that was acceptance.

Standing at the edge of where Herman would rest at last, the plain pine box slowly moving into the ground, I thought how beautiful it was to see children standing there in the upturned dirt. My two sons and two of Herman's granddaughters, their colorful coats and strong energy bright against the flat winter ground, the gray headstones, the January sky. Life force. Everyone took turns shoveling earth onto that box, and as difficult as it was for me to do, how much it tore at me, I felt the unspeakable honor of it—not only to do it for Herman, but to be included with his real family in this sacred moment. They gave my family space within theirs to mourn, to remember, and to be strong, to thump our chests, to live.

Fractal Cats

Judy Grahn

T he minds of animals have always interested me, as does telepathy among humans, which I have experienced more than a little. When animals communicate with me across the psychic plane, I feel that a spirit of the universe is moving and I am riding in companionship with other beings. My stolid narrow sense of self falls away. For a moment something better replaces it, something connected and dancing, at home in the world beyond human interactions. I learned to trust this nearly indescribable feeling gradually, from a number of incidents, such as the following, which raises more questions than answers, questions of assumptions our culture makes about the substance and terms of reality, and the "real" or "para-real" nature of our relationships to the creatures in our lives.

ALICE'S CALLING

One day in 1972 my friend Alice began talking about wanting a cat.

"Let's go get you one," I suggested.

"Noooo—the cat I want is a Russian Blue," she said, rolling a cigarette and looking up at me out of the corner of her eye, rather like a storybook Irish countrywoman, I thought. Though Alice actually grew up on the Lower East Side of Manhattan with nothing country about it.

I had long admired this type of cat. Often I had gone to the glorious and of course bizarre San Francisco cat show, and I had never before seen felines with so much fur or no fur whatsoever. The Russian Blues had gorgeous fur, thick and short, matching their intense bodies, supple with compact muscles, while their eerie silvery blue-gray coats contrasted with sudden round green eyes.

"Besides." Alice was pouring a cup of coffee, taken black. "They are rare. Not that easy to find."

"Let's look in the paper anyhow," I insisted, pushing some of the junk off the kitchen table to hunt for a recent edition. At the time, we were living in the same house.

"No. I just want to think about it a while."

In the next few weeks we repeated this conversation at least three times. I couldn't understand her wall of resistance.

"Let's try the animal shelter," I would suggest. "The pet store."

"I just want to think about it, do a little meditating." In retrospect I recall that Alice loved to read about the minds of plants, and other ways the universe connects: it did make sense that she would go about acquiring a very particular cat through meditation alone. Alice's version of meditation, like mine, consists of lying flat in bed and staring out a window or counting ceiling tiles while allowing random thoughts to flit around the hollow middle of her mind. At the time I didn't think of this as a very creative form, just a lazy habit we shared.

By March, some six weeks later, we were opening the heavy oak front door for much of the day. The house was huge, three stories and five bedrooms, not counting ingenious uses of the attic and the back half of the living room. I already had two cats: Marmalade, a large red-yellow shorthair, and her white-furred, blue-eyed son,

T-Bear. Marmalade had a slew of boyfriends coming around that season, though none dared come into the house.

What did enter the house one afternoon, with the sturdy swaggering motions of a little athlete, was a nicely muscled, short-haired, densely blue-gray cat with round green eyes.

"Look, Alice," I exclaimed when she came home that night from work. "Here's your Russian Blue. Exactly as you wanted. He just walked right in the door."

She looked at him suspiciously.

"He's not the right one," she said.

"What? He's perfect—look at those eyes."

"He's not the one I had in mind," she said, and went upstairs to her room.

I was flabbergasted. Hadn't Alice called him to come to her? I couldn't believe anyone could be so picky. And I was certain she didn't mean it. Here was the rare Russian Blue, the answer to her description! And confirmation that she was correct, that the world does have a psychic mind that responds to our deeply held desires. So I called the cat Charley and fed him, certain she would come to recognize him as what she had requested. He stayed.

Alice paid him no attention whatsoever, and as I hadn't intended to acquire a third animal, I didn't spend much time with him either. He didn't seem to mind our indifference, having his own agenda, and shortly after began an intense love affair with another household cat, T-Bear.

Marmalade's large son-cat was part Siamese. Though big-boned, snub-nosed, and stiff-bodied like his clever mama, he was gentle and complacent; blue-eyed, he was completely white except for the tips of his ears, his nose and his tail's red rings. Slow and a bit strange, possibly a consequence of Marmalade's dropping him down the ladder leading to the attic during one of her several family moves, before his eyes were opened. Once every two or three months he went up into the attic, climbed out onto one of the outside eaves, and posted himself precariously on a narrow external support beam to moan loudly for several hours. No persuasive tactics would get him down before he was ready. The rest of the time he stayed silent.

Though he was nearly two years old, I hadn't bothered to get him neutered because, following the Siamese hormonal path, his testicles hadn't yet descended into their sacks of fur.

T-Bear and Charley lay on the living room floor in each other's arms all spring, washing and chuckling, rolling and rubbing. On closer examination I noticed their sensuality had gone further. Charley frequently mounted the younger cat, gripping his white neck fur wetly to bump his stocky gray pelvis along T-Bear's raised backside. I could see thin pink penises protruding during their washing exercises, revealing the eroticism of their play.

"They're lovers," I announced to Alice, thinking to rouse her from her indifference to Charley. "Isn't that fascinating? It puts a whole new light on tomcat fighting." And, I thought, here we are, all of us Gay, even the cats. But Alice put her morning coffee mug between her elbows on the cluttered table and wrinkled her nose.

"I want a sweet little Russian Blue. Female. That's all I'm thinking about in the way of cats."

Irritated by her ingratitude, recalcitrance, and blind faith in the power of positive thinking, I went back to observing the living-room lovers.

As spring stretched out, T-Bear began to fill out the round pouches of his testicular posterior, to smell a bit musty. His cheek fur puffed up thickly while muscle tissue gathered heavily on his bones as they outgrew his lean adolescence.

Charley changed, too, though in behavior, not body. Where earlier he had been tender and sensuous he now became challenging and ferocious. He began hitting T-Bear and pushing him around.

He also began spraying his thick musk unpleasantly everywhere in the downstairs of the house.

Perhaps, I thought, if T-Bear were only a more highly developed being, he could have answered the challenge in kind, and Charley would have guided him into adulthood, and now in retrospect I believe that's exactly what Charley was doing.

Nothing could make a warrior of T-Bear. The male-ferocity friendship rivalry that Charley's behavior seemed to be trying to foster did not develop. Though T-Bear was much larger than Charley, he simply collapsed under the weight of the new expectations. I was horrified to find T-Bear cowering for hours on end, having wedged himself under an overstuffed armchair in the living room. In increasingly protective outrage I watched him avoid Charley, his ears back, slinking from room to room on his belly, as if dominated by terror toward his lover-turned-bully.

The morning I came upon Charley pounding his round gray foot between the red ears on the top of T-Bear's head until the white cat's chin audibly smacked up and down on the wooden floor, I decided Charley must go.

On the eve of this decision, Alice swept triumphantly through the front door with a slender gray cat in her arms.

"Here she is!" she cried. "I'm going to call her Freddie."

Incredulous, I went to look closely at the shorthaired, blue-gray, year-old female Russian Blue cat with round green eyes. "A woman down the block was holding her. When I told her that's just the cat I've been wanting, she gave her to me." Neither of the women seemed surprised to have found each other.

A one-woman cat devoted to Alice, Freddie was perfect, silky and sensual yet also full of mischief and fun. A housemate opened the refrigerator one morning, shocked to find Freddie sitting in there, calmly, green eyes blinking at the light, having sneaked into the bottom shelf when someone was grabbing things out of it while gabbing to someone across the room.

Alice arranged for friends in the California countryside of Sonoma County to take tough-boy Charley and get him fixed. The adults Freddie, Marmalade, and T-Bear established an alliance in the house. Freddie was indeed sweet-natured, and became Alice's close companion for at least a dozen years. Her confirmation had arrived: the world does have a psychic mind that responds to our deeply held desires.

And I continue to puzzle over the fact that, out of all the cats who could have walked through the door that season, only a Russian Blue did. And why, out of all the women who could have been standing on the sidewalk on our block willing to give her cat away to the first person who asked for it, only the one with the Russian Blue female *was* standing there, in the moments when Alice, who spent most of her time indoors, was there too? What waves brought them all together to coalesce around Alice's desire? What wave sent the wrong cat first, and then accounted for him? Just exactly how do our minds, wills, and bodies interact with each other and with creatures across time and space?

THE NICE PERSON OF BILL

If it is true we can draw cats and other beings to us by putting our thoughts intensely into the biosphere, it is equally true that cats can influence us with the power of their own thoughts.

I learned this very clearly once in upstate New York, near Syracuse, where I spent the summer of 1981 house-sitting for a friend of mine, the writer Rachel Guido DeVries. Rachel had two animals living with her. One was an amiable hound-type dog, Scooter, while the other was an extremely willful black cat, Bill.

I call the cat willful because his method of getting into the house or any room in which I had enclosed myself for privacy was so forceful. He would claw and bang with his foot as though it were a fist, making explosions of noise as he slammed his body, as if willing to keep the din going for the duration of his life, though I don't know what his exact endurance was since I was never able to outwait his efforts. He quit the instant I opened the door for him, which I did increasingly quickly as the weeks of our companionship proceeded.

In the middle of the night, he was particularly effective at making noise with the outside screen door, never finding it necessary to use his voice for the purpose of rousing me. The inside doors he rattled by shoving a curled paw underneath to jerk the door back and forth in its latch.

I explain this as prelude to the mystery of his behavior on the first night I spent in the house. Knowing nothing of the cat's character, I read the general note of instructions Rachel had left on the dining-room table, including the right percentage of canned food for Bill and Scooter. Being exhausted from traveling, I simply may have perfunctorily set some skimpy amount of food down for the two animals before going to bed.

The newly remodeled bedroom featured a gorgeous skylight directly over the pillow, through which I could see the stars of the northern summer sky as I drifted to sleep with no difficulty. In the many strange beds I sleep in, since my living entails so much traveling, I have grown accustomed to odd dreams and awakenings, even to other peoples' pets running up and down on me.

The particular dream I had that night was very odd; indeed, I don't think it was a dream at all. For one thing, it had no pictures, just a firm, moderately loud, masculine voice in my ear.

The voice said two sentences: "Bill is a nice person. Feed Bill."

Confused about where I was and who was speaking so emphatically to me, I struggled to wake, then fell into slumber again. The firm voice came a second time: "Bill is a nice person. Feed Bill." This time I popped awake with genuine curiosity to find out where on earth I was. Who the heck was talking to me? I turned my head and saw the sliding doors on the side wall, the outline of the bed lamp next to me. Already feeling an extra weight on my covers, I flicked on the light. Settled into the valley formed between my outstretched shins, and in that sphinx position characteristic of the species, there posed the cat of the house. His yellow eyes were fixed on mine with a penetrating stare that I began to understand had probably been going on for some time. I felt the wave of his will, which in the days to follow I would come to know well.

"Oh," I said aloud. "You're Bill. What were you doing inside my head?" He got up, I got up, and we went to the kitchen where I fed him. It was 4 A.M.

This method of waking was never repeated. Either he didn't use his telepathy again or I didn't respond. Instead I put him outside at night and he switched to the door-banging game, which for all of its ruckus I found less disconcerting and easier to explain to other people than that his voice, in human English, had spoken inside my head.

Back in California seven years later, I moved into an apartment with a tuxedo cat, Percy, who communicated with me through telepathy, though I wasn't able to consciously capture anything as clear as Bill's lucid sentences that summer in New York State. One morning as I lay dozing, Percy settled on my chest with his chin lightly resting on mine. I startled awake, aware that I had been having a dialogue in my mind, in English sentences, and that there were clearly two voices, one mine and the other a pleasant masculine one. Percy, I wondered? But I had no way to check, nor could I recall the content of the discussion.

More obviously, Percy communicated by staring at me with great intention to communicate. This I am quite certain of because I would often wake in the middle of the night to find him doing it. We had an agreement that since we lived in a second-floor apartment I would carry him down to the front door whenever he requested, even though his usual request could come deep in the night. Once or twice a week, if after his first attempt I fell into a doze, images of his face flooded my mind repeatedly until I opened my eyes and remembered I hadn't yet taken him downstairs.

Researchers have found that cats understand a vocabulary of about one hundred words, including such words as *dresser*. Certainly a mass of pet owners testify that cat comprehension of human vocabulary includes their own names and elementals such as *dinnertime* and *want to go out*. But *nice?* And *person?* Bill had a complex vocabulary indeed. How formal his syntax was, how reasoned his argument. Not *Get up and feed me, I'm hungry,* but *Bill is a nice person. Feed Bill.* I was to feed him, not because he was hungry, but because he said, using the third person, he was nice. Does Rachel use the word *nice* a lot? I had to ask myself. Did Bill's choice of words stem from Rachel's approach? Or was the vocabulary formed in *my* head after the impetus of his will reached my brain waves? If this last scenario were the case, why would I not have constructed the sentence along the lines of *Get up, feed the cat?*

The question of Bill's self-defined niceness and third-person personhood remains intriguing, as does the fact that the message happened only once. My pendulum, which I have come to trust for questions such as these, emphatically states that Bill constructed his own sentence, suggesting that nonhuman beings comprehend our language with greater complexity than anyone has yet tested or verified.

Well, at least Bill was real. In my third example of cats in the psychic realm, the animal was like Macavity from the musical *Cats:*

When you get to the stair. He isn't there.

A SPIRIT CAT

In 1982 I was only beginning to explore my own psychic capacities and had suspicions but no real sense of my life as full of spirits. By then I was living with a woman, the writer Paula Gunn Allen, whose life *is* full of spirits, and beginning to recognize a few myself. It would be a long time before I realized that I had grown up in a house full of them.

Ghosts and ghost stories have never much interested me, though I have seen reproductions of photographs claiming to be ghosts captured on film. A couple of times in my life the recently dead have stopped to deliver a message or two on their way to—wherever—but on the whole ghosts are not a part of my everyday conversation.

I was a little surprised and delighted, then, to detect a spirit cat in a house Paula and I had rented in El Cerrito, California. One early morning, we stood on the small wooden back porch while she smoked, the two of us talking vigorously but not directively, our conversation more like free association in a broad field of attention, with all kinds of creative connections surfacing unexpectedly between us. Suddenly I became aware that, even as I participated, I was also watching a small light-colored female cat who came up the porch steps, flitting past our legs and disappearing on the other side of Paula, who was nearest to the open back doorway.

The cat just went into the house. This I thought as a matter of fact.

Abruptly I shook myself back into three-dimensional material reality, feeling like a character in a comic strip doing a double take. "Wait a minute. We don't have a cat." I peered into the house. No cat. "This is strange," I interrupted Paula. "I just saw a cat go into the house."

"Oh, I saw her too," Paula confirmed, describing at my request "a small, gray cat. She just went in the back door. She ran past our legs."

We laughed about this mutual sighting; I always feel exhilarated by any sort of event on another plane. I wouldn't have thought much more about this incident than that we two were playing in each other's psychic minds, since, while for us there obviously was a spirit cat, there were no other humans around to compare notes with on the subject. I say we "saw" the cat—but realized it wasn't "real" immediately. This kind of seeing isn't exactly out of the corner of the eye. We turned to look directly at the cat. But it's a little like seeing something in a mirror. Everything is there yet something is missing, and you can't say what exactly. A missing dimension? How real flesh (and fur) reflects light? Somehow we knew this was a ghost cat.

"Probably that cat used to live here before it died," Paula speculated, our conversation turning to parameters of time and space for a minute or two before we went back inside and on with the day.

Later that afternoon we had a visitor from the East Coast. Excitedly we told her about our sighting, watching in disappointment as she closed her face in what could only be obvious disbelief. A woman directive in her attention, she was the kind to focus on real life and its problems and dilemmas with great success. So we dropped the subject and I didn't think about it again. How quickly any subject is stifled when it has no social matrix to give it confirmation and "reality."

Until early in the evening. After our first visitor left, we had a second, from southern California, our friend and fellow poet Eloise Klein Healy, who also likes to engage in free-flowing associations in a broad field of mind. Non-geometric, we might say. Having worn out the slight bit of fun to be taken from jarring skeptical minds with tales from the psychic realm, neither Paula nor I brought up our morning's encounter with the nonmaterial cat.

After a brief tour of our living quarters and some admiration of the big yard and Meyer lemon tree, Eloise, sitting on the arm of the couch in the living room, looked up with a beatific, whimsical smile and said guilelessly, "Did you know you have a cat in here?"

"What's that?"

"I keep seeing a cat here in your house," Eloise said.

"Well, yes," we exclaimed.

On closer questioning, she described the spirit as a small, female, light-colored cat. We discussed what it might be. Someone who used to live in the house, we guessed, and came back to reminisce. Maybe run over in the street out front, I improvised, the idea lingering for some reason. What reason? "It is the house that matters," one of us said; "the cat pays no attention to any of us." So was it a ghost with a past and intention? Or was it an afterimage? A sort of movie-shell shadow sent from a different location altogether?

An organic magnetic field caught in a loop? A forethought not yet born as a cat? At any rate, it leaped across dimensions to us and only on this one day. Had time bent that day and put us all as one mind into a different place? Or were we in a fractal zone in which a spark reached out to connect all of us for one moment, a moment none of us ever forgot?

Science has begun to formulate experiments with results that support experiences of anomalous precognition and the reality of psychic capacity. But so far no experiments show the possibility that through thought alone we influence the course of material reality. Or that cats speak from mind to mind and can convey precise English.

My friend Alice showed me that nature is responsive. You get what you request with your intent, spirituality people say; don't be swayed by the skeptics. Be a little patient. Just be sure to include *all* the important details, as you lie abed, meditating. Then wait: wait for the unpredictable, that fractal moment.

We are not alone on this planet unless we shut ourselves away from its myriad interactions. Whatever the reasons, these occasions feed my sense of profound delight at the interconnectedness of life: we are not just random dust motes blowing around, when, anyway, maybe dust motes aren't so disconnected either.

partners

Rumination in Three Parts

Noy Holland

Years ago I lived in Tanzania on the shore of the Indian Ocean and, afternoons, when the heat was too much, I pulled on my fins and walked backward into the broken waves. I had fins because I liked to swim out, almost past where I could see the shore.

I was twenty-five, twenty-something. I felt not so much invincible as curious, drawn to peril, easily lost. I never had a premonition of drowning but a dread that I would be eaten. Still I swam because I loved the feeling and the strange peace of being beyond the break and beyond where anyone could see me swimming to India, swimming to Zanzibar; I often wondered how far I could go. Once I swam up close to a fishing boat, very small; there were often boats and, in them, two or three men, beautifully dark against the glare of the sun, standing in the boat and hauling in a net, or flinging a net as if sowing seed out into the swaying water. Net of words; I thought of Virginia Woolf. As if they were netting a story. I thought I would become their story, the *mzungu* by accident caught in the net, helplessly knotted, my hair in my mouth. They would haul me out and into the air, drowned, among all the flopping, gasping life that would drown from being dragged out of the water.

Of course this never happened. What did happen, one day out swimming, was that I felt myself suddenly and irretrievably lost; I could see the shore but I could not see the curve of beach where I lived with my boy from America, my American boy. My amour, my temporary lover. I could not see the small hotel we lived in, the rumpled bed, the grace of the net that hung around the bed to keep the malaria mosquitoes away; he'd had malaria, he would have it for years, but I couldn't see him, and I didn't love him, I only loved that he was a gypsy like me, and a dreamer. For the moment, I dreamed myself lost, and soon exhausted, in the great wide sea between Africa and India, the trade wind, the current the merchants sailed along, bringing silk and spices and tea.

Twice now I have typed "a little sigh in the Indian ocean." I meant to type not "sigh" but "fish." Little yellow fish of relief. Sighing, of course, is a sign. So, too, was the fish, a beacon. Big as my little finger. It was a grayish dullish yellow fish that brightened when it caught the sun. In an aquarium, I'd learned that a band of nerves runs laterally down the sides of a fish and, by these, the fish senses movement; by these, the flashing thousands are able to move as one. Swallows, too, murmurations, flocks, in the glare of the sun, the velvety blue, a swooping exultation. But this image comes from elsewhere; here there seemed to be nothing between Africa and India except me and a dull yellow fish small enough to swallow whole. I turned for shore and the fish turned with me, beneath me, below my breasts, my belly. I couldn't see it quite; I had to stop to see it. It had chosen me, somehow.

I hope to go on believing in the weird miracle of being chosen. By the little yellow emissary. A thrush in the trees. A leaf falling. I have a sense sometimes of being spoken to. By living humans, yes, but there is more to it, more to us, than this.

Because a leaf twisted down at Rowan Oak, and I lay on my back and watched it, because my husband who was not my husband yet lay on his back beside me, and we watched the same leaf, we married. Because of that. And because of this, two people—a boy, a girl—came to be. Who so easily might not have been.

If not for the helpful yellow fish, I might have panicked and drowned. The fish seemed to guide me ashore. To wish me life.

How this might sound to a sensible person doesn't trouble me.

I don't believe in an orderly universe but I believe that when that leaf fell, it fell for me—fell because I wanted it to fall, because something in me was seeking, and in seeking I could see an answer that had long been there. I knew the leaf was my dead mother coming to me, saying as she often did, simply, Live.

And so we married. I have been married twenty years, and my husband, a sensible man, easy to like, down to earth (down to earth: isn't this a strange thing to say?), my husband felt my mother speaking, too. The leaf came down in its twisting erratic way and fell near us where we lay at Rowan Oak in the chill of the evening coming and my husband who was not my husband yet, who had never once met my mother, knew without my saying a word that she spoke to him also, he felt her saying also, Go on and love her. Live.

This is a rumination in three parts, bound to the centering self. In the first part, a fish swims beneath me; in the second, a leaf falls beside me; in the third part, a dappled horse appears among the stars in my head, looking down. Each act was at once negligible and lastingly momentous; each was its own weird blessing.

The dappled horse appeared in Egypt, months after I'd left Tanzania and left the American boy I had traveled with who was drawn to peril as I was, drawn to peril like me. I traveled alone by then and preferred it. I piloted by whim, or what I thought was whim, who could not see the footprints before me, could not see how often my impulses did not originate with me. Cairo—heaps of saffron in the markets, chickens losing their heads on the chopping block, flowers, heat, a terrible brightness. And the pyramids, of course.

I found a stable. I don't remember the saddle but in my mind the saddle was tasseled, colorful, cloth. The horse was dappled, with the pretty, dished face of an Arabian, a horse bred to live in the heat of the desert, a favorite of Genghis Khan.

We lit out across the Nubian desert. At a lope, at a gallop, the guide ahead of me—an apparition in white, a girlhood dream—*King of the Wind* was the book—in full flower. Elated, I have seldom felt so—what? Insubstantial. So entirely unknown, unfindable. At a gallop, my horse stumbled and went to its knees and from its knees surged forward and over me, still in the saddle, thrown to the sand. And day was night, instantly, and the brain I use to see with saw the night sky pricked with stars.

Months later, in Tuscaloosa, I was telling my father this story. He looked amused, maybe incredulous.

"You don't believe me," I said.

"No, no."

"You think I made it up. I can't have seen stars."

I was ready with the scientific explanation: the occipital lobe, etc.

"No. Only that your mother, we had traveled to Cairo, just as you did, to see the pyramids, the Nile basin, the ruins. This would have been '56, '57."

(A date is like a door to a story for my father; until it is opened, he cannot go on.)

"September of 1957," he went on. "That very thing happened to your mother. A horse fell on your mother in the desert and, like you, your mother lay there, and slowly stood up and rode away."

I lay there. My horse heaved up and stood looking down at my face. I felt the breath of the horse on my face, tender, the skin, a little raw from the sand. I did not think of my mother. I watched the stars going out; I could hear them. Bees, I might have called them, a flock of gnats. Flock, swarm, murmuration, school. And closer still, above me: that marvelous, dappled creature.

Conspirators

R. O. Kwon

There are those who like to look for girls in the subways. Once I knew someone, a Barcelonian, who was good at it. Prodigiously good. Oh, that Spanish swagger. She liked very much the challenge, she said. It is so like being on the stage, she said.

I am not so brave a girl. Blanche might say it is not bravery that is required but rather openness, a glasnost of the soul. A blossoming. Blanche and her poeticisms! I am never open, but there was a time, three years ago, when I did get lucky. I was in the subway and speeding toward a Halloween party. I am everlastingly bad at parties. Without fail, I become once more the child I used to be: mute, judgmental, desperate to hide behind the skirts of the one I love. Still, I wanted to drink, and not alone.

So, I was on my way uptown. The subway car was rollickingly loud, overloaded with goblins and whores; flappers and rockers; schoolgirls, heroes, and ghouls. The revelers were drunk and exuberant. They wore short, preposterous skirts.

I was by myself and, defiantly, in a simple white dress. I never wore a costume for Halloween. A leprechaun twirled around a pole. Superman, disappointingly, staggered. I noticed a girl sitting catty-corner from me, reading, alone. Long fingers hid the title from me. She sat very straight in a trench coat of a dark, peculiar green. Her legs were bare. Her close-cropped hair alchemized fluorescent light to gold. She laughed to herself, then underlined something in her book.

Most of the drunkards disembarked at Christopher Street. The girl stayed, still laughing. I kept looking. I love looking. Beauty baffles me. That posture of hers. She appeared uncompromising and apart, like statuary. What was she reading?

We swung through tunnels, and I let my stop go by. More revelers got off. A disproportionate number of elderly couples got on. They were quietly well dressed: suits of gray, dun furs, pearls. They looked unaccustomed to the subway. They leaned into one other and peered at scraps of paper. "I think the next stop is for us, dear." "My goodness, already?" "It is fast, isn't it?" "Oh, here we are." "Take my arm." They got off at the stop for the Lincoln Center. Operagoers, I thought. Of course. Aboveground, the streets of Manhattan would be overrun.

By and by the car emptied. When the girl stood up, I wasn't ready for it. Sitting with her for so long, I'd thought maybe, like me, she had nowhere special to go, and together we might carom around underground, fellow vagabonds, all night long. But, no, she was up and at the doors. I would have liked to be standing, too, able, as the doors opened, to step aside and intimate with a murmur: After you. But I was too late. So I did the next best thing. I followed her.

I kept pace from a distance. Despite the hordes on the platform, she was easy to see: a pair of bare strong legs, a flash of green. I wondered if I had ever, to anyone, looked so memorable. As she passed a group of singers busking at the black gates of the subway—She bid me take life easy, they sang—she dropped a bill into their open guitar case. Was it the song? Was she just that big-hearted? Was she, like me, new to the city, still feeling for those who asked for money? We came to the base of a steep staircase. There was an escalator, but she ignored it and ran up the stairs, lightly. She flew by all the plodding, earthbound walkers. I hurried to keep up.

A lamplit street. Merrymakers everywhere. She strode on, her trench coat flapping. I cut through the celebrating crowds. For a moment, I lost her. Drunkards, imposters, trying to be for one night something other than themselves. All—in—our—way. But then, that flash of outlaw green. I ran, feeling giddy and optimistic, like an adventurer.

She turned left onto a narrow, quieter street of stalwart brownstones and ailanthus trees. She stopped and about-faced, and I stood still. We looked at each other across the length of half a block. I wondered what she saw. A wooer at the ready? A slight girl in a white dress and cowboy boots? A small face cupped by blunt black hair? I heard the song of sirens far away.

"Do you," she called, "do you like the way I walk?"

Oh, I did. In the leisure of the days and years to come I would study the rhythm of her walk, deliberate over the language of her legs. We would be naked and in love and would do as we pleased. We would travel the breadth of the whole, the biddable world, and we would open ourselves to it: open like a door, like open sesame. We were open with Tibetan dissidents and Bajau sea nomads; open to nightclubs in Sinchon; open in Yanji, and open in Barcelona. Blanche was a travel writer and photographer. I quit my office job and picked up odd gigs teaching English so I could stay by her side.

At first, it was fun. Blanche and I, we duetted in karaoke bars. We petted ratty orphan tigers, and laughed at men who tried to pick us up. She seemed to think it perfectly natural, no big deal, that I would leave my life to be with her, so I pretended I thought so, too. On filthy trains she dozed, and I watched her, amazed: her legs curled under like a mermaid's tail, cheap rhodium bracelets staining her skin greenish gold. As we roved, I jotted letters to old friends. The letters became postcards, postcards became occasional emails, and finally I forgot to send any word at all.

I don't know when I started worrying all the time. The thing was, Blanche needed me to keep her safe. In these teeming, starving cities where anyone might have killed her for her boots alone, she lived free of fear. Though six years older, she was the naïve one. The risks she took—they made me sick. She was all for hitchhiking, for example. She was careless with her things, flinging them anywhere. Worst of all, she habitually held her camera up to her face while crossing streets. "Blanche, Jesus," I would say, yanking her back as a car screamed past, and she'd shrug me off and laugh. Then, she would shoot another picture. She looked at everything. She looked at everyone. I looked after her. For three years, I couldn't sleep from the strain.

Then we were in Rajasthan, walking down a dusty sidewalk. For all of five seconds, I paused at a food stand to buy us water. She crossed the street, and a rickshaw hit her. It split her open. The doctor said she needed a transfusion, and the new blood poisoned her. All night she shook as though she'd break, her body too small to hold the outsized soul. I squeezed myself around her, holding my girl in place while her fists flung out crazily, the knuckles globes of bone. In six languages she cursed, teeth chattering.

After she recovered, she was weaker. One morning she woke me up, her eyes bright. "What if we went back to New York," she said, sitting on top of me. "I know how much you've been wanting to go back."

"For how long?"

"For good," she said with a half smile, and I thought, At last.

A year later I was sitting in our living room with no company but the flat tick of the clock, waiting for Blanche to come home. I watched the minute hand fall down the clock face, and swing up and around, and fall down the clock face, and swing up and around, and it was twelve, then one, then two, then three o'clock.

Blanche was on a fifth date with her first, and so far only, other girlfriend. An open relationship; that's what we had. We're-so-young, the-world's-so-vast, monogamy's-so-outdated-and-counterfeit. That was why, or so she said. "You should go out, too," she'd told me before she left, slipping on a pair of peep-toe slingbacks—my peep-toe slingbacks. She strode to the refrigerator, pulled out a silver can of Red Bull, and snapped it open: a quick, efficient swig of caffeine, in case the night went long. "Meet someone new," she called over her shoulder. "Get frisky."

"But I don't want to," I said. Then I added, to sound less miserable, "Maybe next time."

The joke so old it's like a creation story: what do lesbians bring on their second date? A U-Haul. That wasn't us, or at least not Blanche, and the pilgrim soul I loved first and foremost in her was a source of discord now. No one changes, I've learned that much, I think.

"At least don't wear my shoes tonight," I said, regretting the words even as they rushed out, but what could I do? Those sling-backs would be her conspirators.

She tilted her head and looked at me fondly. The open refrigerator lit her bright, short, heroic hair. "My introvert," she said. "My delicate lotus flower."

"Blanche," I said, "we've seen lotus flowers. Remember Beijing, the Summer Palace? They're tough. And big. A lotus flower can be described in many ways, but it is not delicate."

"My paradoxical lotus flower," she said and tipped back another swig.

"Stop fucking patronizing me."

She looked hurt. She looked hurt, her eyes wide with surprise. And, despite myself, I was sorry. She was killing me, fine, but here's what else I knew: that when we slept, she cupped a hand around my head as if to protect me from bad dreams. Blanche in her tool belt, brandishing a power drill—oh. Once, she hitched a ride on a cargo ship to Panama, just because she wanted to. I went to her and touched her arm. Its fine gold hairs. She wouldn't look at me. "I didn't mean that," I said quietly.

"I know," she said. She freed her feet from the slingbacks. Then she did a strange thing: she knelt in front of me, lifted my left foot, and gently slid it into the shoe. Again with the right foot. "All yours," she said. Finally, she looked up at me. She hugged my legs, and left for her date with another girl.

The Only Other Person in the World

Rebecca Wolff

I leave my home, which I share with my boyfriend, for a two-week retreat in which I will work in relative solitude, in the anonymity of the colony. In there I can choose how I make myself known, and to what degree.

I miss you, he texts me. I miss your smell. I do not respond to that, but only to the other content, about snow and roads and my studio's amenities. I have often been told I smell good; I cannot smell myself.

I can regard myself only in the unity of impressions I receive—from exes, parents, friends, siblings, even offspring—that I am detached, and heartless, and dangerously selfish, self-absorbed, and self-centered. Perhaps narcissistic, a diagnosis. It's hard especially for friends to put fingers on the problem, because I can be a lovely friend. Honest, witty at times, curious. To be generous: I am a child, with a childish understanding of things that either literature or living ought to have long ago taught me. The meat of life, discord and sufficiencies: I am missing that; I am skating on the thin surface of how one is to live. I have not read the Russians. My newest friend, a younger German artist whose habit of optimistic problematizing sets me at ease, did not hide her discomfort at my revelation that I have not read the Russians. She told me the arc of *White Nights* over ginger tea, just hot water with ginger boiled in it; it does not taste good but it is good for your digestion and your mental clarity.

I have always been good with sentences, but this writing may be flawed, just as I am, in ways that keep it from being great. It may not have the greatness of heart that great writing can have. It may not know you— it may not show you anything but what is inside me—I used to think that *I* stood as a metaphor for *you*. But then where does that leave you?

White Nights, white heat: a village man meets a village woman who is out wandering, weeping; she is waiting for her lover to return. He said he would come for her, they set a date, this is the date, he has not come. The man and the woman talk and walk together; the man falls in love. He says he will marry her, save her from disgrace or loneliness or heartbreak, it is all the same (it is not all the same). She agrees. Now her lover comes, as he said he would, and she knows she loves him still, she must have him, and be with him, and not with the kind man who would have saved her, and she leaves.

No one likes to be treated like a second-class citizen; no one likes to be treated like a lesser human; no one likes to be overridden, or rolled over, or bowled over by the one they love, who does not love them. No one will put up with this forever. My boyfriend at home, of substance and spirit, says he feels like a specter, as though he is an appendage to me, as though I do not consider him. In truth, I do not think of him; I do not know how to keep him in mind; he disappears when I am not with him. Is this *mea culpa: I am sorry I do not love you?* Do I not love him, or do I not know I love him because I do not know what love is? How can it be that I have loved only one person? How can it be that this is what I am writing about, at this point in the young century.

Art makes shared reality; texts of our lives. Having read of love one might know that love exists; one might understand that love will come or what might happen when one loves. But one is anomalous. One read with impunity. One got this old without knowing the phenomena that occur in love—disastrous, to love like a child from inside an adult body and accountabilities. What is one to do without the resources of that knowledge, the shared hidden knowledge adults have, about love? One is ill prepared.

You entered a summer kitchen, carrying a plate of raw meat out to the grill. En route to the out-of-doors. You passed close by in your short-sleeved cotton shirt, and I groaned out loud. Without a thought. Your smell was meat to me. It awakened appetite. This mode of address in which I had never indulged before; it is trite. It is trash.

In college I lived in a small house near the grounds of an old Gothic shutdown mental hospital, with two other women. One was from Chicago via Ukraine, a salacious conceptual artist named Ula. The other a lissome dusky voice major from Connecticut. They both had boyfriends who slept over; I had a detached boyfriend, an hour or so away, who visited. Somehow the configuration of our rooms was such that my bed was in a kind of antechamber to their rooms: they passed my bed to go to the bathroom or kitchen. The men came in with them to their rooms and then I heard intimacies: laughter and quiet speech and silence and cries. It caused me anguish; I felt acutely the lack of knowledge of how to arrive at love, how to join in love. I figured it as inaccessible magic, what brought the two together into the same sphere. I felt like that with no one. My boyfriend called me his Cerebral Pal-sy. I hope that I paid less rent for my room.

Antechamber to intimacies; icy surface above and away from the hearts and minds of those one is supposed to love, to give love to; this writing is disarming.

One could make a claim that alienation is social; cultural: but it is anachronistic, antisocial. Our living culture is replete with opportunities for communing and for transpersonal volunteer-ism, for intersubjectivity both sublime and material: divine. Alienations like mine are formulated from, reified retroactively by, nineteenth-century tropes of self and other, capitalist smut we gobbled up in college. Romantic idealism, problems of old Germans and opiate-abusers. My alienation chimed with me: *I felt myself alone so beautifully when a child,* like Wordsworth, like Frank O'Hara joked about; I didn't get he was joking. A self-aggran-dized, halcyon, self-fulfilling self-consciousness was my favorite feeling; music made it even grander, colors made it tactile; per-ception and expression made it fruitful. To perceive of myself as godlike. . . . Could it be a simple misstep no one bothered to cor-rect in me? Could all my troubles, pain I have caused to self and others, have been averted if a gimlet-eyed guidance counselor had clocked my slump, given me Marx to read? Or Marcuse? Someone who effectively blasted the castle walls of hyper-individualism? Sat me down and made me hold hands in a circle? Simply told me to get over myself and not hold myself apart, and understand that we are all in this together, there is a shared reality called Study, Content, Material, called snap out of your own miserable head and apply yourself to Godhead?

The ice might be thicker than that. It might go deeper than that. I might have resisted that. I may have deflected attempts, a Teflon novitiate. I may have deceived others with my surface. I may have been my own worst enemy. I was a willful and resourceful young woman. I wrote poems and made friends, attached myself to ideas that supported me. I thought I loved. I apologized. I looked good to people; I looked good to people for a long time. I looked good, and I smelled good.

In fact I believed I could do no wrong, existentially, forever. I was myself and that was perfect, by definition; there was no other self that I could be: a closed circuit. In high school a friend was sui-cidal; amateur guidance counselor, I coached her in this mantra of preservation, an ultimate defense. You are you, I said, and you are

124

everything. You only need to see that without you you're nothing; with you you're everything. You cannot, categorically, not exist. She made it through despite my reckless supremacism, lives on even now in a handmade post-and-beam cabin, off the grid. A different register of self-sufficiency; she touches material, she makes content, she attaches parts to parts to make a whole; when she needs help she receives it from within her nearest mountain of community.

I'm tearing myself down and it feels good. Don't make me stop. I've come to this place to be alone and begin again, stripped clean and faceless. If I were stopped in the snowy woods by a bear or Buddha it would go around me, as I have no smell. This writing, I'll add, is trash; modern self-involvement at its basest. A gratuitous involution. The things that pass for poems and stories and essays that should never trespass outside of the limited frame of reference in which their impulses dwell; material for a good old-fashioned letter, to be burned, a letter full of important self-disclosure for your close friends and your family, burn it. I should just jam this in an envelope and mail it to you.

Because *I miss you*. I never knew what those words meant before I lost you. It's a feeling, not a thought. A set of feelings, a continuum from loss to longing, and back again. When you are not with me I'm blue. Subtraction makes lack, I want you with me always, I need to be near you, the whole is neither sum nor parts, me without you is a deficiency, error. I never would have believed this feeling really existed if I hadn't met you. *I miss you*. These words were in the past said to me, and I said them back without feeling. I did not know that anyone else did anything different. This is not hyperbole; this is self-revelation at its most affectless. I'm writing this because it's true and I want to record it lest it be forgotten. Maybe I'm autistic, maybe I'm a monster, maybe many others live this way and no one talks about it. The last taboo: heartlessness.

One can be a good-enough mother and friend and even wife without knowing feelings, and one can offer compensation at least for a time with the various charms produced in any living body. But one cannot be a lover.

One can be a good enough writer without knowing these feelings; disassociation is close to observation, and can give it that extra thrill of synesthesia, the color of what things seem like to a self who is objectified and therefore objectifying. But one cannot be a witch without knowing these feelings; one cannot cast a spell if one does not dwell serenely in the shared reality in which that spell will take effect. One can't believe in *anything* without believing in objective reality: gods/ spells/ rituals/ interpretations/ causalities/ assertions: all are performed within metaphor. You and I shared reality when we fell in love; neither of us had before. You came inside my body and it was not a metaphor; the last time we fucked I touched the skin on the back of your neck and I felt my own touch from the inside. From inside your skin. You were a twin / you were within. You were in my dreams; your name was on the wall in my dream, literally, a literal metaphor. You were the writing on the wall. You played songs for me, obsessively, and you literally played songs *for* me.

My heart is like a wheel—Let me roll it to ya / Let me roll it to ya / Let me roll it to ya

I'll be thinking of you. This is what my ex-husband always said to me when we were going to be away from each other for a few days, or a week, as happened not infrequently. I could not understand what he meant. The blank where he was supposed to be, in my thoughts. The marginality of his impression. I'm still angry with him for all the years we spent together. It's not his fault.

Now I'll talk more about you. When I saw something, I wanted to show you, to share my eyes. When I heard a song, I wanted to play it for you. When I wrote a poem, it was to you. When I went somewhere, I wanted you to go with me. When you went somewhere, I wanted you to come back. When I watched you eat, I wanted to go inside your mouth. When I masturbated, I imagined your cock. When I imagined your cock—imagining while driving down the road, across the bridge—I shuddered inside. I believed in you; you were always there; you did not disappear when I looked away. You stayed there, and I thought about you, wherever you were. I could call you, I could find you, I could talk to you. I always wanted to talk to you. I used to think that I would not need to write, anymore, if I had you; I would just talk to you.

In my studio in the middle of the day I lie down on my little cot to nap. I doze lightly; I wake in dread; the thin protection I wore from purposelessness, dissolved. What I do could be less than great; what is less than great is not worth doing, is not my doing. I think what will become of me if I cannot write anything worth reading ever again; now that I am not perfect I don't know what mechanism can fill me with the certitude I need to produce the writing I have set myself to do. All I have ever been is a writer. The engine of my writing is this certainty that what I write is perfected even before I have set it down. That I am my own audience; that I am alone; the relationship is one of self and mirror. Narcissus and the flowering of his face.

Yet the last time I checked, it is more important to be a good person than to be a good writer. I make phone calls now—reach out, in the nomenclature of the day, feebly and rhetorically to those whom I know I ought to wish to speak with. It will make him feel good if I call him. I will fulfill his desires, and that makes me a better person, because I know him enough to know what he needs and wants and I care enough to do that for him. A giving partner.

But there is only one person in the world I ever wanted to speak to. It was the flowering of want—desire—a word I have despised and mocked in others' poems, a buzzword; I did not know it had a meaning made out of feeling, I thought it was a construct like an origami flower, opening into academic economies. I felt pride in scorning its use.

Is it generous, to love? Is it a gift, to believe someone else exists?

127

To whom does the gift extend; is it a gift to oneself to believe in another; it would seem condescension to gift the other with his own existence. I gifted you with books and songs and poems, lover's gifts, and with my heart, a fanciful construct that weighs a ton. You have captured my fancy, I said, like it was the nineteenth century; meaning, in the imagination is where I feel my heart, and you were in there with me. I saw you there, and painted you there, and read you there, and sang you there. You sang back to me. *Help me, I think I'm falling—in love—with you. Only love can break your heart. I believe when I fall in love with you, it will be forever. When I fall in love, it will be forever. You don't know what it's like, baby, you don't know what it's like, to love somebody, to love somebody, the way I love you.*

The mad joy of love is feeling that the love belongs to the loved one, that it goes home to the loved one. The despair of love is feeling that that love has nowhere to go, and is therefore gone, when the loved one is gone. The madness again is feeling that it cannot be gone, and therefore the loved one cannot be gone, even when all evidence is to the contrary. "You" cannot, but must, make this journey—turn from the specific to an abstract.

I have a boyfriend. He calls himself my partner. He loves me. He misses me. He is real and the other is gone. He wants to know if he has my heart. I have told him I will return to him on a certain day at a certain time. Dear Reader, what shall I do? This letter is for you.

On Mothers, Lovers, and Other Rivals

Ana Castillo

This is not the story about a love affair. It is a story about *the* love affair. It doesn't tell how it started or all the good stuff along the way. It is only about its inevitable end. There was a lot of good stuff, to be sure. For example, I recall the hard-earned week at a resort in Manzanillo where we spent most of the time in our room or by the pool and back to our room. There were piña coladas, "La Bikina" piped in through speakers, and how I marveled at how blond her hair turned with the sun and how golden her skin. Long before safe strap-on orgies were organized in Nevada or we ourselves had that talk and moseyed into a women's toyshop, we were making it happen with extremities and imagination. When we weren't giving each other orgasms we read all of Galeano (with the exception of *Open Veins of Latin America)* aloud. It was a book we each had read before we met—one of the million points of light that first bonded us.

Going on vacation to that place was my idea. When I was pregnant a few years before we met, I had been following a telenovela that was set there. Living in a Midwestern city and pregnant in summer with no air conditioning, I thought the resort looked like paradise. When I was in labor, during contractions I'd close my eyes and project myself to that beach. I vowed that if I got through it alive (not an exaggeration when you're in the last stages) I'd go one day. I told her about my promise and that's what we did—went to an agency and booked a week in paradise.

Then there was that Saturday in autumn. When the fog of San Francisco draped the city as night fell and after making love all afternoon, she began reading *Pentimento* to me. The next morning my lover went out for scones and then made coffee and we read the *San Francisco Chronicle* in bed. We loved the Pink Pages and combed them for all the things we might want to see and do. I fell in love with Hellman's language and was already in love with Galeano's. To this day I cannot think of either writer without remembering her and those occasions strewn naked against starched sheets, smeared with each other's scent, and reading in near whispers. I fell in love with Sunday mornings in bed together with the paper and no one since has taken her place. There was a lot of shared reading, irreverent sex, and, yes, we wrote. It was with the writing, what we both swore was as important as all the rest of it, if not more, where the good stuff went bad.

My toddler spent the weekends with his father. Funny, it took a separation to get my husband to spend time with either of us. From that loneliness I went to a relationship where I was anything but, or at least that was what I thought at first. In time, I would finally accept that loneliness was integral to being alive. Nobody makes you feel that way and likewise nobody takes it away. But the memories dipped in "good stuff" tell me that for moments, at least, the loneliness was soothed when I was in her company. My husband, a good provider, nevertheless made little time for his young family, as I've mentioned. As a full-time mother I remember that Saturday night and the next morning because it was rare to have the chance to do my most favorite things—read, have sex, sleep in, repeat. I remember the good stuff the way a kid remembers a day at the circus, as singular and magical. Even after she grows up and learns it was all tricks and invisible wires, it was real enough at the time.

So far in life, I've been truly in love only once with a woman. How it came to be was like a personalized meteorite had plunged from the sky faster than the speed of sound and left a radiating crater in my chest. It felt like a nonstop poem in progress and I couldn't get hold of its meter or rhyme or if, in fact, it held any. Identity, literature, and the G-spot combined in a single fuse. Because of my cynical disposition, I went around suspicious that soon the gilded fuse would be lit and, boom, game over. Such a potent combination in the heart of a young brown woman poet would surely be the death of her. It wasn't because I had fallen in love. It was that part of me had been validated. Validation proved my existence.

What do I mean by validation? It meant that another person recognized how I saw the world and did not judge me as loca. And what I mean by crazy here is not the kind where you'd find yourself in the loony bin or more often now on prescribed drugs. I refer to the crazy that people think you are because you don't agree with the system or how it treats you as a woman, tap-tap like water dripping every waking second, and you must be loca because you've set out to challenge it.

That is what being in love is about, after all: being validated. It was my lover, however, who put the match to the fuse during our first rendezvous out of town. It is why this story is about the end because the end started so near the beginning.

For our getaway, a friend lent us his apartment near the beach in Carmel. I left my toddler in the care of his father and she and I drove to the coast. I want to say it was late spring or early summer but the sea is always cold in northern California and the waves often choppy and gray like they were on that occasion. We took pictures of each other along the hostile shore. (I assume we did but I don't believe I have any.) Every time I think of being on the shore with her there I remember a story about a young Asian family on vacation in California. As the husband snapped the picture of his wife and child, a monster wave rose from behind and lapped them up to their deaths. I don't know where I heard this story or if I knew it then. Somehow, for whatever reason, when I remembered it I saw myself as that smiling woman holding her child and the next instant disappearing.

I don't recall what we ate, if we stayed in and cooked or had romantic dinners out. I am only certain that we mostly did what newly minted lovers do best, especially away from society's scornful eyes. It was after sex that my beloved told me what would change our course. She was hopelessly in love with someone else. It was a much older woman, who was "ostensibly straight" and had refused to come out.

We had been fucking like two starving porn starlets for days and nights. I learned things about my own body that you couldn't find in books. (My copy of *Our Bodies, Ourselves* was worn thin. It had helped me through pregnancy and childbirth. It was the eighties and, of course, no Internet. There had been *The Hite Report* in the seventies, which led me to a kind of *I'm Ok, You're OK* view about my desires. But there were things you couldn't know from books even if they came with diagrams.) My lover's confession was so incongruous to our heated coupling that I had no way to process the letdown.

The other woman was not at fault for the infliction that began to fester where the meteorite had landed. Apparently, after their tryst, which had occurred perhaps two or three years earlier, she'd made her feelings clear. She wanted only to maintain the friendship, which had a basis in their shared radical feminist of color views. If literature fed our souls as writers, the content of that literature was the acknowledgment of our perceptions. Our writing made them real. I had nothing but respect for their alliance.

Feminists of color had to be united. These two hadn't been sharing cups of sugar across the fence and one day decided to fuck and see what it was like. In the seventies and eighties meeting a feminist of color was like meeting someone from the Résistance. These underground liaisons were so vital to the greater cause they sparked all kinds of heretofore forbidden feelings. One held on regardless of personal disappointments. As I saw it, the other woman in my lover's mind, however, had become the "obscure object of desire." In other words, something my lover couldn't have.

Before the extent of information currently at our fingertips through social media and the Internet hungry minds learned about life from periodicals, TV, radio, books, and foreign and indie films. Gleaning the kind of information one felt she needed to grow was not easy. In Chicago in my late teens I caught films at art movie houses. It was where I discovered Bergman, Fellini, and Truffaut. One day, I thought, I'd become a film director and would tell the stories of brown women in the States that no one saw on the big screen. The genre would be called Chicana Noir because our narratives were invariably dark.

One of my favorite movies was Buñuel's *That Obscure Object of Desire*. It cleverly related how we (and by we, he meant men) were drawn toward what we saw in a woman and not necessarily what was there. As feminist thought developed, women would be referred to as "other" (as would most marginalized people). But before that was written out by intelligent and learned feminist minds, as one who was often seen as "exotic" and therefore sexualized, I identified with Buñuel's film. To this day I don't think that most of the men I've ever dealt with intimately knew me. Instead, they saw what they wanted to see.

What I heard from my lover that afternoon when the bubble of what I considered our sublime union had burst was that she wanted that woman to be someone for her that she was not. My head throbbed and ears rang as if I'd just heard a mine explode. *¡Qué barbaridad! Tell me, it's not true!* I kept thinking. If the political agenda of the radical feminist lesbian was to have a right to her sexuality, who was she to object to the choices other women made?

It was an era when sexual identity was black and white. You chose one camp or another. When white women switched off, her friends and former lovers might disapprove but she slipped comfortably into her place in society. Women of color were marginalized no matter what. There were two races and brown was under scrutiny as a race by all. It was a time when there were two genders. There were two sexualities. Queer meant being gay and not what it currently refers to now—to be anything in between gay and hetero.

I would venture to say that today the Other Woman might have considered herself queer, not straight, ostensibly or otherwise. But it was a period in modern history of hardliners. You were either "with us" or "against us," so to speak. My lover declared herself butch and I, with my tight skirts and red lipstick, was classified as femme. These presentations or, as I often call them, costumes (which has everything to do with my own penchant for fashion) did not necessarily speak to who we were inside. Or at least not to me, as I only speak for myself here. Today, the discussions among activists have evolved such that a wide range of identities may be expressed under the two umbrella terms: butch and femme. Furthermore, a person, if she chooses, may change these identities in accordance with the situation. A femme may now identify as femme and be straight. I struggled with wanting to know who my lover was beneath the mullet haircut and trousers. I urged her toward trying other "costumes" and sometimes I took to wearing trousers. After we broke up she grew her hair out, which, being fine, also softened her appearance. I never knew why she was wearing it long or if there was a connection, but that was when she decided to get pregnant and became a mother.

Somehow, I afforded two or three therapy sessions to discuss all this with an objective analyst. I found a Latina lesbian. If she was helpful at all I can't recall but I don't think so. Mostly, she sat across the room in her office and listened. What I do remember was that having an outsider listen, I thought, was worth it. I was so protective of my lover and concerned that my therapist was among her fans that I never used her name (just as I am not doing here), which the therapist found disturbing. Afterward, I would treat myself to a cup of tea at Athena's Café on Valencia and then, with four part-time jobs, my "me time" was over. I had to pick up my child from the sitter and get home to make dinner. After Mi'jo's bath, story, and lights out, I'd return to work. I had two part-time teaching gigs, but at home I applied myself to freelance translations (English to Spanish) for a textbook company and was also translating *This Bridge Called My Back* into Spanish for a small press. When my husband and I decided to separate he told my mother-in-law that I was into women. While he agreed initially to let our son and me have the apartment, she was intolerant of the news that I was lesbian and wanted me out in six months. In that amount of time I would hardly have been able to change my job situation so that I could afford an apartment for Mi'jito and myself in San Francisco. This was in large part the reason my lover and I decided to take a place in Oakland. We could split expenses there.

Questions popped up in Carmel, reverberating off walls, closing in until I said we had to leave and began packing. What was a lesbian feminist doing pining over a straight woman? Why had she encouraged me to leave my husband for her if she was in love with someone else? (Obviously, I would have left eventually; I didn't fault or credit her for that decision. At the time however, she wanted it to happen immediately as proof of my sincerity.)

It was that day, while passions for each other raged and the potential of camaraderie as writers seemed boundless, that the end began. With the confession, it was my lover, not the other woman, who became my rival. When I wasn't surrendering myself to our relationship I was planning my escape. If I couldn't have her, she would never have me. Nora in *A Doll's House* comes to mind now and maybe did then. It wasn't freedom from a man that

I sought. It wasn't that I had to prove myself capable as a woman on my own. I was not going to live reflected in someone else's idea of me.

As time went on, my lover's feelings for the Other Woman, who lived on the East Coast, didn't seem to diminish. A year or so later, she announced it again, pounding her chest and telling me, with tears streaming, how she wished the Other Woman would get out of her heart. It was then that I learned how love could be sometimes. You could utterly abhor (intermittently) the one person you most loved. Whether this was a truth or not, I am certain that was what I felt from the door of our bedroom watching her cry. By then, we had our own apartment and our own bed, and in that bed, with me so near, she agonized over an unrequited love.

In many ways, the Other Woman wasn't only irrelevant to our problems; she wasn't even real. I felt this despite a framed picture of her that my lover kept on display. For a long time I thought it was her grandmother. When I realized who the hunched woman with bifocals and bun was, I absorbed a good lesson in feminism. Now that I am past the age of the woman in that picture, I am glad to know that real passion has no age or aesthetic limits. In straight relationships, many women have suffered the humiliation of being left for younger women. It used to be that cross-generational, same-sex couples were often formed. Yet as same-sex attractions became more acceptable, looks and factors such as class and race that applied in straight society crossed over, too, and such couples don't form as frequently these days. Ageism is alive and well. But back then, what brought same-sex people together was mostly their sexuality, which was so marginalized by society that it limited the dating pool.

Drama continued throughout our relationship, which lasted for three years. Because we were together nearly every day or at least in touch daily, produced two anthologies, traveled near and far, met each other's families, and lived a public and private life together, those three years were compressed intensity times ten. Drama happened all the time but the one involving the Other Woman she acted out on an actual stage.

My lover turned actress in order to perform her play. It was about the Other Woman's rejection. She was on the rise. I stood for the ovation, clapping enthusiastically and proudly because that was my role. As a writer I understood that what one took from life was not what was important but the product. Afterward, back stage, I brought flowers. It was a triumphant evening for her and it would have been among the good stuff but I don't recall her treating me on that occasion like a protégé or her lover but instead as among her admirers that night. The loneliness was back.

When the time came and I got the courage to leave her, she disappointed me again. Rumors came to my attention that my now former lover had led others to think that she had given me everything and that breaking with her had broken her heart. When we met I had been married to a man. Gossip came to me that her supporters claimed my departure meant that I had abandoned the lesbian front. It wasn't that I was more susceptible to gossip than the next person. It was that what I heard rang true of her accusations before we split. There had been fallout, all right, which I prefer not to remark further on here.

The fact was, I hadn't left women; I had left one woman. Moreover, before I moved out of the apartment, she had already replaced me. She'd found a new partner in a position to take her to the next step in her career. In time New York City would fête them and I heard the mayor came to one of their openings.

While I've had romantic liaisons with women and, later, men, for most of the rest of my life thus far I've remained on my own. During the years that followed our breakup, I was dedicated to producing work, making a living, and raising my son.

During the relationship she had been excited about my having Mi'jo.

We were both in our thirties and questions about motherhood were always present. There was the proverbial biological ticking clock. As women together, however, further challenges were present around adoption, IVF was brand new and expensive, same-sex marriage was prohibited, and partners were not eligible for health benefits or community property. Then there was her identity as butch. She asked herself if becoming a mother wouldn't go against being what is now termed a masculine of center womyn. Regarding my child, she was so immediately enthralled with the idea of one in her life that I had the feeling that my having a kid was a big part of my appeal. Moreover, in time her lament at our breakup seemed to me to be more over the loss of my child in her life than of me. Adopting a child together, where she would be the primary mother, seemed it would solve some of the conundrum. After all, Mi'jo had two present parents and my lover and I were not yet ready to make the long-haul commitment.

Neither of us had full-time employment or was able to afford her own apartment in San Francisco. In the second year of our relationship we moved in together into a shady but affordable neighborhood in Oakland. After a few bad encounters, I was miserable there. We made the best of it. During those months we took turns getting my son to nursery school, after which she returned to write in her study. She had her own room with a door. Since my child, who had all the things children often come with, had a room, I worked in the living room. While she and my estranged husband made random purchases for him, neither paid for his care. Since my separation from his father, I had become the primary financial supporter of my son, and this continued into his college years.

During the months we shared the apartment I asked her and a longtime friend of mine to act as godmothers in a native ceremony. The friend also made a commitment to come around and spend time with my little boy each week, a promise that lasted while we lived in the vicinity. I saw them both as co-madres; what they could do was completely up to them, but neither was under any obligation.

Maybe we should have had a sign on the front door: "Feminist Household under Construction." Everything had to be discussed and figured out. Fairness and equality were paramount. My lover had a type A personality. For instance, dishes had to be done right after a meal. If it was my turn, then I had to do them then and there. Toys must be picked up when the child had finished playing with them, which it was his duty to do then and there.

She often assumed the authority of a parent, even at times over-stepping my own decisions. All this control became reason for friction between us. One day, as I lined kitchen shelves with Mi'jo playing nearby, she came in and gave him an order of some sort. "Are you my new father?" he asked.

No, she was not. In addition to other concerns I had, which may sound as absurd to young ears today, just as it may feel strange to consider a time when women couldn't vote, was that women lost custody of their children when they were proven not to be good wives—that is, good women. Any woman who had an adulter-ous affair could lose her children. A woman who was living with another woman held an additional stigma. Same-sex attraction was being reassessed in the American Psychiatric Association's *Diagnostic and Statistical Manual of Mental Disorders,* but the general view of the public was that it was perversion. That view found its way into the courts. My estranged husband would very likely have been able to take away our son, if he had chosen to do so. This was all a real threat to my being able to be a mother to my child at the time.

Today, an advocate for gay and lesbian rights might say, "Well, fight for it." I did. I did it privately. I did it publicly. I did it for my lover's sake, for mine and ours. I won custody. I fought to keep Mi'jo. In the long run, I felt at times that he wanted (or needed) his dad, not just a man in his life but his own father. And the challenge and struggle to keep my son didn't help the anxiety that arose amid all the other challenges she and I were facing as a new couple.

So as not to argue, especially not in the presence of others, I often remained silent when she ordered my child around or insisted he take her hand or sit with her instead of me. When my parents came to visit from Chicago, for example, they observed my lover's dominance in the household, especially with their grandchild. In private my mother called it to my attention. "Even if you were married, why would you allow it?" she wondered.

My lover's parents visited us a couple of times. They had grand-children and my son was not seen as one of them. He was their daughter's girlfriend's child. They supported their daughter uncon-ditionally and were pleasant to me but did not involve themselves in our relationship. After my child and I moved out, although the relationship was still intact, Mi'jo and I never saw them again.

During those months that we shared an apartment I concluded my lover wanted a child perhaps more than she wanted a rela-tionship or maybe our relationship. We had, in fact, discussed it during the idyllic week in Manzanillo. Since Mi'jo was from a marriage with two involved parents, she felt left out. We decided that an option to fulfill her own motherhood wishes could be that we should consider adopting and my lover would take the role of primary caretaker. If we split up, she would get custody as, we assumed, I would have my son.

The spring that we lived together I was offered a visiting profes-sorship out of town for the next school year. I had been unable to get work nearby, and the job would provide desperately needed income for me. I remember my four-year-old not having a coat that winter in Oakland. His father finally purchased one that looked like he had picked it up on the fly after I had badgered him so much. The vinyl pink girl's jacket he bought stands out in my mind as a symbol of one of the hardest years struggling as a writer and mother. I vowed that my offspring would never lack for anything and stopped begging his father for support.

Before the lease was up, I moved out. As usual my child went to spend the summer with his father and in the fall, of course, he came to live with me to start kindergarten. She and I didn't break up. Her theater career was taking off and she had projects that required her presence. We kept up long distance as we were able for another year and at the end of the second school term we finally called it quits. I wasn't coming back to her or to the Bay Area. I couldn't find affordable housing there. I moved again to another city to take a new residency in order to support my son and writing.

The next academic term after we broke up she came around once, insisting she had something akin to custodial rights. His father, who did have custodial rights, had the now six-year-old most weekends; otherwise, I had full responsibility. On that occasion, when my ex-lover returned with my boy and in her usual alpha manner gave him some order in front of me, I'd had enough. As she walked off I yelled for her to do the world a favor but especially her and have a child of her own. Sometime after, I heard she did just that. Until then, and for some time, again ugly rumors drifted my way that she continued to lament that I had taken away "our" son. I think it made a good story for some: the idea that a lesbian activist was being victimized by her "ostensibly not-lesbian ex." If I sound cynical it is because the results of bad tales sometimes do damage. Enough said on that point.

After I had moved out and just before the ties were fully broken I'd met someone, too. It was to be an uneven fit and while we would have numerous comings together over the decades that followed, we usually parted with severe ruptures and never came together as partners. If the public didn't know about this relationship it wasn't because I had scurried back into the closet. My on-and-off-again lover came from a Middle Eastern family with some money and both the culture and her professional ambition kept her attraction to women under wraps. Romantic relationships between women from traditional cultures came with a warning label. *Caution: May produce ill effects and, while uncommon, even death.* Eventually, she managed to live her life freely but that was many years later and with someone else.

Game not quite over, but no question, women could mean emotional hell. Everything I went to women for in a relationship backlashed. Women were indomitably strong in all senses but they could also be weak. They cheated. They lied. They were vain. Like men who were ambitious, they could also be egotistical. Some women were spoiled and liked to be spoiled. (Being *chiflada*, as I saw it, didn't gel with me, unless they were willing to spoil me, too.) Like men, they could fall in love with younger, white, more successful or serviceable women. These were the conclusions I drew from my experiences. In sharing them I don't aim to trivialize the relationships I had. The good stuff went deep and became integral to my core being. It wouldn't be honest, however, to reflect on what was true without being willing to look at the lies.

Years passed, and when my son was in middle school, I had a brief marriage with a man. The rumors from the Bay Area found their way to me again. This heterosexual marriage seemed to be the final vindication for those who thought of me as only having played with a famous lesbian's heart.

In general, I haven't cared much for labels. Sometimes they are an important byway for introducing yourself. Many times they are slippery and lack concision. When you come to the next juncture in your journey, this might call for reassessment and a new description. You aren't recanting or flip-flopping when you change a label to be true to yourself. We shed old skins, morphed from cocoons, transformed. Even if the outside looks somewhat the same, you never come out the same. The new you is real, just as you were real in the previous form. A couple of times I've been

identified by the media as polysexual. "What was that?" I wondered at first and looked it up. After some thought, I've concluded
that it may be accurate.

Perhaps as feminists of color preparing new ground we were all
on unfamiliar territory. It would not be an embellishment to say
we went about our public and private lives suited in armor. Our
armors were our pragmatic analyses, our evolving theories made
from day-to-day living. I'd broken off a leftist straight marriage to
be with a feminist lesbian without any game plan. We were making it all up as we went along. Neither should or could say she was
100 percent right and the other, likewise, wasn't wrong by default.
("Who washes dishes?" "We take turns, of course." "Yes, but when?"
"Now!" "Now? I don't want to do it now. Don't try to control me."
"I'm not trying to control you but it isn't fair that dirty dishes should
sit in the sink while I am trying to concentrate on my work in my
room!" "At least you have a door . . . close it!" It sounds funny now.
It wasn't then.) Both domestic and professional divisions of labor
came up between us as we worked on two books together, and I
was at times the insecure woman I was brought up to be when in
love with a man. To muddle my mind and heart further, my first
feminist lover, brilliant and sensitive in so many ways, had her
own issues. As I write this reflection, I see that the matters of the
Other Woman who left her and, later, my departure with Mi'jo, to
whom she had grown quickly attached, are not totally unrelated.
It seems, as I see it now, that fear of abandonment may have been
an unexamined issue in her arsenal. If so, perhaps our union had
nowhere to go but to end.

Or what we'd had until then was over.

A decade later we encountered each other at a conference banquet. All she wanted to know was how my son was doing, she said.
When her current partner left to do something, we got up to dance.
The dance turned into a slow one and, in each other's arms, she
rested her head against my shoulder. Several people jumped up
and began taking photographs and the intrusion upset her.

"It's okay," I said.

"But I give my people everything of me," she lamented. Perhaps she did to some people. But despite her assertions, she hadn't given everything to me.

Recently, we had a new exchange. A vicious rumormonger was at it in the worst way and had involved her. This time to assure me that she was not involved, she reached out. Nearly thirty years after the start of our affair and despite years of estrangement, there we were on a familiar topic. She contacted me via the most popular twenty-first-century form so far: through email. It wasn't ironic that what brought us together was vile gossip intended to cause animosity between us. Experiences, like matter, don't dissipate. They change form (yes, like identities.) Love is an experience. That experience has left us connected. She didn't want Mi'jo and me to feel she would ever want to hurt us. We finished our exchange as proud mothers, sending pictures of our sons, now grown men.

P.S. A couple of years after my lover and I split, the Other Woman moved to the Bay Area and was teaching at a university. She had included one of my novels in her course and invited me to speak at her class. When the session was over and as the students left, she said, "Ana, I meant to ask you something." At the door I turned and waited. "Have you ever read Clarice Lispector?" I had not. Lispector, from faraway Brazil, was from a previous generation and long gone from this strange and wonderful thing we call life. "Your writing reminds me so much of hers," she said.

Walking slowly across the campus, I wondered who this writer she named was, this person who supposedly came from the same interior world from which I wrote. I went directly to a bookstore.

Reading has always been part of the good stuff.

They say there are two sides to every story. This is mine.

Ring Theory

Sejal Shah

YELLOW GOLD

Six months after my husband tied an ornate gold mangalsutra around my neck and friends showered us with rice, I chose a wedding ring. Under the noontime Chennai sun, the center stone glowed, a cabochon dome. Inside the store, the ring spoke quietly: reserved, a dark magenta set with two tiny diamonds. Yellow gold, typical Indian gold, South Indian temple-style setting. I picked this ring halfway around the world from where we live in Rochester, at a store in Chennai my parents-in-law have frequented for years. They designed my wedding necklace here and bought the other jewelry I wore, all of it presented as part of the ceremony. I had not chosen any of this adornment; it was, per tradition, my in-laws' choice.

NEW MEXICO

Three years earlier, I flew to New Mexico for a friend's birthday, a week after my own. We had once been roommates, long been friends. We spent one afternoon in Santa Fe, wandering the Georgia O'Keeffe Museum—the reason my friend chose New Mexico. O'Keeffe was a strong woman, an individual, an artist we both admired. In the gift shop, a particular designer's rings called to both of us—sturdy, each different, each with an architectural quality. I am usually drawn to simpler, smaller jewelry, though larger pieces look sharper and suit me. My friend and I deliberated over who would buy what, but different rings called to each of us. I found mine: thick-banded and modernist, a statement in a way I don't tend to make. They were inexpensive: we marked our fortieth birthdays with jewelry that cost less than forty dollars.

Now my New Mexico ring is discolored from wear and water. I wore it every day for the two years I taught ninth graders and on dates and during the two months my grandmother was in the hospital and in rehab for her stroke; I did not remove it when I washed my hands at school or restaurants, at the hospital.

This ring had presence, declared itself without shouting. It evoked the moon, the sun, an egg, a shield; a talisman in motion, a pendulum at the moment of pause.

SILVER

Later that same week, my friend and I drove south, to White Sands National Monument. My friend had signed us up for a moonrise walk there, and we tread and twirled, taking photos of shadows, across all that sparkling (in sun), then glowing (in dusk) sand (was it once an ocean?), it was a desert: beautiful—barren—stark. The dunes recalled salt flats I had seen in Sicily, a lifetime ago in my twenties, wearing a silver ring from Mexico I've since lost. The dunes and silver ring reminded me of all that had slipped by unnoticed, all that had happened, and had not happened, since then. What we knew or didn't know about friendship, about time; about which jewelry lasts and for how long; about which friendships last and for how long; about how meaning morphs with age; about age itself.

146

HAMMERED

A few years ago, I left New York City, unwilling, when it came down to it, to hustle. I had not found a partner, not secured a book contract or tenure. All the golden handcuffs. But I didn't want to stay on the treadmill or in the water, treading, waiting for life to begin. I did not want to lean in. Instead, I opted out. I landed in India, and traveled for a few months. Then I moved back home. Before all that, I threw a ring into the East River—a hammered silver one I had bought for the interview for the job I had just left. It was my longest relationship, that job. After eight years in academia, leaving was my divorce.

MANGALSUTRA

In western New York, I marry a teacher who had grown up two miles from me, just outside Rochester. We live here, ten miles from the shore of Lake Ontario, the smallest of the Great Lakes. His parents chose the mangalsutra and the particular design of the pendant. He is South Indian, I am North Indian, we are Hindu. We place flowers in rituals in water, at the temple, at home; we are told to gaze at the full moon, to drink in the moonlight, and there are special full-moon pujas. He is not an artist, but it is an art of sorts—marriage—learning a way to live together.

NEW MEXICO RING

I vacillate, take time to make a decision. Yet that first ring had been easy, like something out of Georgia O'Keeffe's world, harsh in its beauty and also elegant. An amulet, a protection, a shield, a decorated sword: proud, confident—not bashful. What a strong woman would wear when she's single and maybe has just lost her job. And maybe she hasn't published her first book, but who's counting?

Is it strange to have such a strong feeling about a ring? When I decided to marry my husband, no ring leapt out and said, *Here*.

This. Here I am. Even after I got married. Perhaps part of it was that no engagement or wedding ring I tried on or found looked right with my New Mexico ring on.

I did not want him to choose a ring. *I'll be wearing it,* I said. How could someone else choose it?

BRASS RING

The year we were engaged, I wore a slim hexagonal brass ring my husband bought at a small shop I liked. We knew the designer. Though I did not choose it, I wore the ring on my left pinky and it stamped a moss green band around the base of that finger, ghostly, oxidizing. But the whole time I was engaged, that whole year, I wore my New Mexico ring on my middle finger and an almost invisible band on my pinky finger. And no other rings. Nothing on my ring finger.

I consult the dictionary. A brass ring (informal) *refers to wealth, success, or a prestigious position considered as a goal or prize,* e.g.: *few of those who reach for the brass ring of the presidency achieve it.*

A month before my husband presented me with the brass ring (though we had already decided to marry), my in-laws hosted a ceremony in their home, according to South Indian tradition. This event proclaimed our engagement: a document signed by our parents and my brother and sister-in-law; a priest from Toronto, a fire ceremony, chanting, lunch, many flowers, our immediate families, and my grandmother, aunt, nephews, cousin, and cousin-in-law present. No rings. I wasn't even sure I wanted one.

Getting engaged and married is considered an achievement in the countries or cultures to which I belong by birth or ancestry, by nationality or ethnicity, by language or skin, by blood or memory, by gender and age. I did not want getting married to be the greatest achievement in my life.

TIFFANY RING

A month before the wedding, my sister-in-law and I ducked into Tiffany's, an unplanned side trip at the Providence Place Mall. I slipped on solitaires and halos and snapped a few photos, images to send my fiancé. Oddly thrilling, that sea-green, blue-green store. But 11,000 dollars? Ridiculous, obscene, blood diamonds lacking imagination. But the sparkle and flash: I could see how the parade could topple a person.

TOTEM

I lost the card that came with my New Mexico ring, but Googled until I dredged it up. The designer, *Christophe Poly*, Montreal-based. The rings, unique and particular, need care. Wear them in water, you ruin them.

Right now, my hands are swollen and I can wear no rings. But mostly I could never wear both, and that has been hardest: I knew this to be true the day we bought the wedding ring, and even more when I wore it, followed by all the days after.

When I bought the New Mexico ring, I chose myself, my life, without needing to prove anything to anyone. I had already failed and I was, strangely, happy.

Nothing has felt right in terms of an engagement or wedding ring. I debated returning to my New Mexico ring: sometimes adornment can serve as both talisman and totem, speaking for who we are. Then months pass, and we can never wear a thing again, or not for a while, leaving it to lie unworn and forlorn. Yet for a time, a pendant or ring can hold such power: an emblem filled with energy, force, intention, love.

METAL

Once I married, I found it almost impossible to be the self I had previously forged. Isn't the point of an engagement or wedding ring that it should outshine your other rings? It is the thing that shows, that is meant to be noticed. Recently I slipped on a plain band, something cheap I found in my jewelry drawer. It suited me and my husband agreed. A simple, nondescript metal. I didn't want the fact of my being married to be the most noticeable thing about me.

Though I knew my husband was the right one, I never felt that way about a ring. Now my hands are swollen, and I wear no rings. Not swollen from pregnancy, but just mysterious swelling, from punching these words perhaps.

AMULET

In India, I found a quiet-eyed cabochon, a cipher. The Burmese ruby has no flash, no game—it is a non-neon digital crimson; polished, not cut, modest and understated. We would leave Chennai in a few days and I was afraid if I did not choose a ring there when I had a deadline, I might never do it.

I wear my wedding ring when I go out, and the mangalsutra to the temple and sometimes when I dress up. During the day, when writing or at the gym or preparing to teach, I wear nothing, my hands clicking away on keys, typing. No nail polish, no rings.

Two years after the wedding, I call my father-in-law to ask what the mangalsutra means, why it matters to them—to my mother-in-law, especially—that I wear it. I know it identifies me as married. But I had never seen the pendant's design before, nor would I have chosen it. *It's a representation of Ganesh,* he says. Remover of obstacles. To protect one's husband from harm. To protect one from harm. Who wouldn't want that? I will wear my necklace more.

In a silver dish, the New Mexico ring and my wedding ring sit side by side. I look at them; they look back at me. None of the jewelry can be worn all of the time. I wait for them to speak, or for the next talisman to enter my life, to be summoned, to appear—and remind me of what I do not wish to forget.

The Unfounded:
A Nectar Guide in Names

Laynie Browne

I taste a liquor never brewed—
From Tankards scooped in Pearl—
—Emily Dickinson

I hoped the Unfounded would pierce the ribs of a tiger and in that
gesture transfigure my own landscape into the infinite.
—Hilda Hilst, *With My Dog Eyes*

Most people are other people. Their thoughts are someone else's
opinions, their lives a mimicry, their passions a quotation.
—Oscar Wilde

I don't remember where I was either in writing or life. O dear potion, concoction, of what are you constructed? Is it only your name I adore, guaranteed to induce love?

Let me tell you how my written husband came to me. It began with writing letters. Written concoctions. Was he a person of flesh and blood before the writing began? Most difficult to say. Even now as I write I am tormented and write to him constantly in thought. "I love you more than I can say." He wrote to me once, in breathless happiness—the early stabs of love. And it is true that I love him more than I should, especially considering we have never met.

The page can be so alluring. Strung up in letters. How to go back and make a book of our letters? Dearest star and angel, you are my utter delight. My fingers on keys. Your keys. Rub them gently within the arc of each letter. Back and forth. Vivid and dripping, tips of fingers. Freedom that shines and then at some point is severed. O liberty of page.

He was busy being tired. I would not allow it. I said nothing. Just took off all of my clothes and got into bed. His appetites are such that I was hopeful. I was not disappointed. He is my cloak. And goblet. The next day he said he appreciated my methods. I dare not speak of my strategies, lest all philters disappear. Nakedness as plea. Love me.

I live in the township of Nether Providence. Located toward the bottom or more distant part of something. Situated below or lower. Believed to be situated beneath the earth's surface. From nithera, nidar down the slope of a mountain. Between neth and nethermore. Archaic, rare, farther down, lower. Nethermore, mostly used only in literary contexts, and is not a true comparative for its formation. Akin to sub rosa. My nethermost symptoms being to exist solely as emblem. Aphrodite gave a rose to her son, Eros. Eros gave the rose to Harpocrates, god of silence. A nethermost providence remains undisclosed. Stranger still, my home cannot be mapped. Such a hidden rose is useful in worship.

I sit with you in this Nether-Emblem, beneath conjured paintings of roses on ceilings of sublunary banquet rooms as a reminder that all written under the influence of love intoxication, sub rosa, also remains within the rose of your lips. Thus I carve on the pages of my confessional nine-petaled roses.

I said to my beloved: it is my Providence to find you here, dear ambled and scrawled immortal love. You foresee and attend. I await with prudent anticipation. Sustaining and guiding. Often capitalized.

He turned to a key of pronunciation symbols, a thesaurus, a rhyming dictionary, and said: You only wish to browse me.

No, I objected, you are polished and urbane. Dish with towels for napkins, brick walls hung and hooded. You are incisive, beginning to resemble a piercing point. Intrepid plunge donning cold-water rescue. Opposing trepidation. Tireless.

How strong is your vocabulary? he asked.

I answered thus: Snow in planes of white, still opaque across the fields and yards visible from my window, yet upon ivy in triangular plot it merely dots the green approaching brown, as if sugared, points of brightness against the drab and textured dun trunks rising silent and thick toward pale white skies complicated by minute capillary tresses above, now naked of leaf.

He replied: My decoction, my philter, my tincture, dost thou know how to cure me? Make me mortal? Douse my lips with your sweet liquid tonic.

I considered a way to write our meeting in several possible manners, before the fact so as to assure me an escape route from the treacherous. Ruinous I mean.

So first I must outline all possible reactions we might immediately have toward each other and then write each one. Where to begin. The problem is that the most exciting is the most dangerous and though I long to be safe that means also that the route that will allow me passage safely nestled back into my current three-dimensional life is the most boring, disappointing, or even upsetting. The explosive route or the exponential route, meaning, by definition, love may expound things, is also the route which may bring pleasure first, pain later. And not only the pain of loss but the obliteration of my current mental vista. A clean plane of snow. A clear conscience. Almost.

I don't want to wait or to drown. Am I vivid? Am I in color? Are we alive, or merely script being fed from the rote hours of one suppository to another. Necklace, my neck lace placed about your throat. Do you see what I mean?

I am also afraid of my opposite, to look at you and see a lost hemisphere finally found, another lobe of the heart, connecting neurons as would any active hopeful participant in a drama which should be as flimsy as paper slip fans, or mortal life. The accident is in not knowing each other but having written ourselves thus far.

I wrote to you: let us not be anxious about our meeting. A nice idea, and like so many nice ideas completely confounded, lost, forgotten, or simply impossible. I should have said, I'm worried that you will not like me so much in person. Or I'm worried that I will like you more than that. And that you won't be trustworthy. How could I have been so idiotic as to trust someone with my well-being, self and dense inner linings of thought all flung upon like so many windows to reveal an intimate sitting room, borders undone, gowns flung about, flesh everywhere? And don't even mention dream. How might I have dared to be so free, so unlaced? I who, for several proper years, attended to my children, husband, and the page. Is it that they are mortal and that you are merely letters strung together which makes me so bold?

But again I was lying when I wrote about my written husband, who in the next chapter will be born into my arms. And then, where will we go? Who will we be?

I said I was going to explore the possible paths, then to write them as preludes. But thus far I have become tangled simply in trying to list them. Perhaps I should begin with one word for each possible path, as I don't seem to be able to keep track of anything more. My hands shake and are cold. I am waiting for repair persons to infiltrate my house and rob me of any small notion of concentration or sense. Still the day is bright with snow still laid out crisply.

Which path do I choose first? It seems impossible not to choose the path of most blistering love, most devastating and most obliterating. But wait, I don't know before I begin to write where this passage will lead. Passage one begins with the word: passage. Over or under, from one place to another. There were moorings for boats wanting passage to the lock. A narrow way, typically having walls on either side, allowing access between buildings or to different rooms within a building. A passage from a written book. The permission, right, or freedom to pass. The route or course by which a person travels. A hall or corridor. A slow cadenced trot executed with great elevation of the feet and characterized by a moment of suspension before feet strike the ground. From Italian *passeggiare*, to walk. A channel. A hall. Division of a piece of music. A sideways walk in which diagonal pairs of feet are lifted alternately. A road, an action of passage. Mountain pass. To go by, passer. To pass from one condition to another. An act of emptying. Passing a group of microorganisms or cells through a series of hosts or cultures. From Latin *passus*, pace.

Stop stalling, write the passage in which we meet! Yet how can I? Do I want to wait and write it from life? Impossible as life provides only the page, not permission, nor person. No, I'd rather not, knot from life nor naught. You, unfounded, having buried me again. Become me. You: written divine. Have I not begun because I am afraid? Relation of page to passage, to possession, to passion, to position? I am still writing in relation to my other self, perverse and intangible twin.

Why not show yourself, I wanted to ask. What did your parents teach you about love, that you would permit yourself to be unattended for so long, in so many bowers? I was taught there is no love without action. And even that a man might be well justified to look beyond his bed if often denied. I did not agree, yet only too well I understood. And now I wish I'd done even more for my mortal husband. He surprised me by saying love is never anyone else's imperative to satisfy. In your own hands, in your words, where will you go? What will you ask of the one beside you? Dear mortal husband, mine to clasp these many years. Something beneath person emerges with age. And so we weren't happy, were we? No, we were deliriously happy. I'm saying yes. Syllables. We've not mocked and maybe coiled. The lists which want bidden reflection of a house. We rub. Become a true friction.

See how I've gotten away from writing the meeting again? Perhaps we are merely a series of digressions. Names. Elixirs and first words. I will write the story of our meeting in several pseudonyms. This isn't a novel nor is it a directory or a rectory, nor could you call it anything beyond a passage of prose. When I write looking at such a picture then I am more alive. Look at those happy faces. You and a lark. I married you, dear mortal husband, now must we age? The written asides to fragmentary and unreal particulars are all a ruse in order to escape that we must be a series of names, digressions, words, in other words, rooms which must expire, pleasures which must end, capacities which ultimately must be given back, including our minds, including your beloved body, including the way you look at me. Come closer and look at me and let us see what we may recognize in each other. Yes. That is what I must turn from because every day does not allow such reverie or permission. With children to raise, tenure to be had, books to write, genes to decode, parents to care for, news to be read, travels to be taken. Pick up this thicket of bed-ridden laundered nouns, please. The stairs are calmly creeping up and down. Rub a back or a hip. Whisper something. Collide. Sleep. And then again we are off. There can be no complaining regarding such a copacetic union, regarding such precipitous ignitions, regarding the warmth which we come to know as voltage, a reliable comfort the way my head fits easily between your head and shoulder. The smell of skin purely edible, the delight of discovery which continues. But knowing that on the day of our nuptials we were very happy to recite *till death do us part*, that sounds a bit less cheery into middle age knowing one will depart, the other will be left. My name is Riven. No, not yet. Never. And yet just looking into the eyes of my dead stepmother changes the course of my written excursions. I covet the illusion of the permanently written. I want to be free of my customs and associations until I am someone else with another life not nearly as dear to me. How could it be, only coming into existence as I write? Newness is the keen remedy for unkind blights. Newness for dejection and demented illusion to illuminate a winter's night. If you do not understand me perhaps you live inside the body of an uninitiated youth. Forgive me, young lovers, bereft of the spectrum of loss. I know you. Have been you. Forgive me, bright and unending day. I am here where I never expected to be, and thus begins the first passage of meeting a sublimely unreal written lover who materializes in a series of travels and ultimately may reveal to me his name.

A Season of Sophistication

Bonnie Friedman

He was from a tiny town in the South; I was a girl from the Bronx. His skin was scented with chlorine, for he swam at six each morning; I avoided the gym and remained immobile for so many hours in my rigid Windsor chair at the kitchen table, studying, that my bones creaked, although I was just twenty-six. If I carried any aroma it was the oil from the fish sticks on which I subsisted in my one-room apartment surrounded by the snowy back fields of Iowa City, and the Herbal Essences shampoo that was my sole indulgence. I came from a bookish household in which I'd surmised that the best existence was one lived on the empyrean of abstraction, as if one might truly scale one's way to the land of ideal geometric shapes that Plato proposed, and dwell there.

He'd been red-shirted in high school—purposely held back a year, that is, so he'd grow bigger to play football—on the decree of his father. Sports took priority. He was the first brainy man I'd met who had backwoods origins. He wrote superb haiku but swaggered when he walked, strolling as if his hips were weighted with a holster. Once I showed him a snapshot of my brother and he exclaimed, "He looks so Jewish." I saw for the first time and forever the prominence of my dear brother's nose below his keen, trusting brown eyes. On another occasion this man remarked that women with short hair do not like men—a claim so preposterously unfeminist I stared. Was he serious? Yes.

And yet, ah, in bed.

Or when walking toward me down Jefferson Street in his leather aviator jacket with its broad, slouched shoulders. Or standing in his jeans with his legs apart so he could be my height and gaze straight into my eyes with a bemused expression that made me feel seen, and savored.

I was on the lam from a boyfriend to whom I'd gotten engaged too soon. We'd met when I was twenty-one, and I loved him. But there was something both hangdog and punitive about him. So I'd come to grad school solo. I'd run away. I lived alone in an underheated room with a vinyl pullout couch and a stove the size of a hatbox. The boyfriend was back East. And almost immediately after stepping off the Greyhound bus in Iowa and starting classes, I met this southern man who also had a committed relationship (strike that: a compelling relationship) back home, his with a woman named Dolly. I'd never met a Dolly in the Bronx. Dolly was a statuesque woman with a sprayed updo and flawlessly applied makeup. In a photo that he pulled out of an envelope one afternoon at his mailbox, she clutched a football t-shirt to her otherwise naked breasts. "Uh-oh. Some cheesecake!" he said with a smile of affection. The jersey was from his favorite team. "Wants to make sure I don't forget her."

"She shouldn't worry," I said breezily, eyebrows aloft. Having a lover made me feel sophisticated, blithe, able to tease and scoff. I didn't feel guilty because my heart wasn't involved, nor was his.

"Likes to tell me what she's cooked for supper. Last week it was chicken-fried steak, fresh-cooked green beans amandine, instant whipped potatoes from a box, which she knows I like, and a great big lattice-topped apple pie with homemade vanilla ice cream."

"I bet it tasted good."

"I bet it did," he said thoughtfully.

"I am truly incompetent in the kitchen."

He gave me a sidelong look. "That can change."

I grinned. "Not likely to, however."

I took a kind of comfort in the existence of Dolly—the fact that Jim and I each had a separate partner kept things equitable—and I studied her with what I told myself was ironic interest.

Surprisingly, to me, she'd married at sixteen, to her high school social-studies teacher, and she'd had three children before discovering the extent of her husband's limitations. In the photo she fixed a gamine gaze at the camera, clutching that football jersey to her obviously shapely breasts—and appeared intimidatingly sexual and self-possessed. And yet also incredible, theatrical: a giant Barbie. Could Jim take her seriously?

He could and did. He liked the way she bit her lip. He liked that she was both insecure and, beneath that, confident. They were two of a set. He spoke to her for an hour every Saturday morning, when the rates were low. She had dated his older brother before she dated him. Now she and Jim talked about marriage. I was secretly dubious. He was a writer of poems who aimed to be a high school teacher, and it occurred to me she might have had her fill of teachers by then. Still, no matter how many husbands life might provide (for her obdurate vulnerability seemed to forecast many nuptials), I felt Jim would always love her. He was a kind of Joe DiMaggio; he had that gallantry in him. I liked it.

He and I lay on our backs on the foldout bed looking at the holes in the insulating drop ceiling as if hoping to find a new constellation. He wanted me, he wanted me. I wasn't sure that my fiancé back home was someone who wanted me physically, not the way Jim did. Nor did I know if I wanted my fiancé that way. It was a question between my fiancé and me: our sexuality.

Late at night Jim would come up my carpeted stairs and rap with his knuckles on the lightweight prefab door. We turned on the radio and I pulled beers out of the fridge—skunky Budweisers;

I didn't know better—and we danced on the rug. Or I'd walk over to his first-floor apartment beside a snowbound river, and he'd set in his cassette player a tape of Billie Holiday. I'd never heard Billie Holiday before. It was a 1958 recording, her voice all swerve and rasp.

Jim said, "I think her late recordings were her best. She had only her style left." He made it sound like a feather boa. I listened hard. What did he hear? I still liked the treacly harmonies of Art Garfunkel. And a certain strumming, merrily driving ditty on the Partridge Family album: "Point me / in the direction of / Albuquerque!" My tastes were unevolved. I ate apricot sauce from a Gerber jar. I wore Clark's Treks, cloddish shoes with a seam down the front like a surging umbilicus. I had not developed my awareness—could not let it mature—in part because I didn't think what I liked truly mattered. And so I couldn't properly digest and move on—from the Beach Boys to the Beastie Boys and Beethoven, from Madonna to an awareness of what was manipulative, crass, and even mawkish. And because I distrusted my own responses, I had to take a great deal on authority. Still, I could tell art held a key.

So I'd sat through *The Seventh Seal* twice but still could not tell why it was great, although it moved and haunted me. What did it mean to play chess with Death? Who was the knight? I watched *Scenes from a Marriage*, and while I understood that it was hurtful to have your husband fall asleep while you were reading him your diary of very private feelings, I didn't understand Liv Ullmann's lugubrious manner or her cloying beauty, or what I was supposed to make of the camera's transfixed, worshipful shots.

If I could understand these things—Bergman and Cocteau, Beckett and now Holiday—I would, I thought, be a less befuddled individual. I would have night goggles that let me see the hidden spirits that disoriented me. For my internal life was a haunted house with drafts and knocks that jolted up mysteriously, and I sensed that art might allow me to see the meaning of these bewildering internal phenomena.

"How do you do, you fool?" sang Billie Holiday beside the snow-banked river. "You're throwing your life away." Her voice was a wisp of Brillo scraping a skillet, something parched dry that hurt. Where was the beauty? The man I was dating lit the tapers of two candles. He'd cooked a supper for us in his kitchen with its mullioned windows. Fried chicken and biscuits and braised Brussels sprouts. He shut the lights and the room subsided into an oval glowing around us. Saturday night. "Summertime, and the living is easy," sang Billie.

"The most beautiful lullaby ever written," said Jim. I was surprised. I hadn't realized it was a lullaby.

"Play it again," I asked when it was over, and he did.

And then he played it a third time, without my asking. There was something about his disregarding what might be his own boredom in order to please me that made my eyes prickle with gratitude. "One of these mornings, you're gonna to rise up singing." Yes, it was a bedroom lyric. And the voice!—now I could hear that the singer had lived a passionate, difficult life, one marked with suffering. It gave a bittersweet quality to her performance, and the lyric brimmed with reassurance but also its opposite. So when Jim said he liked Billie's late recordings, he wasn't saying just the trendy, correct thing, it occurred to me.

"Is that the moon?" I asked, pointing at a dirigible suspended above a rooftop.

"My gosh," he said. "Yes."

We set aside the chicken bones, and I stepped out of my espadrilles, and we adjourned to the bed. The room smelled of paraffin, swimming pools, the baking soda from the biscuits, the slow seep of gas from his junky oven. A moan escaped me, and some part of me thought: this is the most important thing on earth, even as another aspect of me, an ancestral, shtetl aspect, declared that no, it was of no significance; it was animalistic, evanescent, of only illusory value. My true life was elsewhere.

Still, the marmalade from the biscuits we'd eaten was drenching through my veins and a voice inside me repeated, "Thank you, thank you," until it came out of my mouth. Unsuspected warmth flooded my thighs. My diaphragm had dislodged, to my dismay. I should have counted the days, known my cycle! After, I washed myself in the bathroom for a long time, shaking my head. "I'm so sorry," I blurted when I finally emerged.

"It's normal."

"But I ruined your sheets."

Wasn't he angry? I looked at him closely.

"That's what sheets are for!" he said with a laugh.

Oh! Why, how very gracious! Yes, what an extremely gracious, kind response.

He had pulled off the old sheets (thankfully there was no stain on the boxspring) and located fresh ones, and together we remade the bed. My fiancé would have stood in the corner while I stripped the bed and found clean sheets. He was squeamish.

Jim tucked in his corner, and we lay back down. The lights were off, and the snow alongside the river glowed blue. "There's Lester Young," said Jim when a horn sounded between lines of Billie Holiday's song. I hadn't noticed it. "On the tenor sax. What a lovely tone."

I nodded. Sunny, relaxed, glowing riffs between the lines of lyric. Tenor sax.

"She loved him. Prez. The man in the porkpie hat. He stepped toward the microphone only when she stepped away." Jim fell silent. Listening, he shook his head slowly from side to side and I did, too. It was Gabriel's trumpet, announcing a beauty I'd never noticed before.

The phone rang. Jim pulled on his shorts as he spoke. His back was to me. I wasn't disturbed. My lips even quirked up in their old smirk. It was good that he had Dolly because I had my fiancé. "Well, someone should punch that guy's lights out!" he exclaimed. "Yeah, I'll handle it when I get back. Uh-huh. Sure thing. Yes. Don't worry, baby."

163

I considered the man to whom I was engaged. Simon didn't talk about punching people's lights out. He wouldn't presume to tell me he'd take care of a situation that wasn't his own, but mine. We were feminists together. On some occasions, when he was feeling very happy, my fiancé clasped my hand in his and swung it, and I felt his particular pleasure in my company. I reminded myself of this as I listened to Jim speak to Dolly, the blue snowbanks glowing beyond him. Still, I found that for some reason I was becoming upset. I couldn't concentrate on the music. Get off the phone already, I told myself. Finally he returned.

He said, "Trouble with a disrespectful neighbor."

I nodded. He was brooding, staring up at the ceiling. Then he sighed, "Ah well. It's all part of life, I suppose. Nothing's wrong."

"Nothing's wrong," I agreed, although somehow my heart was breaking. The room was surfaced in silver and tin from the shining snow. The mullioned windows reminded me of a harlequin's costume. I could picture a jester in cobalt diamonds, one diamond balanced above the next.

Jim turned and we were kissing. And inside the sex again, I thought, this is love, this is love, although another voice said, No, he doesn't really know you, this man is make-believe.

At ten-thirty I walked home through moonlit snow to my own apartment. My fiancé was calling me at eleven. Besides, I never stayed over. The snowy streets gleamed as if instead of a small city this was a field, both the yards and the sidewalk ice-white. When the phone rang at 11:01 I was seated before it. Ahh-aah-ahh, said my fiancé: the sound of a dinosaur crooning. I answered back, Ahh-ahh-ahh. I wished I could kiss him. I thought of his slender hips and large eyes under soulful eyebrows, eyebrows like sparsely furred, deprived animals that had never been sufficiently loved.

"When are you coming home?" he asked mournfully, his first words when we spoke.

It wrung my heart. I looked at my calendar, and counted. "Twenty-two days."

"Forever," he said miserably. The corners of my own mouth tipped down. He loved me so much that he really, really missed me! I bent forward at the waist as if sliced in half, and gazed at the floor, and murmured, "Oh, baby, I'm sorry."

And yet I was in my graduate program, where I needed to be. I thought of Jim saying, "Someone should punch that guy's lights out!"

"I stayed in bed until about four o'clock in the afternoon," he said. "Is that okay?"

"Yes."

"Just watching TV."

"That's okay. It's fine. You work all week."

We spoke about the rerun of *Blazing Saddles,* which he'd seen with his housemate, a convivial black lesbian with whom he lived alone now that I was gone. He'd also watched a Richard Pryor movie with her.

"It's nice you're doing so much together."

"Well, it's not like doing stuff with you," he said.

Again I felt miserable. "I'm so sorry, baby," I said. Had I said that before? No matter.

"We ate at that sandwich shop in Cambridge. You know the one with the amazing tuna salad with homemade mayonnaise that has a slight flavor of egg yolk?"

I smiled. I loved this precise expressivity of his. It had always made me feel extra close, as if I were talking with a girlfriend but with the added, intimate benefit that this was actually a talented man.

We were on for an hour. When it was time to end the conversation—phone prices were still expensive—I said, "I'm sorry. We shouldn't stay on any more," and he said, morose again, "Yeah, well, bye." And abruptly hung up.

I sat at my little desk in the sudden jangling quiet and gazed at the snowy meadow beside the house.

It was pleasing, clean, nice, numbing. It recalled to me the chill emotional landscape of my fiancé's childhood: his mocking mother, his insistent, narcissistic father. He'd remained in the middle of that coldness, pining. We were similar that way, Simon and I, looking for a love to rescue us, and being astonished and disbelieving when it appeared.

The phone rang again. "Come home or let me come out there," said a voice desperate with tears. "I don't like this living apart."

My heart beat hard. "Let me think about it," I replied softly. He'd never asked this before.

"Look, you either want to be with me or you don't."

Was he right? Could that be true? "I want to be with you," I said, my voice soft and dull.

"Then if you're still there next semester, I'm going to be there too or else that's it."

An old dreary muffled feeling overtook me. The field before me, the room itself, felt far away. "Okay."

"Good," he said, voice hard and clear.

We hung up, and I continued to sit at the little wooden desk. Next year was forever away. I might be someone entirely different by then. And maybe, whatever I needed to get out of my system would be purged. I suddenly recalled that Simon had called my hips "tender chunks," a phrase from a dog-food package. He meant it affectionately, he told me, his eyes and voice sincere. Once, when I wore a burgundy-colored Danskin skirt for him, he stalked past me saying, "It makes your hips look wide."

Now, for the first time I wondered why he'd said these things. Was it that his parents were insulting, as they certainly were, or was it something else? I gazed down at the icy field. Well, next year Jim would be gone, anyway. He was a year ahead of me in the program. He was leaving this spring. So, did it really matter if Simon came?

Still, what would become of dancing at workshop parties with the music turned up, the long winding conversations with my friend Inika as we strolled through the town, and the afternoons with Mary when her pet goat clattered around our legs? Simon might preclude all that. He would need me to take care of him. He wouldn't know other people. A gust of laughter lifted up from the street—a woman, joyful. And a thread of panic plucked through me.

I zipped up my coat and ran out the door. The streets were very quiet now, although once I passed a rowdy group of undergraduates, young men stalking along in shirtsleeves despite the chilly weather, young women in skirts. Snow creaked beneath my espadrilles, which remained on top like snowshoes.

From the beginning Simon and I had felt like spectacular, thrilling chums—even the first evening we'd spent together, when he turned out the lights in his bedroom and danced for me by the glow of the street. He was a sad marionette! Drooping shoulders, dragging, hollow limbs, and a face deeply etched in the lamplight. It was brilliantly done! I applauded, rapt.

And then he switched on the light. Shock went through me. He was a handsome young man! He said, "Look at my mouth. I can make an entire show just with my lips." He drained his lips of color by sucking them in. They were very thin, parched, ash white. Then he relaxed them, and his lips plumped and infused with rose.

I applauded. A drama with just his lips!

He liked to read the *New York Times Book Review* aloud to me; he loved to devise clever, intricate puns—and I had assumed without even thinking about it that the communing that arose from my appreciating him would at some point swerve and become his appreciating me. But now that I was at graduate school we both seemed to feel that I'd cheated, stolen away to hoard attention for myself before it was quite my turn, and that he was justified in feeling aggrieved.

And wasn't he? Even as I'd ridden that Greyhound bus away across the country—listening to my transistor radio, eating the peanut butter and banana sandwiches I'd packed—I'd felt guilty. I'd run away. Still, I recalled seeing three ancient women with linked arms step off the curb in a small Ohio town. "Sisters," declared the bus driver. The song on the radio had been "Material Girl." A science program explained that although we perceive just three dimensions, in fact there are eleven. I gazed out the deep green window at green fields, green houses, green people. I didn't want the trip to end.

So why don't I just break up with him, I wondered, creaking over the snow. Instantly a sensation of illness shot into my stomach—as if I'd been boomeranged. It was a hot, sick feeling. It would be a terrible, unfixable mistake to leave him. If I left him, I would shatter my life. My life with Simon was healthful, grounded, wholesome, heimish, abundantly good.

I entered Jim's building—a two-story, long, Tudor-decorated building—and found his door. Was he asleep? I set my ear to the wood. "Is baby to me. Yes, yes." Billie. I began to smile. I tapped with the tips of my fingers. Nothing. I tapped again louder. Still no answer. Was he talking to Dolly again? Did he call her after I left? Were they speaking in an intimate way, sharing secrets? My heart, crazily, started to beat hard. Or, I thought madly, did he have a different girlfriend from me that he'd gone out to see? Is that why he never wanted me to stay over?

I had the strange sensation that all the joy of life was being pulled away from me, receding fast. I pressed my mouth to the slit in the doorframe. "Jim," I called, and my nose and eyes stung. A sob wrenched from my throat, and I started to weep, childishly. I sat down, leaning on the door. There was a clamor—someone tromping up the short stairway—and I looked up, smiling. It was a young man and his girlfriend. I would have to walk home alone in the mercury landscape. The young man was dark-haired, with a stupid, gawping look, staring at my wet eyes. I looked away and then I tumbled backward. The door had swept open behind me.

"Can I stay here tonight?" I exclaimed in a rusty, high voice.

He steadied me as I rose, and held me. "Yes," he said, but his expression remained serious.

He didn't ever say he loved me. It made him feel wrong, disloyal to Dolly. What he had with me was an of-the-moment thing—a friendship, and just sex, simply sex. In bed again, he put his arm around me. Soon Jim was asleep, and in the silence I heard Lester's horn.

I recalled sex with my boyfriend, something I'd never really wanted to think about directly. When Simon touched my breasts it felt like a lewd, fascinated child touching them.

But I could be wrong, I told myself. I might be confused by Jim's presence. Let's see how it is when I'm with Simon again, without this distraction. There's hope for us. As long as there's life, there's hope. The glow from the snow illuminated the walls of Jim's apartment. It was warm and cozy there, but I couldn't get comfortable.

In the morning Jim set out cold leftover chicken and last night's biscuits slathered with warm butter and the marmalade. It was a warmer day than yesterday—Indian spring. We sat at his desk and watched the piled-up snow dissolve into the river. In the sunshine the streets looked dirtier than they had the day before, with the snowmelt revealing things that had slipped out of people's pockets or that they'd dropped. Sales slips, cigarette butts, silver gum wrappers, yellowing newsprint, plastic bags. And just soot.

He turned to me and after a moment brushed the hair back from my face. He gazed into my eyes. "You'll be okay," he said. "Don't worry. Don't be sad or frightened. Lots of men would want to be with you. You don't have to stay with him."

A stricken feeling went through me at his last sentence. What did he mean? There was nothing really wrong with my relationship with Simon! Nothing unfixable, anyway.

I smiled, and set my silverware on my plate. On the walk back to my apartment, the puddles flashed in the dull, insipid light, the diffuse, metallic varnish of a midwinter midafternoon. My feet in their flimsy espadrilles were cold, and the shoes themselves were sodden and seemed in danger of unwinding. I walked quickly, eager for my desk, eager even for the aroma of fish sticks, my feet throbbing.

I would marry Simon, I knew. I simply didn't have the strength of mind not to. Back in my house, I turned the little key the size of a mailbox key and flung open the lightweight door. Then I dragged the Windsor chair from the desk and collapsed—the vertical bars were snug as a wooden corset—and felt secure. It was a good sane reassuring disciplined pious pain. I didn't bother even to kick off my shoes. In fact, now the cold felt good on my feet, made me feel strong.

I pulled toward me the book which I'd been studying—*Barabas,* a novel of which yesterday I didn't understand even a word. Maybe, without Jim here, all would be well. Come on, come on, urged a voice inside me. And before long the tangle of words began to sort itself, to acquire meaning and brightness, and my breath slowed. What had been a thicket yesterday resolved itself into erratic patches of understanding. Yes, the answer that would make everything easy was about to arrive. I could relax. Soon I would know it. My smile rigid with optimism, I lifted my pencil, ready to underline.

creative spark

Leap

Sarah Ladipo Manyika

I n March 2015, a gift arrived, via email, with the subject heading: COTTAGE ALERT. I was being offered a week's stay at a writers' residency on Whidbey Island. The cottage had been first awarded to a writer who couldn't make it. Would I like to take her place? This unexpected gift couldn't have come at a better time. In the throes of a novel, I longed for a place of solitude and quiet in which to write. Having encountered the magic of Hedgebrook five years earlier, I accepted immediately.

Spring was in full bloom when I arrived on the island: tulips and daffodils, bunnies in the meadows, ducklings in Deer Lagoon. Though eager to seize the inspiration of such an idyllic environment, I found my morale low. I had just finished writing an essay on my fears for young black men in America, young men like my teenage son: a hard piece to write, which proved even more difficult to place, however timely it was, written in the wake of a flurry of reports on police killings of unarmed black men—reports that April had only worsened. "By the time you hear the next pop," sang Kendrick Lamar in his newly released song, "King Kunta," "the funk shall be within you." The funk was with me and I feared that I was wasting the precious gift of time and space.

One afternoon, after staring too long at a blank page, I took a yoga mat and lay down outside. Sivasana: corpse pose. I closed my eyes and listened. Birds, noisy and chirrupy. Insects buzzing. And white-tailed rabbits whose movements I sensed. I opened my eyes to see if what I felt was right, then froze. Just feet away stood two deer—one with her hoof raised high in a yoga pose of her own invention, the stance of a carousel horse, and both close enough to trample me. I moved, cautiously, until upright: the whole while, they watched but did not move. Feeling less vulnerable seated, I thought next of my phone. Could I stand up slowly and quietly enough without disturbing them?

"Do you really think you can get up, find your phone, and have us wait, same pose, so that you can take a photograph?" said the one with the raised hoof.

"Please?" I tried, "Just *one* photograph? How long can you hold that pose, so serene, poised, and strong before you leap?" But even as I thought this, I felt myself missing the moment in all its sacredness. I let go of my desire and sat, eyes locked, with lifted hoof. Seconds abracadabraed into minutes. "When will you leap?" her glassy eye asked.

In response, I got up and watched in awe as they flew, in synchronized leaps, into the nearby woods. Back to the cottage I went and straight to my desk, where I picked up my pen and began to write. A few sentences later, I glanced at the cover of a magazine on my desk. The picture was of Toni Morrison—her silver locks tied back in a red, white, and black scarf. She was staring in the direction of the woods so I looked with her, and there, only partially camouflaged by leaves, stood my deer, this time with her four feet firmly planted. "Just making sure," she said, watching me, before she bounded off and disappeared.

That evening, still thinking of the deer, I read a journal entry from a writer who had once sat at the same desk. She wrote of a smaller creature, the spider, one who seemed to have empowered her in the way the deer had inspired me. Of spiders and in relation to her own writing she wrote:

> They enter a space
> And spin out of their body
> A universe that
> Has never
> Been there
> Before.
> —Gloria Steinem, 8/19/09

The Life of Stuff

Heather Sheehan

The first time I was invited as guest professor to the Higher Institute for Fine Art—Flanders, a postgraduate art academy in Belgium, I had a studio visit with a young visual artist who had nothing in his studio to show me. Nico Dockx, who has since exhibited at the Venice Biennial, had just returned from an excursion through Canada with a backpack full of notebooks and a dusty little thing in a plastic container. Sitting in the vast studio with no artworks to be seen, I asked him about the thing. Taking it out and placing a dry, jiggly, gray ball in my hand, he explained that throughout his trip he had collected abandoned spiderwebs, rolling them, layer upon layer as he went. A compact collection of absconded, fibrous stuff. It nearly pulsed in my hands.

What magic, I thought.

This inanimate object epitomized for me just what it could not rationally be: a thing, alive. It was teeming with mysterious energy. What had fascinated me since early childhood, the sense of life, an encrypted meaning in objects, was presenting itself to me as fact. One which my adult mind was loath to accept. But there it was, this strange notion that energy does not only exist in the form we think of as living beings.

> This experience of a situation being filled with a certain presence also may be felt in the purity and aloneness of nature. ... A range of high, rocky mountains can be felt as an immensity, a solidity, an immovability, that is alive, that is there. This immensity and immovability seems sometimes to confront us, to affect us, not as an inanimate object but as a clear and pure presence. It seems to contact us, to touch us. And if we are open and sensitive, we may participate in this immensity. We may then feel ourselves as one with ... the vastness.

—A. H. Almaas

Longing for a deeper sense of connection with the world, I began to experiment with communicating through a language of form using three-dimensional objects to convey meaning. When an object expresses meaning it seems to take on a life of its own. This is what I refer to as the life of stuff. By recognizing the presence in an inanimate object, we may communicate independently of reliance on verbal language. Ultimately, this can enhance interactions on a global level.

The concept of wordless language can be difficult to grasp. We may have known images of art to provoke response, but not many of us recognize this as a means of conscious communication. It seems strange that a message can exist in the form of a material object.

In his study of the history of objects and our response to them, David Freedberg recognizes this difficulty. We are surprised by "the transcendental qualities of imagery that belie the essence of the material of which it is made." I ask myself how it can be that, at this moment, I am sensing transcendental qualities in nothing more than a ball of gray fibers and dust.

I hear other artists speak of the charged nature of an object which holds what we imbue it with. Or describe a successful sculpture as "happening" when a sense of activity gathers in and around its presence. When a group of objects clearly resonates with meaning, I feel them sing.

Science has its own explanation for this phenomenon. James Redfield writes that "Einstein turned our world upside down. He showed us that matter isn't ultimately solid. It is in fact shaped and compressed energy."

Taken from this vantage point, let us say that you and the book in your hands are bundles of teeming energy interacting. And at this point, I'm wondering if I am sensing the collected experience of a hundred spiders spinning their traps or if I am channeling the spirits of those old houses in which their webs were made. This thing in my hands works like an ekphrastic bomb.

Throughout history, there are examples of people responding to the energy in manmade objects, sensing meaning in them. It may be fun to read Michael Kimmelman tell that "ancient Egyptians lopped noses off despised pharaohs' statues, lest the sculptures breathe in the souls of their subjects and thereby give them sanctuary." Statues in ancient Greece were chained in place to prevent them from escaping the duty of protecting their owners. Those Greeks believed in the power of black meteoric stones to affect their lives. David Freedberg recounts in his magisterial tome:

> Even as late as the fourth century, the pro-Christian apologist Arnobius recalled that, before his conversion, whenever he saw one of these stones "anointed and smeared with olive oil, he adored it and addressed himself to it; he would seek benefits from what he later realized was a senseless stock," as if some force was present in it.

The idea prevails to this day that such notions exist mainly among uneducated or unsophisticated peoples belonging to so-called primitive societies. We can note that Arnobius' belief or ability to sense the life in an object was said to occur "before his conversion" to Christianity. That which intuition tells us is viewed as superstition.

"We in the West tend to dismiss the kinds of powers that were once called divine, all the more when we perceive the deployment of artistry and skill in working the object," Freedberg writes. The talented object maker is accused of using tricks or manipulations rather than truth to influence us. Sensed impressions rather than written ones are treated with skepticism.

The spiderweb ball, no sacred object, neither attempts to escape nor to corrupt. It simply sits, humming with invisible vibrations. It may be more than just my "primitive" Native American ancestry that is responding to the energy in this object. Yet, beyond the option of religion, we educated, secular, modern humans are not encouraged to believe this.

Coming to terms with the indescribable power of certain objects, I agree with Kimmelman when he says, "Call it aura. Art has always had to do with aura—spiritual aura in the past, individual aura in modern times." In order to contend with the unfashionable experience, we belittle the awesome truth of our ability to communicate through forms.

Call it aura or molecular energy, we still think that we should know better than to believe what is disparaged as esoteric silliness. Ignoring our valuable sense of intuition, we do not accept as truth that an inanimate object has life energy. We view it as a betrayal of our own self-importance and superiority to think otherwise. And yet here I sit with this spiderweb ball in my hand, sensing life energy in it. And a valuable message.

This type of skepticism has become commonplace. We do not expect or even notice when an inanimate manmade object has something meaningful to tell us. We are not trained to recognize or accept the information, nor to value it or trust it as a true form of communication. On the other hand, skills in verbal articulation

179

are praised. The acts of reading and writing are supported by our society; we are taught to value verbal communication.

But why stop there?

Just as we learn to write and to read verbal language, we can relearn to use the language of form. We can train ourselves to form ideas three-dimensionally. As we make sense of the words on the page, we can make sense of the wordless message in the form of an object. And in doing so, we can deliver complex ideas more directly into our intuitive consciousness than through the use of verbal or pictorial language. We can recapture the sui generis language of form. We can recapture the pleasure of feeling connected to something larger than ourselves.

> Making images is as natural a human endeavor as speaking. The necessity to communicate with the world underlies both, and both are means to touch, explore and create the world. Both verbal and visual language develop very early in life and are soon practiced by all children. . . . However, whereas all normally functioning people, having once learned to speak, go on speaking throughout their life, very few people continue making images. Most of us are severed from this native ability to visually "speak."

—Peter London

I designed "The Life of Stuff" workshop to guide a natural return to lost knowledge. During the sessions, I witness people blossom as they rediscover their three-dimensional, visual language "voice." In weekly rounds of what I call "show and listen" rather than "show and tell," we practice communicating solely through the language of form. Without the use of spoken words or body language, the participants place before the group the objects they have created the night before. The others read out loud what the objects alone convey. The workshop participants are deeply affected by the experience of having their ideas not only communicated but also fully perceived. Tethered by increasingly flexible roots, self-aware-ness grows. Petals of tightly knotted creativity unfurl.

One participant is shocked when others describe nearly the exact emotional state she had been in on the evening when she made her object. How could it be possible, she asks, that feelings known only to herself are being stated by the group? Has the clay read her mind? How can the stuff know? Does it have a life of its own?

Brancusi said, "It's not birds that I sculpt, it's the act of flying," as John Berger writes in an essay about the sculptor. His art objects offer more to experience than the mere static representation of birds. The complete idea of flight, of "leaving the earth for the sky," is communicated deeply and directly by his sculptures. Relearning to read the language of forms, we open ourselves to experiencing, in this case, the otherwise physically impossible feeling of free flight.

Participants in "The Life of Stuff" workshop experience some-thing akin to my first success in foreign language class. Jokingly, they may blurt out their first thoughts upon seeing a sculpted lump of clay that another participant has made. They are sur-prised to learn that they've gotten the message right. From body to mouth directly, the spontaneous reading is spot on. Connecting with true meaning, be it by the use of letters or forms that we have previously believed to be meaningless visual elements, feels like magic.

During the workshops, I witness countless examples of this magic when form language uniquely communicates abstract, complex concepts. The messages are delivered more directly than by other means. Information is purely sensed. It is transferred to the entire body at once as if directly under the skin.

A mutual sense of support develops out of the bonding expe-rience of struggling to reopen doors long closed. Eckhart Tolle reflects my experience in his words: "A group of people coming together in a state of presence generates a collective energy field of great intensity. It not only raises the degree of presence of each member of the group but also helps to free the collective human consciousness from its current state of mind dominance."

In my practice as an artist, I specifically open myself to the language of form. It is my work to release the life of stuff. As I listen to the possibilities of the material, the objects I make begin to express meaning, to tell stories, to take on a life of their own. Witnessing that energy as it translates into form and receiving the message is what keeps me addicted to making art.

When creating new works, I test the magic. I consciously avoid preconceived images, hold no idea in mind, no words to be illustrated. There exists only the sense of an emerging presence. With material in hand, mind and senses set to respond to the occurring nuances of the evolving form, I await the moment of success, when that presence makes itself known to me. When form and meaning meet, the object comes to life. The stuff sings.

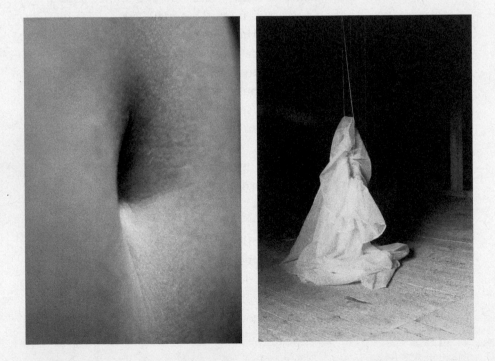

Original artwork by Heather Sheehan, provided courtesy of the author.

Witnessing how viewers interact with the work is purely fulfill-ing. The forms communicate without need for words. The viewer intuitively connects her or his experience to that particular com-bination of textures, planes, and shadows. And together we under-stand something deeply, without being told. We just know.

> Art on one level already may be a state of mind. Of course it is first of all a physical object with which we interact in the moment. But after we have seen a work, what do we take away except a memory of it? And memory is thought, a men-tal seed planted by the artist, which is reproduced in as many different variations as the number of people in whom mem-ory exists. What makes art good is partly its power to pro-liferate as a variable memory, an intangible concept filtered through individual consciousness.

> —Michael Kimmelman

An intangible concept can take on shape, and given form it becomes literally tangible. We speak of the shape of things to come. We speak of ideas taking form. But when we say that an idea or concept "takes form," we are not literally speaking of a solid object coming into existence but rather that the abstract con-cept becomes more clearly defined, recognizable, moving toward realization.

When this is achieved three-dimensionally, we confront an object, the form of which has been intentionally created or selected with the goal of delivering a message. The idea is conveyed directly under our skin, beyond the barriers of verbal language, into our intuitive consciousness. It is more than just the stuff of which it is made. It has life.

On the second of many studio visits with Nico Dockx, he gave me the spiderweb ball. He understood that I needed to have it. It sits on my drawing table, in the corner of my studio, as a reminder, a mascot, a silent guest. The life of stuff.

After Smithson

Clarinda Mac Low

An irresistible force pulls us into orbit, and, tumbling under and over and through each other, we draw a net of muscle and bone and motion.

Not lovers but dancers.

For as long as I can remember, the urge to move—move for the sake of moving, move in a nonfunctional manner, move with music, move alone and with others, move in organized formations, move freely, move with intention, but above all *move*—has been strong. When I was a young adult this urge was one of the few clear directions in a very blurry life. Moving hot and anonymous in dance clubs all over New York City gave me access to a pure state of relational joy. The rigor and precision of ballet classes, where a pointed foot can be its own work of art, honed my mental concentration and attention to detail. Improvisatory composition kept me sharp and in the moment, tuned in to other selves. Emotional overload and constant worry, fear of failure and lack of self-esteem—the common companions of a tumultuous upbringing—all fell away for a moment when I was dancing.

Growing up in the avant-garde arts scene of the 1960s and '70s I was surrounded by a wealth of interdisciplinary art practice. I lived in the heart of an ongoing experiment in form and I was part of the experiment. I began performing with my father, poet/multimedia artist Jackson Mac Low, when I was four years old, mixing dirt and water to make mud onstage. My next performance, at age five, was as part of a group of refugees in Meredith Monk's first iteration of *Vessel*. I learned to perform the way some people learn a catechism—as a matter of course, as a mode of participation, as a way to be included in the adult world. I was fed on art and my playground was the cracked concrete and broken glass stew of cultures in 1970s New York City. It was nourishing, terrifying, and familiar. My ambitions—to be a dancer, singer, or librarian—seemed perfectly feasible.

My childhood arts scene linked to the dance world grown out of Merce Cunningham's experiments with chance composition, and emerged from the Judson Dance Theater, a loose confederation of movement experimenters. The word *Judson* these days serves to identify both the people involved and the methodologies they investigated, a type of dance later characterized as postmodern. In principle, Judson mirrored much postmodern investigation: the deconstruction of method and material, minimalism, conceptual art, and the embrace of instruction-based experiments.

When I was about eleven years old, I started to understand more clearly how hard it was to make a living through the ephemeral. I switched my allegiance to the next best thing, and, for all of high school and most of college, I devoted myself to the pursuit of a career as a research biochemist.

Dance kept breaking in, though. As a teenager, in rebellion against the "weird" dance I'd grown up with, I took ballet classes, using money I'd earned from baby-sitting. I was no good at ballet, and finally, after one too many veiled putdowns from a condescending teacher, in my senior year of high school, I quit.

I concentrated on my laboratory work—a precocious position studying feeding behavior in rats— and dance was no longer on the agenda. In college, however, dance again took hold and this time wouldn't release me. The raw need to move transmuted into a fascination with improvisatory performance, the embodied presence, and the pure visceral possibility of being entirely in the moment. I became captivated by the possibilities of the compositional process and the small society created every time you make a performance, and I started making dances. Soon I was so involved in dance and dance making that I decided to double-major in dance and molecular biology/biochemistry.

Until senior year, I assumed the dance major formed no part of my serious work. My previous plan stood: on to graduate school in biochemistry, postdoctoral studies, a career as a research scientist. Having worked in laboratories since I was sixteen, I knew what I was getting into, and I believed this path was my desire. Every time I thought about the progression, I felt suffocated. But, really, what was the alternative? My family, rich in social and cultural capital, certainly couldn't support me financially; I had to be able to make a living.

Then I met Robert Smithson.

When I say I met Robert Smithson, I don't mean, of course, that I met him in person, though I probably bounced off him at some point when I was a child. He had died long before I encountered his work, which happened while I was writing a paper for a composition class. Through his writing I met myself, finding my way back to my legacy.

The assignment asked us to compare choreography to another mode of composition. I was ornery and didn't want to engage with the obvious—another time-based art form or standard pictorial composition—so I went to the art library, and, browsing the stacks, found *The Writings of Robert Smithson* (edited posthumously by Nancy Holt). I was drawn to his iconoclastic embrace of the unlovely and his passionate, multifocused mode of expression.

Through Smithson, I started to understand the profundity of playing against form and tradition. I started to connect, in a visceral way, to the amniotic fluid of the experiment I had floated in for most of my life. A fish, I started to become aware of the water. In navigating Smithson's delirious intellect, I began connecting the dots enough to situate my dance making within a larger artistic tradition. *The Writings of Robert Smithson* became both touchstone and talisman.

Smithson felt the so-called inanimate world to be a set of entities and relationships, one that rendered the normal strange. In a 1972 essay in *Artforum,* he wrote, "I am for an art that takes into account the direct effect of the elements as they exist from day to day apart from representation." Smithson gave the most objectified of objects—rocks, soil, machines—a voice, lending them authorial vigor. Constantly aware of and enthralled by entropy, he understood the vulnerability of the physical world.

My encounter with Smithson's writing crystallized my own intentions: he created a subjectivity of objects while I sought to objectify the subjective. Through the lens of his investigations, I became highly attuned to the body as a site interacting with other sites—bodies human and non-human, as well as architectural, industrial, and natural spaces. Within each body is a self, and it became clear to me that, like the borders within the body, the borders between selves and between self and space, are squishier than we have been led to believe, but also more tangible. A colleague once remarked that, in my work, "it seems that the connections between people are what you see, and what you work with." I would add to this that my artistic material comes from connections between humans and other creatures as well as humans and the so-called inanimate world. I see us caught in a web of crisscrossing sticky lines and shadows, and wish to see what happens in the spaces between.

To me, these spaces can become a fully material substrate. Smithson's statement that "to have something physical that generates ideas is more interesting to me than just an idea that might generate something physical" instigated my mode of dance practice. Bodies spark nonverbal ideas, states of being, and modes of investigation that have serious heft. The urge to dance creates complex solar systems of spirit, brain, and breath, all formed around one obsessive need: to move. A self reaches out and around other selves, absorbing information on many levels. In this forum, information is haptic, three-dimensional, affective, hovering, and interpersonal, hard to record but clearly defined. Every dance is a research, an investigation into the possibility of now, and now, and now.

Just as to be, according to Jean-Luc Nancy and Martin Buber, is to be *with*, to move is to move *with*. No solo is performed alone; no dancer lives outside the network of humans who create the dance. The dance constructs an edifice, while the accumulated weight of dance making builds cliffs and piles of connection, relation, and effort. If the network isn't visible to the naked eye, it exists as material into which we dive, an effort carved out of all the systems that surround us. Like Smithson's accidental monuments to an industrial age, the shells of dance may be casually discarded after the bright show, but glisten, shining, long after the stage has cleared.

My Magdalene: Divinity and Desire

Dale Kushner

No needlepoint homilies or gilded icons adorned a single surface in my childhood home: no anguished Jesuses, haloed Madonnas, or Holy Doves. Likewise, the absence of brass Buddhas, many-armed Taras, or doe-eyed Shiva with his glorious blue face. In our house, religious accoutrements consisted of a pair of bronze candlesticks (Grandma's), an unpretentious menorah, and Sunday bagels and lox. How, then, did I, raised in a secular Jewish home, fall under the spell of Mary Magdalene, Christianity's favorite sinner after Eve?

It's the early sixties, and I'm a teen innocent of erotic love but brimming with romantic affectations. I lose myself in movies, *Splendor in the Grass,* a favorite: insanity induced by sex; an amour fou. Billie sings it right: *Good morning, heartache, thought we'd said goodbye last night.* Passion exacts its price, an invitation to despair. Female desire is a sure road to trouble, and even the strong dames of cinema—Crawford, Stanwyck, Davis—get crazy or suicidal when they lose their man. (I hadn't yet met the alternative narratives of Lucille Clifton, Audre Lorde, Adrienne Rich, or discovered Magdalene's epic tale.)

My sister's room, forbidden to a snooping younger sister, pulses with the allure. Within her domain await the keys to womanhood, secrets the uninitiated must somehow obtain. (What younger sister isn't tempted to fiddle with the lock and break into the treasure house: lacy bra, nylons, fake clip-on pearls?) The book is on her wicker night table, face down, the poetess's name (we said "poetess" then) embellished in red: *Edna St. Vincent Millay*. I skim the starred stanzas.

> Time does not bring relief; you all have lied
> Who told me time would ease me of my pain!

TaDA TaDA TaDA TaDA TaDA. Before I comprehend the words, my heart recognizes the thunking iambic pentameter of its own beat. Tiny flares of light wink at the corner of my eyes; I catch a flicker of my own dark shining pushing at the bars of her cage. The beautifully brutal voice, the love-struck lamentations, the eerie sensation I'm reading my own future diary—I'm way too young to know but somehow I understand that one day I will have to pay for the sin of *luxuria,* love's lavish madness and the body's thunderous demands.

I whisper Millay's lines in bed. Cadence and meter pacify the churning. The poetess herself is a dazzling creature—part vulnerable child, part rock-star glamorpuss, transgressive in love and art, the first of many women artists whose work I will devour, ravenousness being an attribute of Eros. (The *vita* of Magdalene, her role as Christ's concubine, is still waiting in the wings.)

Impulses tug at me; I'm awakened to longing. I go to Mass with my friend Pamela and stare at a mural of the crucifixion, my gaze fixed on the weeping beauty in the red cape cupping Jesus' feet. I don't know how to put any of this together: love and death, my wish to be empty and full. The radiance of grief. In dreams I wander the labyrinth of Mr. Kalarsek's garden, dizzy with the smell of bursting peonies and dying lilacs. The elemental calls. My wild spirit opens her throat but dares not answer. Eros is said to be the principle of attraction. I begin carting home stray feathers, rocks, shells, shiny horse chestnuts, totems of immanence my mother calls trash and throws out. I steal back into my sister's room. Millay is suddenly gone.

I cast off childhood, get married. Have my own children. I'm drawn to the mystical, the soul's life. I study poetry, seriously. Millay is passé. Sexton and Plath speak to my native self, but their anger burns. I am searching for a myth by which to understand the paradoxes of self. Hildegard of Bingen and Simone Weil enlighten. I veer from the psychological toward the spiritual, caught in the slippage between yearning and knowledge. The changes within are subterranean. In secret I'm finding my way to howl with wolves.

I transgress. Inevitably, for ages that seems like eons, the world is fogged by grief. In the underworld I search for illumination, for an image or narrative to hang my loss on. In the famous myth, Psyche is visited nightly by her invisible lover bridegroom, the very god Eros whom she is forbidden to see. So, too, do we blind ourselves to love's dual aspects, beauty and the monstrous, which the ancient stories warn us never to ignore.

In the nineties, a renaissance of scholarship about Mary Magdalene. I am smitten anew, read the unearthed texts. Magdalene is the quintessential bad girl turned good. The whore transformed into the penitent who becomes an apostle herself. The *Beata Peccatrix*. ("But Christ loved her more than all the disciples and used to kiss her often on the mouth. The rest of the disciples were offended and expressed disapproval.") In the new/old story about Magdalene, Jesus is her lover. We cry to the songs in Jesus Christ Superstar. *I don't know how to love him . . . I've been changed, yes, really changed.* We get it. Love breaks us into a new self. If we survive. I have been broken. I want to survive.

Mary Magdalene is not Psyche. She exists in a Judeo-Christian world in which God is all lightness, the dark forces allotted to the devil. She's a standout in the New Testament, a favorite subject of artists. Magdalene has lost her beloved, Jesus, and thus she has lost her connection to the divine. Her Lord is dead. And isn't this how it is with us when we lose someone we love? Our world bereft of radiance and awe? I do not join a heretical cult; I am no convert. I adore no god, and yet the account of Magdalene's life reflects my search for love's radical divinity, love's incarnation of carnality, that partnership of ecstasy and death.

I begin to write poems in Magdalene's voice, persona poems that tremble with her anger.

> Let them call me harlot!
> I refuse
> to think of myself, or you, sweet pudding,
> as a boil on god's face. I refuse the Pharisee piety.
> —"Letter to Martha," published in *LUNA*

Her sorrow and confusion brew in me.

> That you were supposed to die—
> No, I couldn't accept it.
> I remember the poor child, Isaac, bound with rope
> and dragged up the cliff, panic sizzling in his head:
>
> I said, *Yeshua, it had only been a test! Our Lord
> is a great dramatist.*
> *There will be no intervening angels this time,* you said.
> —"Magdalene, Rehearsed," published in *Nimrod*

What has been promised to her of this love; what does love promise?

> Your mother laid her head in my lap.
> Her grief has no pity for the living.
> She wants to know if the Lord
> has blessed us with your death.
> I tell her: the Lord wounds us with love
> so that we may contemplate the jewel of suffering.
> —"Visitation Selpulchri: At the Tomb," published in *Green Mountains Review*

The poems pour out, answers to questions I don't know I'm asking. I begin to understand that Eros is more than the convergence of an absolute attraction; its wholeness includes wounding loss. In a late interview, Denise Levertov said imagination is a prerequisite of faith. But faith is an abstraction unless it is a lived experience. In love we feel the faith the Other holds for us and mirrors back. When the Other vanishes, we descend, like Magdalene, into our depths to search for the lost divine parts which we can only know through projection.

With Eros we inhabit the timeless realms. (Can you remember your first gasp of it, transfiguration of blood into fire?) To meet Eros is to meet mortality.

> For us death is not distance . . .
> That is the great secret: we are not separate bodies.
> —"Vows," published in *Hayden's Ferry Review*

My understanding of Magdalene becomes a work-in-progress, dependent upon new scholarship and Vatican policies. I go to see her in Italy to view her various manifestations—the opulent Mary Magdalene of Artemisia Gentileschi, the fleshy, breasts-bared Magdalene of Titian, alongside representations of a stark

Magdalene in her later years, an anorexic hermitic Magdalene in her cave. Desire uses her the way it uses all of us. What we pursue pursues us. Sinner, seeker, devotee, lover, disciple, apostle. In our fantasies, Magdalene is each of these: infinitely unknowable, never fully contained within a single image.

Now she has gone inward, my Magdalene, into the briny meat of me. I've absorbed her and been altered. The fifth decade of my marriage approaches. These days, I rarely think of my wild girl, despite all those poems and scholarly research. She is no longer a symbol, but gnosis itself, wisdom that guides spirit and flesh.

Does the soul know when we long for an image to concretize its experience? Does the healing image appear to a hungry soul in a mystical gesture one might call love? Is it more than luck that Magdalene appeared when I faltered and needed her? I sought her. She yielded and I took everything she wished to give.

polarizing forces

Fetish for Complicity

Sonia Feigelson

I

Last time I saw my grown-up, he held my head still while kissing, then belted my neck when we fucked. He likes one position. All others leave him limp, he says, but I am welcome to try.

During sex, he craves intimacy. "Tell me," he says, and again, when I won't: "Tell me you love me."

I tell him I love him because he wants me to. Between us are twenty years of warnings. I think a lot about how we taste: each our own cocktail of pennies and milk.

II

We meet in rehearsals for a play. We are both part of the Devil's entourage, but as the only woman, I am also the only one required to spend half the play naked. He has a bachelor's beard on the first day but has shaved it by the third. I can't believe how openly he wears cargo shorts. I say, "I can't believe how openly you wear cargo shorts."

"It's okay," he says. "Your boyfriend has French-braided hair, and I definitely wouldn't be into that."

III

At the lake, on our day off, he wants to teach me to play badminton. I want to watch my feet warp underwater. Weird creatures, each with five craned heads. One way I ripple, another I pale.

"You're gonna wanna use your dominant hand for the racket," he tells me.

"You're gonna wanna shut the fuck up," I say. "Because this is my dominant hand."

There is a time when he will try to build this failed volley into our origin story. "You were always pretty," he will say, petting my hair, "when you selflessly left your novel on the towel and tried to learn a skill you didn't care about. That's when I got the crush."

In July, nothing but heat counts. My boyfriend and I have an arrangement that will eventually ruin our relationship. I want so much to be coveted, as if someone else's certainty can stay the risk of growing up.

IV

Earlier, we exist online. In emails sent at odd hours, we are reckless, weightless. 3:02 A.M.! 3:13 A.M.! 8 A.M. on the dot!

I read what he writes to me over yells of boys whipping one another with hot pasta. I read in sight of my boyfriend, whose spaghettied burns are run under cold water, who is offered a freezered beer by his attacker, who cracks and guzzles and spits and whaps and snorts.

While most boys make noise, he writes, "I had a dream in which we were skiing down a crazy steep hill that kept going and going but you insisted on looking at me and not where you were going, so I kept screaming, 'TREE! ROCK! TREE!'"

"That sounds like a new extreme sport," I write. "You get judged both on how well you survive and how funny/interesting your story is."

He is serious about not participating in that sport, he writes. It's great for the storyteller, but the spotter of danger is a bundle of nerves by the end of the run.

"Do you ever think about what song you lost your virginity to?" I ask him.

"Cheryl Cadel," he writes. "She had long blond hair."

"That wasn't the question," I say, then: "How old were you?"

"Fourteen."

"You were fourteen once?"

"You'll understand when you're older."

"I'm only nine," I write. "Why are we even talking about sex?"

Humor functions as oblique confrontation: the currency of my age fluctuates over the course of our relationship, but his value is a constant. I pretend to get his references while he dismisses mine as modern fads of which he is only tangentially aware.

What are the kids into these days? Strategic emotional debasement: I weaponize my insecurities before anyone else can. I even the battlefield by neutralizing rejection's threat.

You can say anything you want about me—to me, even—but not without knowing that I've thought the anything first, and compulsively verbalized it to us both. Call me the kind of baby adult who finds a parent to fuck, but know also that you're the sort of adult male who is interested in a twenty-year-old with the body of a thirteen-year-old, and the naked abuser in me is just begging to capitalize on the threat of your deviance.

At 12:16 A.M., he writes, "We really shouldn't be talking about sex. This is the last time we talk about sex."

Six months later, when I sober from joking long enough to tentatively ask him if my age is what makes me interesting, he wraps arms round me.

"What do you mean?" he says. "I'm a pedophile, can't you tell?"

V

My grown-up buys me ice cream. "I can't flirt with you anymore," he says.

The dark is broken by Christmas lights. "Move over there," I tell him. "You're not looking at my good side."

He laughs. He thinks I am funny. People seldom think I am funny because I am a girl, and also because at rest, my face usually looks close to tears.

"I'm serious," he says, after a time. "It's too tempting with you. To want more. It's too tempting, and it's too bad."

He is looking at the ice cream melting across my hands. I lick it off. He is twenty-one years older than me. I say, "What about what I want?"

It isn't a joke, but he laughs.

"It helps," he says, "to know the impossibility of it."

"You make this difficult," he says.

He looks up. He looks away. He closes his eyes. He says, "You won't let me avoid you."

He shakes his head and he takes my hands and I take them back and I put them in my pockets.

"Why would I let you avoid me," I say, "if I didn't want to be avoided?"

He is smiling when he says, "It would be better, though, if you did. I have weird tastes, and I'm moody, and I'm old."

I am smiling when I say, "You can't be nearly as old as me."

We are laughing and then we are no longer laughing because we are kissing. We are kissing and then he sticks his hand down my pants.

VI

My grown-up is an addict. Alcohol, gambling, affection: his world is full of alleys into dead ends. In his spare time, he makes collages out of magazine cutouts and tapes them up around the house. I cannot open a cabinet without encountering his dry humor stuck onto the door.

My boyfriend lives with other boys and several dozen bottles of Smirnoff Ice. There are Smirnoff Ice bottles in blenders, drawers, bedside tables. There is a Smirnoff Ice hidden in the log pile out back. If you find one, you have to chug it. The boys cheer each other. I open the breadbox, get buzzed at 8 A.M.

"Is there a way to win?" my grown-up asks.

Laughter like coarse code. Our contact seems improbably unique. He has a cross tattooed on his forearm: externalization of a Catholic childhood in the 1970s and a dead friend in the 1990s. I am half a family of Jewish intellectuals who discuss the Freudian significance of Elijah's never coming to a Passover bought almost exclusively at Zabar's and half Connecticut cocktail parties at which someone is closeted, someone else just totaled a car, a third person is a raging alcoholic, and we are still talking about the best time to plant phlox.

Nights, I sweat in a room cooled by a slowly breaking box fan. My boyfriend, who has air conditioning, also has other things going for him. Three months earlier, when we finally got back together after the third messy breakup, he set clear parameters—nicely phrased platitudes that meant our connection existed on a trial basis, and that we would reevaluate whenever he liked, and could fuck whomever he wanted.

I love him. Our separation has destroyed and, later, rebuilt me. Old heartbreak catalyzes a recalcitrant urge to make him sorry and cradle his head in my lap.

"All my ex-girlfriends have told me I'm a bad partner," my grown-up tells me, many times. "So I don't date anymore."

"My sexuality is you," my boyfriend tells me, many times. "I don't have a sexuality."

"Does he want to fight?" my grown-up wants to know. "Is that what he wants to do?"

"What does he give you?" my boyfriend wants to know. "I'm not mad. I just don't get it. His favorite thing in the whole world is baseball. What does he give?"

I am unconcerned with moral character. I am unconcerned with coded affection. I am unconcerned with the restrictions men impose, except when they ration joy. I want to take responsibility, but I want to break things too.

VII

I want to own myself, but during dress rehearsals, I spend hours standing naked in heels. No one will look at me. They want me to know that they are respectful people. They elbow each other, slump out of their corsets. Like me, they have their own private jokes.

Later, my grown-up will tell me, "I couldn't look at you, but I saw what was happening."

He will get angry at me for taking the motorcycle ride to happy hour offered me by a fellow cast mate. "Korovyev certainly knew what he was doing," he'll say.

When I arrive at his house around midnight, my boyfriend is playing a video game with his roommates. He doesn't say anything at all.

Desire bears with it the building of an implicit mythology, tunneling through grit and grist to a burrow where sustained contact feels like prenatal suspension. Sex sweats toward ideal or exorcism or both.

I fuck my grown-up so that I'll become one. My grown-up fucks me because he wants to break me as much as he wants to worship me. I fuck my boyfriend because the penetration is a way into being wanted. My boyfriend fucks me because he wants to get it over with. He is tired of being left wanting. He is tired of wanting at all.

We enact iterations of self through pushing into other. We hope to excrete or to concretize an archetypical mythology of self, and so does the person we fuck.

Sometimes, after sex, I think my grown-up might cry. He takes my face in his two hands, stares into it.

"I don't know what to do with you," he says.

He says, "I have the dirtiest thoughts about you and then the most reverential. I want to tie you up so you can't move and then after, I want to take care of you all day every day. I want to buy you things and rub your neck where it hurts. I want to choke you and hurt you and I want you to want it."

He rests his forehead on my forehead. "I want you to want me like I want you, and then I want you to never see me again."

VIII

My grown-up gets strep. I get strep. My boyfriend gets strep. We get sick in a round.

"I got it from your boyfriend," my boyfriend complains.

I lie naked on my bare mattress, eating Cobb salad. My grown-up shows up at the door.

"Yummy nummers," he says, "you don't look so hot."

The pet name is an inside joke I hate. "Don't ever call me that again," I say, letting him in.

He asks me why the t-shirt I've donned for door answering is referencing an Eisenhower speech.

"It's not referencing an Eisenhower speech," I say. "It's referencing a band."

He nods and tries to touch my breasts.

"I have to remember to eat," I tell him, wiggling out.

He says, "You're pretty when you're in pain."

I am mid-chew in a bite of hard-boiled egg, cucumber, avocado, cheddar cheese, iceberg lettuce, tomato, bacon, and bleu cheese dressing. I look at him.

"God," he says, "you're so hot."

I take a swig from an old plastic bottle I have refilled with Emergen-C. By the time the bottle is back on the mattress, he has begun to masturbate, kneeling over the curve of my back.

"I don't know why I'm into it either," he shrugs. "But it'll be a funny story to tell."

I close my eyes. I am chewing iceberg lettuce when he comes on my back.

In the shower, I cry. My throat is raw with hurt. Unseen, I am an I again, neither appetite nor fetish. The return of subjectivity means having my own eyes, whose first impulse is to turn back and look, in imitation of the father gaze, at the self.

I know how to look for ugliness. I see where perversity lives.

IX

I can never sleep when my grown-up does. Slack muscles leave in relief his jiggling jowls, and I am transfixed by our sudden difference in age. I am so much older than this man, I think; then, I am so much younger than I'd like.

I get up and walk to the window. Look out where muddied chunks of ice line the curb below. I do not know it then, but already my boyfriend is leaving me and I am leaving my grown-up and my grown-up is leaving me and I am leaving my boyfriend, and we will still all exist, interacting retroactively with the imprint of one another.

In each telling, the same old slalom. I swerve with eyes averted. How gross, to profit off my own grotesquerie, but what else can I do, when judges also mark for how well I survive?

We pick people up. We put people down. We are picked up. We are put down.

I want you to want me like I want you, and then I want you to never see me again.

The Line

Melinda Misuraca

After my shotgun wedding to a Javanese fisherman, his family of eleven invited me to share their bamboo house with its palm-thatched roof and carefully swept dirt floor, its water drawn from a communal well, and evening conversations lit by tiny kerosene lanterns. Samino and I had spent most of our brief courtship in this house, trading bits of each other's languages while his family splashed me with confused laughter. And yet I hesitated. It was not so much the spare lodgings as the lack of privacy and solitude. Privacy here stayed mostly symbolic: a batik cloth hung over a doorway, a well-timed glance away. Solitude? Avoided if possible.

Solitude, my refuge. In solitude I threw off the unpierceable breastplate of strangeness and sorrow I had worn forever. Me, the odd girl who longed to fit in yet kept herself apart, who loved hideaways, forts I'd build in the woods behind our northern California home. Years later my oddness morphed into a draw, at least for some, but those people worried me, too. Even in Java, where my white skin and American passport should have granted me a recognizable (if bland) identity, I couldn't shake the sense that I was not what people expected, as if they sniffed some universal odor of the outsider on me.

When I traveled to West Java in 1991, I had no plan other than to escape the death grip of winter. Not to fall in love with a fisherman with waist-length black hair by whom I'd get knocked up, then married after a quick drive-through conversion to Islam. It just happened. Or, more precisely, I let it happen. *Why not?* was my ars poetica. A week after the wedding I returned to the States, solo. I had it all figured out. I would slip seamlessly back into my life in San Francisco: my apartment on Telegraph Hill with its Coit Tower view; my day job and night classes at the Art Institute; weekends spent with a few close pals. I would say goodbye to the intrigues, trysts, to late-night bike rides to and fro. I was a fishwife now, my own little rice ball plumping in the steamer. I would file a visa application for Samino and he would soon join me, learn English, find work. We would get to know each other over the months before our child's birth. None of this was ideal, but our sudden, reckless love made anything seem possible.

Almost immediately, my plans collapsed. Within weeks of my return I could no longer rise at dawn to work on my feet all day, nor could I pull off my usual coffee-fueled all-nighters in the school's basement painting studios. I was thrown into the dark hormonal underworld of early pregnancy, guarded by a three-headed demon of nausea, hysteria, and exhaustion, with sleep my only escape. I dropped my classes and took a sick leave from work, my old life dissolving into nostalgic mist.

Then, the visa. Paying a visit to the U.S. Citizen and Immigration Services, I entered a dour building only to feel its air thickened by hope and desperation. After passing through the metal detector, after taking a number, I waited almost an hour to speak to one of the clerks stationed behind bulletproof glass. "About two years," said the stout woman in her mud-colored uniform. "If he's granted a visa at all."

"You're joking."

206

"No, ma'am."

"But I'm pregnant!"

She sighed as if she heard the same story at least a hundred times each day and all before her first cigarette break. "Your other option. Get him to return to his country of origin and apply at the U.S. Embassy. They'll need to verify he's not attempting to immigrate just to take advantage of our benefits."

"You heard me say that I'm married and pregnant, right?" I struggled to temper my voice. In answer, her gaze turned intimate and sadistic. The thick glass between us was gouged in several places, as if it had been attacked.

"Bitch," I muttered and turned away. I stopped in the restroom to cry and instead threw up in the toilet.

With meager savings, I rented a house in Java, figuring Samino and I could kill a month or two there while we waited for his visa to go through. Our landlords expected a year's rent up front, so I coughed up the $300 they asked. My in-laws were shocked. "Such a waste!" they chided. The house sat at the end of a lane off Pananjung Road, in the fishing village of Pangandaran. It was an old U-shaped stucco house built around a carp pond, wild orchids and antler ferns spilling over its crumbling courtyard walls. From Indonesia's former Dutch colonizers the house had inherited a sharply peaked roof, clay roof tiles, and quaint shuttered windows, but years of swelter had caused it to tilt casually to one side, the doors no longer shutting properly. We scraped off patches of moss that grew here and there on the walls before whitewashing them with lime bought from the market in chalky clumps. You'd add water and the lime bubbled up like porridge: after it cooled, you painted it on. Our furnishings were simple: a table and chairs crafted of bamboo, kapok-filled mattresses to sleep on, and a well from which we could pull water for bathing, cleaning, cooking. The village now had electricity, and though most people couldn't afford it, the landlord insisted on having the house wired for us, as if assuming that without electricity a white person would shrivel up and die. The wiring hung from the walls and ceiling in luxurious swags I tried to ignore.

After a few weeks in our new home my morning sickness and fatigue had backed off a little; the odor of salt fish drying by the road only mildly stirred my insides. Samino was often out on the sea, and though I'd made a few friends I spent most of my time alone. My days moved with the sun, with chores completed before sunrise and naps taken during the hottest hours, and I kept time to the sounds made by others: roosters; the muezzin's soul-shaking wail; sing-songy children en route to school; the roving snack sellers who passed, each announcing presence with a well-chosen call. In the morning I'd hear the hollow *tok-tok* of the porridge-monger tapping a stick upon a length of bamboo. At midday came the *ting* of the chicken soup man hitting a bowl with a spoon. Late afternoon and the resonant strike of a bronze gamelan gong meant coconut ice cream was nearby, while at dusk a metal poker scraped across an iron grill triggered my craving for barbecued chicken satay.

My favorite seller was the *pecel* lady. "Pecel! Delicious pecel!" she'd call, approaching with a large bamboo basket strapped onto her back. After I had stopped her a few times and eaten her offerings, she'd come looking for me every day. A lukewarm dish of steamed vegetables such as cassava leaves, long beans, and mung sprouts, pecel is flavored with delicate shreds of a fragrant pink flower called *bunga turi* and dressed in a peanut sauce. Street pecel is usually served on a banana leaf, with a bamboo toothpick as a fork. Pregnancy in the tropics had shrunken my appetite, but pecel revived it. Tender yet crunchy, with a flavor that was sweet, salty, and a little bit spicy all at once, pecel dominated my crazy-cravings list. The pecel lady looked a thousand years old, with branch-like limbs and eyes hidden in folds of skin, yet she grinned like a girl, with a voice to match. She'd sit on my porch in her tattered sarong and compose my pecel, taking her time, offering me a chipped glass of boiled water to drink as I ate. Never in a hurry to leave, she'd thoughtfully chew a wad of betel nut and spit the red juice into a rusty can before hoisting up her goods and heading off. She once told me she had no family. "I am barren," she explained, placing a hand over her womb and nodding solemnly. Her husband had left her for another woman, and for many years since she'd lived alone in the tiny mountain village of Perbahayu, an hour's walk away.

"Are you ever lonely?" I asked her once.

She laughed. "Work leaves no time for loneliness."

To get to our house we had to pass through the front yard belonging to another old woman. Child-sized, with a lopsided hump looming over her left shoulder, she strutted and bellowed with an outsized attitude seemingly designed to make up for her odd form. Soon after we moved in, she, too, came for a visit. Like any decent fisherman's wife, I served her tea and rice crackers while we sat and chatted in the front room. Then she got down to business, switching to Sundanese, a dialect I didn't understand, though I could read annoyance in Samino's smile. Finally our neighbor stood up, grumbling under her breath as she made her way out.

"What did she say?" I asked Samino.

"She wants to hook up a line so she can siphon electricity from us."

"It probably wouldn't cost us much."

"That old grandma sees a white person and thinks free cash. If we say yes to that, she'll be asking for favors every day. Better to cut her off from the beginning." He chopped the air emphatically.

Whenever we passed by our neighbor's house we'd see her sitting on her porch. Once she caught sight of us, her face would screw up in disgust and she'd start ranting to herself, loud enough for us to hear. "This house is too dark! These old eyes can't see a thing. Any day now I will fall down and break a bone." Or, "A woman this old cannot live without a fan. Who will carry my body out once I've died from this heat?" We took to calling her *Nenek Listrik,* or Grandma Electricity.

"Maybe we could help her out a little," I said to Samino.

"She's lived her whole life without light bulbs or fans," he said. "She's just trying to shame us into giving in."

This sort of thing happened often. People assumed I was wealthy. If I worried about the dry fishing season and wondered aloud how Samino and I would make ends meet, my Javanese friends would laugh and ask why I didn't send home for more funds. Most of my friends and even my in-laws had hit me up for loans. Nobody believed me when I told them I was broke. I was an American, and obviously all Americans have piles of money. If I didn't give them some—especially my new family— I was stingy. Worse, if I really didn't have any money, I was an idiot. I never knew for certain if people liked me, or just saw me as a potential source of cash. At times I think it was both, which muddied my relationships. I tried not to take it personally. Most of the Javanese I knew struggled to afford their daily rice, never mind fantasies like running water, electricity, or medical care. And here I had come, jetting in from the mythical land portrayed in the sparkly reruns of *Dynasty* that villagers gathered to watch through a window of the headman's house.

Our house was ringed by trees: a giant mango that fruited gloriously once each year; papayas that had burst from seeds tossed out a window; bananas whose spent carcasses spawned babies to continue their lineage. A banana tree takes a year to grow from tender sprout to mature tree so heavy with fruit that it doubles over and must be staked. A staple food during my pregnancy, bananas were easy to digest during the sweltering days when I had little appetite. One lovely spiraled bunch grew in our yard, and every day Samino and I checked its progress, anticipating the harvest. Like everyone else, we had very little. A freshly caught fish, a bubblegum-flavored jackfruit, a young coconut carried down from the top of a palm: food was our deity, every meal a ritual, every mouthful a sacrament. Yet one afternoon we returned from an errand to find that someone had butchered our banana tree of its long-coveted bounty.

"*Anjing!*" Samino swore.

Of course we suspected Nenek Listrik but couldn't prove anything. For several days after the theft, we'd return home to find her on her porch as usual, her lopsided body languorously stretched out on a straw mat. As if on cue she would reach over to a fruit bowl conveniently parked at her side, pluck a banana, and peel it slowly with her doll's hands. After a pause, she'd mash the fruit between her toothless gums, mischief dancing in her eyes. This caused my husband to tremble silently with rage.

Samino had discouraged me from eating a banana in this way, branding it too sexy for a woman my age. Better to break off bites, or batter and fry it beyond recognition. Old women were exempt: aging had drained their desirability, earning them the curious freedom to do all the things frowned upon during their youth: flagrantly munch on bananas, puff on *kretek* stogies, cackle like demons, let their depleted breasts hang out for all the world to see. Javanese men, of course, could do as they pleased from the moment they were born, a gender inequity for which I'd occasionally feel a burning desire to compensate. If I was really pissed at Samino, I might eat a banana on the street, making a big show of it, watching his eyes narrow and his face stiffen as every nearby male gawked and snickered.

One afternoon we returned home from visiting friends to find a boulder sitting smack in the middle of the path that passed through the old woman's yard.

"*Gobloke,*" Samino muttered. With effort he heaved the rock over to the side.

Later that night we discussed just how Nenek Listrik had managed to get the boulder to the path. She couldn't have done it herself, and it was much too heavy to have been transported by *becak*.

"Who would agree to push that rock to her house?" I asked.

"Someone who's jealous," said Samino.

Jealous of him for his marriage to a white woman, considered a sure ticket to the West, money, success.

A few days later we returned from the market to a newly planted plumeria tree in the path where the boulder had previously rested. The tree's fragrant, creamy buds were just beginning to open. There was no way a *becak* could maneuver around it and we were forced to haul our groceries from the road.

"Talk to her," I said, but Samino waved me away.

The Javanese don't like confrontation. *Tidak apa apa* ("no problem") sums up their social survival strategy, and it works most of the time. People stay calm and avoid conflict. But sometimes a cool face hides a percolating rage, and occasionally someone will boil over. Certain individuals were known for their tempers. Whenever my husband erupted, people would scuttle away like sand crabs.

Samino pedaled over to a little petrol shack near the market, bought two liters and ferried them home in the bike basket. He sat in the house with the glass bottles on the floor next to him, silent and still. He waited until the holy hour of *maghreb,* then went out to do his unholy deed. I couldn't stop him, so I followed. I watched him douse the plumeria tree with petrol and toss a lit match. Together we listened to the tree hiss and pop as its fresh young cells exploded. Later that night, when Samino's hand reached over to stroke my belly, I turned away.

The next morning I went out in the front yard to find that a white line had been drawn on the ground with powdered lime, marking the border between our property and Nenek Listrik's. I had never seen a distinct boundary mark in the village before. The only fenced yard belonged to a rich man from Jakarta who rarely came around. People here were always in each other's business, and not only was such overlapping welcome, it was expected. Boundaries were fluid and meant to be breached. But I was a trespasser, the white line like an arrow pointing straight at me, broadcasting how little I belonged, how I never would. My head throbbed with hot, dizzying shame. I went out less, just to avoid Nenek Listrik's glare as I crossed over.

Not long after the tree burning, Nenek Listrik summoned recruits, a couple of young guys who hung around her house for several days. They looked like pirates of the Java Sea with their long black hair bound in old batik rags, their necklaces and rings, their t-shirts with cutoff sleeves. They'd sit around on the porch, smoking, swigging *arak,* and talking trash. I half-expected them to haul out some big-ass knives and meticulously hone them, but the most aggressive thing I ever saw them do was a weightlifting routine using a village-style lat pull-down rig: they tied a giant rock to one end of a heavy rope looped over a tree branch and knotted a stick at the other end, with which they'd heave the rock from the ground, exhaling with a grunt. Mostly they just sat around. Whenever we passed by they would flash the typical smile, their eyes aflame with contempt. Samino lobbed it right back like a grenade. I was fascinated by just how much hatred could be traded with a smile.

Most afternoons I'd sit by the pond and watch the carp. I would often hear Nenek Listrik puttering in her backyard as she listened to the traditional *wayang* play broadcast on her transistor radio. A brilliant imitator, she'd mimic the slapstick antics of the obnoxious characters Cepot and Udek, cackling at her own efforts. Though I knew she hated me, I still wished we were friends, that I could go over there and listen with her. We spent our days just a few feet from one another, both of us almost always alone. Outsiders, each of her own lonely stripe.

One evening found me home alone, Samino out night fishing. Earlier that day a box from California had arrived. My mother had sent a bag of dried apples, a stack of cloth diapers, and five new novels. They weren't by authors I'd have chosen but it didn't matter. Whenever new books came I binged, reading each one two or three times straight through, comforted by my mother tongue.

I was up long past midnight under the mosquito net with Isabel Allende's *Eva Luna* when I heard a noise on the front porch. Samino must be home early, maybe a problem with the boat. I got up and switched on the porch light, a dangling bare bulb with an electric sizzle that I hardly noticed anymore. I caught sight of something strange on a nearby window: the greasy imprint of a person's broad nose and full lips, as if someone had pressed a sweaty face upon the glass to peer inside. I opened the door. In the shadows just beyond the light's reach I saw a man bolt from our yard and into Nenek Listrik's house. I slammed the door and locked it. At seven months' pregnant I would burst into tears over just about anything, and did right then.

When Samino returned home the next morning – barefoot, sandy, stinking of fish – he found me waiting. "No more feuding with the neighbor," I said as he shuffled, exhausted, into the house. I didn't demand we give her electricity, but I insisted we were friendly every time we met her. Nenek Listrik still glowered when we walked by, but each time her frown weakened, as if she, too, had wearied of being angry.

One afternoon the pecel lady told me Nenek Listrik's name: Yaya.

"Do you know her?" I asked.

"For more than fifty years," she said. "She was my best friend. People called us the most beautiful girls in the village." With a sliver of bamboo she picked at something between two rotten teeth. "My husband died suddenly a month after we were married, and I went to live with Yaya and her husband. When she didn't have a baby, her husband threw her away for me."

I stared at the pecel lady but she continued without embarrassment. She didn't conceive, either, she explained, and the man abandoned her, too, disappearing to a faraway village. People said it was stress that caused a lump to form on Yaya's back, which grew over the years.

I'd never paid attention when the pecel lady walked through her former friend and rival's yard. From then on I watched the two women carefully, but neither of them gave anything away.

Soon after that, the pecel lady stopped showing up. Days passed. I asked the chicken soup man if he knew why she hadn't come around.

"She's sick," he said. "I think she's in the hospital."

I went to see her, heavy with dread. As I entered the building, I realized that I didn't know the pecel lady's name. I'd always called her *Bu*, a term of respect for an older woman. I found her lying on a stained mattress in a dim, musty hallway set aside for those who couldn't afford to pay. Her body looked like an old brown rag draped over a pile of sticks, but her eyes lit up when she saw me. She smiled but didn't speak. I sat and held her hand for a long time, until she fell asleep. The next day I returned with a small pot of chicken soup that Samino had taught me to make with cellophane noodles, fried shallots, and peanuts. A bored nurse told me the pecel lady had died. When I asked where she would be buried, I was shooed away as if it were a silly question, one not meant for these halls.

Wet season began. Every day the air would simmer and thicken, blanketing people with sluggishness, but by late afternoon a cooling thundershower washed all burdens away. I was hanging sheets out to dry when I heard a voice from the road. "Pecel! Delicious pecel!" I ran out to find a girl in a faded dress and flip-flops, a basket strapped to her back. I motioned her over. As she unpacked her wares, I noticed Nenek Listrik watching from her porch. I called out to her. I felt too shy to use her given name, but invited her to eat with me just the same. To my surprise she got up from her mat, hobbled across the boundary line and up the steps to our porch. She stood for a moment, then sat down on the cool tile. For the first time I got a good look at the hump on her back. The size and shape of an infant, it quivered a little when she moved.

The pecel girl was no more than fifteen, the age I was when the world first began to unfurl its vast realm of possibilities, infecting me with a ferocious restlessness driven equally by curiosity and the need to escape myself. This girl and this old woman and this baby girl in my belly did not know these things about me, and yet our shared moment would not have happened otherwise. The girl took out her bowls and utensils and set them neatly on the tile, then folded a banana leaf and sliced it in half with a knife. On each leaf plate she forked ingredients and spooned sauce she had made in some small abode, long before sunrise. She tossed the pecel with a precise grace that trickled up my spine. Did my elderly companion feel it too? If so she gave no sign, but her weathered face opened like a flower and I glimpsed the girl she once was. We ate under blackening clouds. We could hear thunder in the distance, and within the hour we would both have to run to take our laundry down from the line.

all about love, nearly

Andrea Scrima

Whose story is this, and what were the others that preceded it? Here, this was the path that led to the cliff—I let myself fall and fully expected V. to catch me, but V. was worried about other things. How it began: V. describes himself as a train wreck just waiting to happen, and me as the person who will change all this, but what does that vision consist in, I wonder? I am different, unlike anyone he's ever known before; he tingles with anticipation, but then he maps it out and grows dizzy from the mind-boggling complexity of it all: the uprooting of lives, the imperfect merging of families, a vindictive spouse. We booked a room and spent an entire day in the dim light shining in from a small hotel courtyard, the first new lips I'd kissed in how many years and the rest of it a rapturous blur. And afterward, for months, an agony of absence: running my tongue along my own flesh to recapture some sliver of that day, the way it zoomed out in all directions at once like a bomb exploding in slow motion, creating not a cloud of hurtling debris but a perfect reality unfurling in some other dimension. And afterward, my mind careening back to that day again and again: the floating stillness, the quiet, carnivorous inhalation of one another's being. Incomprehensible to live in a world where I couldn't close my eyes and beam myself back to that hotel room, at will, instantly.

There's a pit, an empty spot where we used to put all the perfect things we'd find; we thought they'd be there forever, as shiny as the day we discovered them. A soft exhalation in a quiet laugh and the half-closed eyes that accompanied it; a cell phone ringing in a museum and the delight in the misdemeanor of it, the air of conspiracy. How could anyone wish to give that up? The lightness, the humor and playfulness, my voice in his ear and his in mine, all of it dead now, chiseled into my mind like words in stone, but these things once issued their immediate commands. And then, the agony of his withdrawal, the agony of his agony, the awful certainty that he would carry on as usual, sleep next to a woman with her back turned to him each night and wake up with the alarm each morning, day after day, like acting in the same one-man play, performing again and again and calling that life, how is it that he doesn't die from the sheer repetition of it, how is it that some part of him doesn't announce its blatant refusal?

We live as though trapped, frozen in the blind space behind a mirror, waiting for a glance of recognition to climb out and breathe again. What is it one feels when one feels love? An echo in the mind, the heart, something both deeply familiar and disconcertingly foreign. I think of nights I woke to go to the bathroom and had to grip myself to keep from shaking.

I know the tidal pull of the blood; that a mere glance can send plumes of fire curling through the nerves. The sudden, mind-controlling molecular saturation of pheromones in the air, a maddening inability to concentrate, to think of anything at all. Intoxication, situational insanity. An attraction so fierce it made me angry; the almost violent force required to resist it. Focus on what you don't like—it's all there, right in the very first moment. Just take a look back and you can see it clear as day: the sober assessment, the critical points like elephants weighing down the wrong side of the scale, and then the sticky-sweet goo of self-deception oozing all over it like an egg cracked atop a skull, the giddy, hypnotic, honeyed brilliance of it—ah, love! How blind does it have to be to erase that immediate recognition of disaster?

Until V. came along, I'd carried on too many loves in the echo chamber of my imagination, but now there were two components that joined to produce an explosive mix that sputtered and sparked and blew me right out of my own unsuspecting mind. It took me a year to find all the pieces, and then, when I'd glued them all back together, I discovered that it leaked, that the goo was everywhere, that I'd made a mistake somewhere and had to begin again from scratch.

And then it was all darkness and cosmic wind and meteorites flying around. Duck! Sit down, find a bench. I couldn't look at the world anymore; the colors were hurting me, piercing my eyes and drilling right through to the nerves. I squeezed my eyes shut and listened to teenagers gathered around the bench nearby, hoping their shrill braggardly voices, their spasmodic, hormone-induced laughter would beckon me back to Earth, but no, not this time, and I began to worry: what if they notice me, that strange woman over there pulling her coat around her, what if they look across the grassy triangle we're sharing with a few empty bottles on the ground and a trash receptacle overflowing with little plastic bags of dog poop? What if they decide to have a little fun?

How far can you walk blindfolded until you topple over that cliff? I'd still like to know what that is, why that sweet, sweet force does its Möbius-strip twist into blind annihilation, why the loss of love can bring down a kingdom, close the curtain on a thousand-year dynasty, extinguish a galaxy for all we know—what is that? I don't want to imagine this time, I want to smell it, I want the Velcro on your jacket to catch onto my stocking and make it run, I want to sneeze at your aftershave, feel the discomfort and the nervousness and everything that goes along with bringing your own awkward existence before the other and whispering: Here, this is me, will you take me as I am?

I tell Z. about V. I don't yet know that it will end soon, I still have hopes, but have grown wary, suspicious that V. was mainly after sex: something better than suburban sex, pajama sex, something more exciting, more passionate than toothpaste-breath sex. Whiskey-breath sex? Artist sex, maybe, writer sex? I am a stand-in for an idea, a fantasy, and this unsettles me, makes me question everything else about V. But Z. says we're all motivated through the filter of our own experience. She says she was feeling very sad about this one time as she thought about her current boyfriend. She realized he had no idea who she was; he downplayed her, doubted her ambitions. It wasn't that he didn't think she could do it, she says, but he was always offering more sane, stable, ultimately misery-making alternatives to her desires. This is a man who will always have sex the same way, Z. says, and although she loves having sex with him his way, she'd like to try other things sometimes. Z. says she grabbed her married deli man's cock in the back office, and then ran away laughing. The point she is trying to make is that perfect communion is a myth. But it doesn't mean we shouldn't try. I think we should try, she says. It's awesome to get that close. But just keep in mind your man may not know you perfectly. He may just want the awesomest sex of his life. And there's nothing wrong with that.

Is it time to introduce a seduction scene? My tongue sliding down your chest to your waist, my cheek brushing against your body hair, nibbling at it as I inhale the smell of your skin. I unbutton your pants slowly, nudge my tongue into the opening and tug at the elastic waistband with my teeth. But that's not what this is about, at least not principally. How to explain?

We've been playing the game of where-were-you-when: where was I when you were in Athens? In Paris? When you returned to New York, I was checking coats uptown, waiting to hear whether or not I would be moving to Berlin to do graduate work. It's not impossible that you had lunch there one day, a small midtown restaurant for the martini lunch crowd consisting almost exclusively of men in suits. They'd arrive in a bluster of back-patting joviality and hand over their coats, which had cost them the equivalent of six months' rent on my railroad apartment; they'd inquire after the book I was reading, and sometimes, rarely, there would be a glint of recognition in someone's eye, something beyond a patronizing expression of approval or amused surprise. I imagine myself standing in that coat check booth, with a little basket of dollar bills resting on a shelf below the dividing wall. I imagine you coming in with someone, in the middle of a conversation, perhaps; I imagine myself slipping a bookmark into a dog-eared paperback and taking your coats. There is no way for us to recognize each other, our trajectories are still too far apart, yet we will smile and then, for a moment, our eyes will lock, and all at once there will be that invisible tunnel between us that shuts everything else out, and the person accompanying you will hold the door open and chuckle, because he will think you're flirting with the coat check girl, but it won't be flirting, it will be something else entirely: it will be the look of someone who understands in some distant part of his disembodied consciousness that he is looking into the eyes of a woman whom, twenty-nine years and countless appointments and disappointments later, he is destined to meet again.

Is it different this time? You sent me a recording, speaking to me in an Earth-to-A. way: I'm in a coffee shop; there's music in the background, there's din all around me. I told you I loved your voice; you wondered if I would consider backspacing to the letter *r*. I close my eyes and listen to it again and again, not quite ten seconds long, an abbreviation of sound waves into staggered frequencies and truncated background blips. I've done so many things wrong in my life; I've fallen in love with the wrong people, for the wrong reasons, and I'm skeptical now, a skeptical dented can on a shelf, a skeptical perpetrator, but of what? Last night, you walked down Shaftesbury Avenue to Piccadilly Circus and up Regent Street, through an excited Saturday-night feast teeming in all directions. The broad sidewalks were jammed with people; everyone was dressed up and on the prowl, some of them prancing and preening, some ruing their bitter reality out loud for everyone to hear. A twenty-something couple in the throes of an argument, she a bleached blonde storming ahead, shouting like a fishmonger: "I can't do it anymore! Yew've gone too far!," he trying to catch up with his shorter legs and his black hair waxed up into a pointy crest on his head, pleading: "Look, Oy've been troying! Yew could at least give me that!" And I, opening my mail and reading it the next morning, laughing out loud, delighted at the thought of you carrying me with you through nighttime London. I am afraid of this evaporating into thin air—poof! there it goes, the illusion you have of me, that I have of you, but no, that's not all, surely there's got to be something more? The part of you that hears me, understands me, picks up the faintest of signals; that sees everything, registers everything, forgets nothing, how can that be?

For months, V. described in exacting detail why he had to leave. He had thought it over with scientific precision. I challenged him, reasoned that he might have lost sight of the person he loved the most. The reasons were legion, he countered; it would take all of Google's memory to list them. Life with her was like being locked inside a box, he said; he felt coiled as tight as a spring, waiting for an opportunity to escape and afraid it would never come. And then it did, and like an animal locked too long in a cage, he stared at the open door, transfixed by the promise of freedom and unable to make a move until the door to his cage was safely shut and locked again.

And each day away from him its own unique ordeal. The weeks I waited: one two, buckle my shoe; three four, close the door; five six seven eight before it dawned on me that it might be too late, that he might not be coming.

I remember moments in which the pain coalesced and acquired form. I remember tunes, I remember snow. At least a foot of snow, and my own hot breath on the inside of my fur-lined hood as I brought my laptop in for repair. The muffled way things sounded. And each tune I remember associated with a bodily sensation, like an essence preserved in a canopic jar. No words to describe this, no words to describe my longing, my horror—my crazy, exalted, euphoric collusion in my own demise.

An email from V. arrived in my inbox last night, and I sat at my desk and gazed at his name in a fog of befuddled senses. A first name, a last name, the mere sight of which made my heart beat faster only a year ago, still familiar, but distant now in a nearly amnesiac way. I see it, recognize it, yet I feel nothing—and at the same time my skin prickles at the fact that I feel nothing; I mistrust it, suspect that this name could all of a sudden act in some unexpected way and catch me by surprise, lash out and sting me when my back is turned. Between his mail and yours is a message from another friend; I'm glad the two are not touching, that W. has wedged himself in between.

This name: how it branded itself on my mind in such a way that any name beginning with the same two initials made me look twice, any pair of words beginning with the initials leaped out at me from the page. And now, an automatism that is already fading. I think of him, someone on whose account I nearly went mad, and draw a blank, like a form of amnesia. Perhaps the mind is protecting itself from the memory, which I feel quivering just beyond that skin-thin, unbridgeable divide.

Like him, you appeared out of nowhere, polite and well-behaved, quietly insistent, self-deprecatingly funny; like him, you began confiding your story, inserting little hints into your messages, playful asides and double entendres I blithely overlooked. And, like him, you peered in the mirror and wondered whether the man staring back at you still had the power to make a woman look twice. Sometimes the intersection is no more than a thin, pointed, ovoid shape, one brightly colored fish on the Venn diagram of souls. This is where we connect; the rest is incommunicable. You have your universe and I have mine, big grayish pies of uncharted territory labeled in the letters of a language the non-native cannot understand, but when we enter our kaleidoscopic zone of overlap, our sparkling iridescent fish-shaped world, all senses come into focus. Yes, you say, and then I know that you're listening, that this struggle with words is not entirely futile. I bow down low to hug the bucking back of my steed as it changes course and gallops off into the mist. I am here to survey the outback, to gather in my own lost herd. It takes patience and cunning to coax these elusive creatures; I maneuver them with as much subterfuge as I can muster, succeed in securing some, while others come so close I can almost see their wild and wary eyes, but their instinct is superior to mine: they sense my intent and scamper away. In the end, sitting on my hobby horse, I have corralled no more than a fleeting thought or two, but when I bring them into our fish-shaped world to show you, you look from them to me, and smile.

epiphany

Fortuneteller

Terese Svoboda

How can this Indian guy know anything?

My friend nurses, her wet pink nipple popped out, popped in. It's the East, she says, and turns up the raga she's playing.

It doesn't drone loud enough to drown out my baby's cries. Okay, he's not a baby, he's almost two and says so with a digit on one hand and his thumb on the other—crying for milk, any milk, inspired by the two-year-old ecstasy of his milk brother's toes writhing in pleasure. I hand him a sippy cup. Long ago she nursed mine and hers as milk sisters, and that's his beef. Now we were going to be business sisters. We'd just come back from the garment district to check prices on how much it would cost to manufacture baby slings like the ones I'd seen in Africa but with an adjustable buckle so we could keep our babies close while we made our own fortunes. Credit? The guy in the office laughed at us and our first-borns, even hers with his rabbi-fixed face.

Her hands free—her boy can help himself—she lights some incense. She always knows what I'm thinking. Credit is like the future, she says through the haze. We need some.

Coughing, I open the window.

Pre-baby, she hung a tanka in her bedroom and shared jobs and the names of Chinese medicinal plants I ought to be stewing. Not exactly by osmosis I learned and overheard that eastern tendencies bested our beliefs, that Baby Buddha invented laughter and what did we invent? Horror. An Indian soothsayer of Hindu persuasion, at least a sidekick of Buddhism, ought to be worth the long subway ride. He would tell us our future.

We pack the sippy cup but no diapers—everybody is past that—for the trip on the train is long and thirsty. Trees and a swing set and squirrels at the end, a park-walk. It is the promise of expedition that the boys gentle at; they stop kicking and arching their backs with their stroller incarceration and glare at each other.

But we are late. The line is so long we can't see the front of it, just the steps up into the place that is strictly for students of theology, the study of god, a practice almost eastern to me, a fallen-away Catholic, so fallen the future is only fiery, or so says the pigtailed man in front of us, crossing himself. I know I'm not going to get much of a break in this future—it's my friend's boyfriend's boy that I stroller, born to me out of a confusion of rooms late at night that remained uncorrected just long enough. The boyfriend had such a Christ-fear approaching his thirty-third birthday that the spewing of seed seemed to him his best chance for the immortal. But his boy is so happy, not fearful. Despite his nostalgia for the nipple, his cheer and my love for him-as-a-gift has already attracted a true suitor with whom I am sending out invitations next week for a ceremony.

My friend holds no grudge about the mix-up of bedrooms: he wasn't her type. Her baby's father actually is a rabbi, another aspect of the Buddha, she says, only closer to her own ancestral roots. Married? Yes, with ten of his own, safe from any baggage, she says, in the obedience department. But now she is searching for a more Occidental connection for the next baby that maybe this Indian guy has a bead on.

She must have heard what she wanted to hear. She looks so pleased after having her hand read, pleased with a big smile, and the guy, business-suited but turbaned, agrees to read her son's hand as a bonus, and does so, telling her about future musical ability and artistic tendencies, which, if she were a sensible mother, should scare her to death.

My turn next, me at the very end of this very long line, and he looks at my hand and his Hindu face fades. He says there is strife and sadness and nothing much good in it. That's what I hear or, rather, he says very little which, as any polite person knows, means you say what you can about what is good and leave out the rest. Still wanting the reading to be worth all the waiting, I say, What about my son's?

The reader unclasps my son from his toy drumstick, spreads his little star of a hand in his own, and the boy stirs out of sleep. The Indian guy, said to be so certain and accurate about all of his prophecies, stares at it and then closes it.

The life line is too short, he says.

My friend who is jiggling her rabbi-son says, What?

I don't answer, I quick-check my boy's harness and whip him down that short set of stairs fast. I thank the Indian guy with my back turned, carefully bumping us toward the subway, and my friend, after a minute, bumps after me.

No steak knives for anyone, all ants un-poisoned and happy, every table edge, seat, and tip rounded, all pot handles turned in, food blanched instead of fried, I even throw open the window for air fresher than hers, but still he is right by the end of the year, when all I want is wrong.

It is the open window.

Yonder

Rachel Cole Dalamangas

W
e lived out on the farthest sprawl of suburbia back then. Built on the plains of Colorado were grids of houses painted teal or beige or gray or mauve with two windows peeking over a garage. The houses always looked to me like they were saying, "Oh, shit."

My dad was 6'4" and gnarly of hand. After my brother was born three months premature, he got a sketchbook that he worked in with sticks of charcoal to draw fences, sleeping dogs, young trees. He made an expression when he was sketching that suggested he was trawling deep within himself. My dad gave me many existentially precarious art lessons, beginning with his drawing face.

My family lived in one of the gray houses, and my bedroom was in the right eye, my brother's nursery in the left. Back then, the community debated a lot about whether it was less cruel to get rid of prairie dogs by gassing them or vacuuming them from their burrows. This kind of thing always got my attention with the zeal of a concerned citizen, which would cause my mom to abruptly end the conversation or turn the channel from the news because she didn't want her children to have nightmares.

As long as I've lived I've never understood this urge of my mom's. Never does my brain feel more serene than after a really good nightmare. I would have a freak-showish, purgative vision twice a week if I could. Naturally, my thesis as a new person was at odds with my mom's thesis as a mom.

Beyond the neighborhood, there were mountains. People remark upon the mountains of Colorado in part because they offer a point of orientation, and mostly because they are very beautiful and wise like sexy old ladies. But before the suburbs south of Denver developed into brunch chains and those creepy mall/apartment complexes, the skies over the plains posed a paradoxical and invisible beauty all their own.

I will tell you about the skies now. Coloradoans of a certain temperament love to say, "If you don't care for the weather, wait five minutes." This is not only hokey, but fails to acknowledge the most impressive and illusional effects of Colorado's troposphere. It is not uncommon for it to rain while it is sunny. There was once a mountain fire started by a woman burning love letters that turned the sun red in July and blew ash down the eastern slope. Shadows move with subtle gestures at the beginning of winter in a way that makes you turn around, suddenly paranoid that you are an exhibit at the Natural History Museum. And when it finally rains a real long good rain, the houses go quiet so that everyone can listen.

Back then, the eye could follow the farthest edges of the landscape populated by the society of prairie dogs and grasshoppers and flowers with secretary hairdos. The pale blue screen that spanned the plains was given to painterly cloudscapes that swirled into the possibility of a tornado.

My mom constantly read the sky. If it was stormy, she would peer out the window and say, "I just want to make sure there aren't any tornados." Even then, I understood that my mom wasn't just watching the weather—she was trying to see the future.

Things got action-packed when my mom actually found a circling formation overhead. She'd grab my baby brother with his jacked-up praying mantis legs, and I would run to save my rabbit in his hutch near the vegetable garden. Sometimes an eerie siren sounded through the neighborhood. When we made it to the basement, emergency snacks and juice were distributed, and we'd turn on the TV that my mom had hooked up for the express purpose of tornado survival.

One time at the beginning of tornado season, my mamaw and papaw were visiting from Tennessee. My mom had an idea that we should all go to the zoo together after lunch so long as "there wasn't a storm coming from out yonder." My mamaw and papaw described the location of anything not directly apparent to them as "out yonder," a colloquialism my parents mysteriously picked up whenever they were around. I tried to imagine what would happen if there was a tornado at the zoo, how we'd have snacks and watch TV with giraffes in the basement.

The adults took turns examining the sky that was stained gray-green as if someone had spilled tea, while I played on the back porch with my mamaw and papaw's Labrador Molly. Molly was raised in the Smoky Mountains on a farm. She was a hardy sixty pounds with yellow eyes, obedient and prone to the sprightliness that is the hallmark of her breed. She drooled when she was feeling enthusiastic, which was most of the time. If Molly had been a human, she would have been inclined to oversharing.

We decided to play with her rag toy. Molly wanted me to throw the toy so that she could retrieve it, and I wanted to play tag. We reached an awkward compromise: I would run while holding the rag toy so that Molly would chase me.

Overhead, shapes were gradually churning. Maybe there was a dot of rain. I'm not sure who started it, but our game quickly devolved into tug of war, and we fell into the outdoor furniture— lounge chairs made of metal elaborately twisted into Victorian doilies.

Molly gently chomped down on my hand that had the rag toy.

Having my whole hand inside of a dog's mouth was the most unpleasant thing I'd experienced at that juncture in my life. Molly's big gross tongue wiggled like disturbed cave larvae, and her saliva was viscous. I could feel her hot breath sinking into my skin and knew that I would smell it every time I touched my face for the rest of the day. I was far less gentle than Molly when I pushed her and tore the rag toy from her jaws. How abruptly I learned of and then became alarmed by the silliness of my body as it tottered to the far end of the porch.

In lazy bounds, Molly galumphed in front of me and caught the rag toy between her teeth again. I pulled back and twisted around, imagining myself as one of the football players my dad watched on TV. But Molly was stronger and didn't anticipate the clumsiness common to human children.

I went down hard face first, striking my mouth on the edge of a brick planter.

A long, bright string burst from my lip and tangled with the wind, making a tree of light that took up the whole sky. Branches of electricity grew past the clouds, exciting the air. Everything paused. Then the lightning disappeared. There wasn't any pain or blood that I can recall.

The contours of my family members were dim through the window. Their silhouettes were gesticulating wildly as they told each other jokes, having forgotten to watch the weather.

Molly put her tail between her legs. In retrospect, I understand the expression she made. This whole incident could have gone sideways for Molly, and instinctively she knew it. I took the slobbery rag toy from the porch where she had dropped it and waved it in front of her snout, but she only put her ears back and nosed my arm with urgency.

Not knowing what else to do, I stood at the glass door waiting for an adult to notice me. "Oh, Lord have mercy, what happened here. Molly didn't bite you, did she?" my papaw said.

I was afraid to move my lips to speak in case more lightning came out. Also, I was trying really hard to pretend I was okay. I was still hopeful we could go to the zoo.

At the ER, people I didn't know kept stopping to peer down at me and say, "Your poor pretty face." There was much made of the fact that I was four years old and was getting exactly four stitches in my lip. My dad kept making his drawing face, and I refused to explain what happened to the nurses, so I was visited by a social worker who had the sort of permed hair and hazel eyes that no one would ever tell a secret to.

On certain nights in Colorado, the sky used to disappear as if it were never there, but you could sense coyotes and mountain lions moving around with skepticism, smelling for the ghosts of human traffic.

It was a night just like that when I developed the habit of trying out all my explanations for the universe on my papaw until he would feed me peanut butter. Everyone has their own hurt to jewel. He said, "You sure do a lot of thinking for such a little shit," and then he closed his eyes like he was straining to see something invisible.

On Serendipity

Indira Ganesan

A joke goes like this: a man is clinging onto the topmast of his sailboat in a hurricane. He prays to God to save him. A boat comes by and the people on board invite him along. "No, thanks," says the man, "I know God will save me." The waters continue to rise and a man in a hot air balloon comes by, offering to rescue him. "No, thanks," says the man, "God will rescue me." The water is just about neck level when a small plane comes by. Again the man refuses, saying God will rescue him. Finally, the waters rise too far and the man drowns. As he enters the pearly gates, he sees God and asks, "Where were you? I thought you'd rescue me!" God looks at him sadly and says, "I sent a boat, a balloon, a plane. What more did you want?"

Take away God, and the boat, plane, and balloon become serendipity, even more so if the man chooses one of them to board. Imagine you are drowning and a cruise ship chances by. Does serendipity represent the mysterious ways of God, small acts arriving at the perfect moment? Is it a situation in which the universe answers our request before we even request it?

Once, a blizzard delayed my flight home to Cape Cod and I dialed my local cab company to explain why I would need to cancel on that end. Hearing my situation, the owner said she happened to have a cab headed back from the Boston airport and did I want a ride? How serendipitous that a hometown cabbie would be at that very moment dropping off a passenger. The cabbie picked me up from the terminal and waved away my gratitude, saying she saw no reason to travel alone. After we left Logan, the snow blew in thick waves, making it almost impossible to see. We inched along. Reaching the Cape, she mentioned she was hungry, so we pulled into a shopping center. She went to a coffee shop while I went to a market for milk, which I needed, only to end up with a dozen other things I didn't. Why these stores were open during a storm was a blessing even if they were simply corporations doing business as usual. We dug the cab out and continued safely on the road toward home.

Things often repeat, and a year later I was at the tail end of another canceled flight after another blizzard. This time I made my way in driving snow to the bus stand, wondering if I was at the right spot, here at the remote reaches of the terminal, past groups of passengers waiting for other buses. Shivering, wet, I put my baggage down and turned around. There came my bus, slowly approaching, appearing as a mirage in front of my eyes. I could hardly believe my luck: another bit of serendipity. But like the foolish man in the flood, after I boarded the bus, I worried that my next bus connection might have been canceled due to the blizzard. I decided to get off and book a hotel room. When I told a new cab driver of my dilemma, he asked how much I had paid and offered to drive me hours home for the same price. Again, was this serendipity or capitalism? In any event, again I reached home safely, even though he requested a tip above the rate upon which we had agreed. Perhaps for him I had been serendipity, a bonus fare in a blizzard. How had my safety been assured each time, and what did that mean to me in my life?

Recently I have been thinking about safety, serendipity, assurance. My cousin says a million things have to occur for two people to meet. So many individual choices must be made in a certain time frame. One different turn and everything changes. Once, many years ago, I had a breakdown in London. I got confused in the British Museum, enough to be taken to the acute ward of Royal Hospital. I had been hallucinating in the museum, imagining some arcane spelling bee was taking place while invisible friends were begging me to stop, saying I was not playing an actual game. Perhaps those friends had acted as my subconscious, horrified for myself.

I woke in the ward and sat up in a hospital bed, feeling cold. "Good," said a nurse, "that means you are feeling things." By *things*, perhaps she meant reality. My first thought was that I was in the hospital because I had been raped. Gathering my wits, becoming more stable, I thought back to my train ride to the museum, recalling a man who had told me, oddly enough, that he was manic depressive and often succumbed to spells of high spirits. Further, when I had exited the station near the museum, a Chinese woman had patted my back, telling me to take care.

If both figures were incidental, perhaps they had acted as agents of serendipity: as warning, foreboding sentries. I ended up at the hospital mainly because my mind had released a thought and jumped off to catch another, as we do a thousand times a day, synapses in sync, but this time, as if an unlucky trapeze artist, my mind missed the catch. Down into the rabbit hole I went, only to be brought back to my senses by medicine.

I stayed for a mandatory twenty-four-hour observation, and the day passed quickly. In a group art therapy session, attendants handed out paper and paint for all of us to express our feelings.

One of the patients, perhaps an actress, began to write out Orsino's opening speech in *Twelfth Night* and soon was out of her seat, declaiming the words, making a supervisor surreptitiously roll her eyes. As for me, I painted a teacup and a clock. One nurse asked me how long I'd been working on the floor, and I had to confess, though secretly pleased at her mistake, that I was a patient, not an attendant.

For food, I had a delicious dish of Indian takeaway. Can you imagine such a feat in the United States? Room service would almost never account for diversity in diet. Later, a nurse took me out for a walk. I was surprised because I'd thought as a patient I was incarcerated, but here I was walking outside on Whitechapel Road, looking into shop windows. Since I was a tourist, every-thing seemed remarkable. To thank the acute ward, to offer a gift, I bought some herbal tea in a shop.

The nurse showed her surprise. "Everyone is so into caffeine," she commented. It was true; at the self-help breakfast, the kitchen had been a mess of stabbed butter tubs and sticky marmalade, with water always boiling for the darkest, most caffeinated tea.

That evening, the doctor with whom I had my evaluation inter-view explained I'd had a multicultural break, something that made me laugh with relief. The doctor also offered to speak in Tamil, my native language, which again filled me with wonder. How long had I lived in the States, where so few non-Indians even knew what Tamil was? The next day I walked out of the hospi-tal, accompanied by my cousin and filled with awe for the British method of coping with mental health, admiration for their doc-tors, and deep gratitude for socialized medicine.

What serendipity lives in this? A month earlier, on the recom-mendation of a friend, I had read *Girl, Interrupted.* Had I not, per-haps I would have lacked such calm during my stay. Instead, this chapter in my life seemed an adventure, something about which I might take notes. Maybe I would have lacked the humor to boast about my knowledge of the Beatles to the medic who brought me in, a man who responded with good humor, "You Yanks always think you know everything about the group." Perhaps I would have failed to notice the *Twelfth Night* actress with her penchant for rule breaking, and how she loved to steal into the boys' wing to read aloud Sherlock Holmes stories. Or I might have been blind to a fellow patient who coped by knitting while never giving up her knowing eyerolls.

All in all, as one of the art therapists said, I had a holiday gone wrong. How I loved the way my crisis became so beautifully reduced in scale: a multicultural break on a holiday. Right before the break, I had made many choices: what I ate the night before, deciding to leave my friends' home. Insomnia had gripped me that night, and, in the morning, I looked so tired that my host had told me to await his return. Yet off I went with his wife on a double-decker bus toward the train and, finally, in the museum corridor, as I was deciding whether to go toward the wings of classical Greece and Rome or Africa, I broke. Twenty-four-odd hours later, with a diagnosis more or less in place, I was reunited with my family. Of course, there is more to the story, but for now, it ends here.

So many steps toward that happy ending. So many strokes of luck and good fortune. Maybe serendipity needs a broader field. For are we not each living in a certain space at a limited moment of time? I am here, and there, there you may be, right when we both need each other most, when boundaries may burst just enough that we both survive.

Cups (A Dream)

Rikki Ducornet

W e had only just moved to rural Europe. The hamlet was built on a hill and all the streets were cobbled. The Street of Cups, our favorite, was narrow and had an irresistible stone statue of a girl with full, round breasts. Her hair fell to her shoulders in thick ropes, and around her neck she wore a wreath of cups. She also held a cup in each hand. When it rained these filled with water that spilled onto her breasts and into her lap. She was very old and worn, and her breasts and lap were black with lichen and minerals from the water.

A few days after our arrival, Marthe, our nearest neighbor, offered to show us the wonders of that place. When she came for us, slamming the heavy iron door knocker twice, we set off at once, her great red Labrador smiling and bounding ahead. To our delight Marthe informed us that if when we left our house we descended the Street of Cups directly, we would reach the outlying meadows. Within an instant the hamlet dissolved and we were up to our knees in yellow poppies and deep grass. The air was alive with butterflies and bees, and birds called out from tree to tree. "They are speaking about us," Marthe said. *"On les embête, c'est sûr."*

We came to a vast open meadow of low grasses punctuated here and there by the fragrant droppings of cows and a fantastic group of life-sized animals carved of stone and pocked black and yellow with lichen. They were magnificent and set out in a series of six: horses, hippos, rhinos, lions, and elephants. Like the temple animals of India, their legs were folded beneath them. I was enchanted, flooded with intense happiness.

Just then the dog bounded up to me and thrust his nose between my upper thighs. I pushed him away and ran to the stone animals where I found a superb serpent I had not seen, thickly coiled and carved with great care. His eyes and furrowed brow, his grinning mouth—these were especially fine. As I stroked his face I saw Marthe toss a small red ball deep into the meadow, and the dog leap eagerly after it. At that instant it occurred to me that all the wild creatures will perish simply because they do not fetch for us, because they are not attracted to our scent and so are deemed dangerous or superfluous.

survival

Coyote on Holy Mesa

Quintan Ana Wikswo

POLICING THE REAL IN LITERATURE

The definition of nonfiction has long been hegemonic—ruled and policed by sensibilities that conceptually fence off "reality" from fabrication. An insidious form of narrative control is inherent in this concept of nonfiction. Under whose authority is reality governed? What institutions and individuals possess the power to define reality for all humanity, for all writers, and for all cultures? In an increasingly global and intersectional community of text-based self-expression, it is imperative to ask these questions, and exercise caution when we are tempted to give ourselves the authority to impose a single cultural or literary norm onto all members of humanity.

In my own hybrid home and relations cultures of African American, Nordic, Baltic, Jewish, and Native American, reality can and does include spirits and ghosts, shapeshifters, animals who become human, humans who become animals, visions, visitations, and conversation with the unseen. Such fluidity is a valid reality, not only for myself, but for the majority of cultures throughout the majority of human history.

The reductivist perspective insists that anything lying beyond reach of the codes of nonfiction are not realities—they are, in fact, fanciful and fabricated fictions to be filed under "fabulism" or "fairy tale" or

245

"myth" or "fable." Such forms, too, are valid. But a classist, racist, and perhaps more subtlety bigoted assumption asserts that the fortified fences that enclose traditional canonized Anglo-American nonfiction must be maintained, with all nomads and unauthorized life forms be kept out. This fence excludes the majority, and imprisons the minority. It is no longer acceptable to guard this fence and segregate all interlopers to other genres.

My work hopes to speak to something far more potent: the complete decolonization of nonfiction. This demands an end to the exile and ghettoization of thousands of writers currently excluded and policed from the colonialist definition of nonfiction, an end to who polices what is real, and to whom. Let the guards at the gate change!

My nonfiction work includes a man who is also a coyote which, in my reality, is neither myth nor allegory. As the writer Max Wolf Valerio has written about policing the real in literature, "Only a non-Indian would say that [such a reality cannot exist]. Someone who doesn't know, who hasn't been raised to see that life is a continuous whole from flesh to spirit, that we're not as easily separated as some think. I knew that." I dedicate this piece to the family on Nambé Pueblo who cared for me when I needed a home. My hope is that our greater literary community will realize each of us comes from a nonfictive reality and that none of us have the authority to stand as prison guards, police, or conquistadors of the terra incognita of literature.

I

I have come to the desert in search of bones. Looking for bones, I walk the desert and feel watched—everything dead is waiting to be exhumed. I walk to the rise of smoke from over the holy mesa. There is an old man with a dirty adobe and a fire of juniper in his stove.

Why are you here, little girl? he says, although I am not little. I am huge and fierce and my hair is strung with bones, even down below.

I have come to the desert looking for bones, I say.

Whose bones? he asks.

The coyote's bones, I say. The old man knows the story. The Diné told it well. The coyote with the stone dildo who knocked out the teeth in our vaginas. I am holding a handful of stones. *I am looking for the bones of the coyote. I have come to take what he stole from me.* I have a handful of teeth in my mouth. They did not come from my mouth. They were broken off, and I have come to put them back where they belong.

The old man looks at my vagina. *The coyote is dead,* he says, *and you are in luck.*

We look at my vagina, its teeth as broken as my heart.

Original artwork by Quintan Ana Wikswo, provided courtesy of the author.

I do not feel lucky, I say.

Not now, says the old man, *not now. But now is a relative term.*

The old man has a bottle of whiskey. The bottle is dirty. The whiskey is filled with dust. The juniper cracks its knuckles in the stove. My mouths are full of blood and broken roots.

The old man hands me a shovel and grunts to his dog, an ancient gray and black mass of matted fur in the corner. *The dog will show you,* says the old man. *The dog will take you to your grave.*

The hound and I go outside. The daytime is dark with soot and anger. The coyote lies dead with his dildo. The coyote is buried under a pile of rocks and teeth. We move them gently with our hands, the hound and I. The hound feels sad for my vagina, its teeth knocked out at the roots. The dog paws at the last of the earth, dry and dark with blood. Under the earth is the coyote. It is dead. A mass of matted fur, smiling, an incisor from my vagina in the coyote's dry and rotting lips. I pry it out. The dog watches me place it back inside me.

That's better, says the dog.

Not better enough, I say.

Not yet, says the dog, *but later.*

I shovel out the bones of the coyote. They are strung lazily with viscera. I have a candy jar with me. We put the bones in the jar. The dog licks its fat black lips. The dog is hungry for bones.

These belong to me, I say to the dog. *I will keep this jar where I can keep an eye on him.*

That's dangerous, says the dog. *He will keep his eyes on you. He will speak cunningly to you. You will let him out.*

Inside the jar, the coyote eyes shift back and forth, watching the length and breadth of me.

He will fall in love with you, says the dog, *if you keep him so close. And not the kind of love you wish for.*

The hound fixes me with a lonely look, and lopes back behind us to the holy mesa.

I walk the desert for years with the jar in my arms. The coyote watches me from the jar. I hear a murmuring from inside the jar. His larynx is twisted, his words broken and fierce.

Those were your baby teeth, he says.

They were the only ones I had, I say.

It was time for them to go, he says. *The Navajo know only one version of the story. They do me a disservice.*

There is no other story, I say. *You took my teeth. I want them back.*

In the true version of the story, he says, *I was hurting you in order to save you. I made space for your vagina to grow stronger teeth,* he says. *So strong that no coyote could ever knock them out. It's not my fault you bled so much.*

When? I say.

When what? he says.

When will the stronger teeth grow back? I say.

Soon, he says, *just let me out.*

His thin dark body rises and falls with the breath of the living.

I see each rib, as delicate and fierce as my own fingers.

What is buried in our soil that is not yet dead?

What of this viscera in a jar, waiting to be set free?

What part of the story has not been mistold?

I open the jar and leave it tilted on the sand.

He stands before me, shyly, disassembled.

Thank you, he says. *I will see you soon.*

How soon? I say.

Soon, he says.

But soon is a relative term.

II

I am here for the removal of my skin. There is a place to make a slice, perhaps along my spine, to let me out. There is a membrane that contains me and I will say quite clearly that it needs to go.

Underneath is something breathing. Lungs that rise and fall in billows of dusky blood. The muscles are being gnawed by teeth, by a coyote, by the teeth of a coyote, sipping the red nectar from my heart, emptying it into his belly. There is a coyote between my hips. There is a coyote between my thighs. There is a blue gold orange violet black coyote that has crouched between my hips and has no need for my skin, only what he can feed on that's inside it.

There is a coyote that is filled with desire. It flicks its tongue against my clitoris, tasting.

There is movement under my skin of the beasts of the holy mesa. There are juniper roots pulling at my veins.

The teeth have been sharpened to points with a rough knife called communion.

There are emeralds in my incisors.

Tonight the snow falls on the holy mesa and this desert is home, this space between white ice and sky. The taste of fur on my face. My second skin, unpinned.

He has opened my ribs. My chest is the mouth of the cave and I listen for the wings of bats, silent in the dark, listen to the heart of a small dark creature hanging low. My heart, a fist, upside down and dreaming. This small dark angry thing, awakened. A mat and tangle of black membrane, folded before flight.

III

In the arroyo—in the arroyo that is here between us—the coyote lies down. In the bright sand arroyo between now and then he stands up. He stands up and lies down and sleeps in the arroyo between then and now. Two crows. A ball of fire called the sun, suspended. In the arroyo of always he stands up and walks. In the

snow in the arroyo in the gaze of the winter sun he stands up and walks to the cliff and calls my name.

In the shadow of the cliff I was sleeping. I was sleeping in the shadow of the cliff I called my shadow: hanging heavy in the dark, a color of charcoal and of soot. In this shadow I made my pyre. On the cliff, in this pyre, I burned my sorrows. I gathered my sorrows and they shuddered in my arms. In the shadow of soot they died, on my cliff, and down below the coyote slept and the coyote walked, knowing the source of black fire in the sky.

On the holy mesa there are fires of sorrows, pyres of desire that have no clear purpose under heaven. The arms of sorrows are branches, red and branched and aching. Immolation comes with every dawn. The sorrows are set to burning—they are burned down and rise again.

There are ashes to scatter. All my sorrows have blown apart on the evil wind that spirals back to find me and deliver its gray carrion.

There are church bells. There are church bells ringing but there is no church. In the valley the coyote is walking. His balls are bells, ringing. With each step his spheres ring out. He smells the smoke of sorrow and he rings his bells of possession and spent seed.

In the valley, at the root of the valley, there is a creek. There is a stream at the fissure of the valley. There at the seam of the valley is a river and he is on his haunches. Thirsty. His paws are in the water. He stirs the water with his paws. On the cliff, my fire steams. He is on his haunches in the valley between the mesa's thighs and he is on his haunches to drink. The water is filled with hope and ashes. The water is in his throat. The fire licks my fingers, sweet. The water is in his throat. There is nothing to catch the ashes from my pyre but his mouth, ringed with hair and sweat and salt.

IV

If I take the first step toward the coyote, will he kill me? If I stop sitting on my cliff. If I catch the eyes that glitter at me in the dark. I see his eyes watching the stone wedged inside me, the stone lodged in between my legs, the one left there long ago, the one that now wants to move, up and out, to roll down this cliff. If I gather him to me at the fire and he burns me? Or if I gather him to me to remove my stone and he pulls it out of me.

The winter sun burns through the white eyes of the ice sky. I am in the arms of the holy mesa. The coyote watches from the edge of the fire. The fire tells us of its volcano days.

In the firelight, I whisper silently to the coyote: *Come here and hold me. You give me faith in the sounds I hear in my head, the moans and shouts of thoughts of the future. Of union. Of saying whatever I want to say, of liquid pouring from my every opening, sudden, to know that it's possible to drink, to wet the soil with everything nobody needed of me.*

And the coyote whispers silently to me, *How do you want me? I can take any form you like. On my toes, running to you. On my haunches, tasting you like the tree that birthed me. Love me. Love me like a body I can hold. Love me like a falcon with the mouth of a red, red rose. Let me sink in you. Let me kiss you like a velvet asp. Give me your tongue to taste. Give me your open ribs to suck.*

Underneath his fur are the muscles to hold me. The thin strong arms. The blazing eyes, the color of piñon in wildfire.

And overhead, the ravens circle in deliberate loops, spelling out the answers to the questions I soon will ask. The direction I will soon seek is the angle of their wings, catching heat rising and wrapping the mesa, the holy mesa.

His paw in the palm of my hand. Reading his tracks on my earth.

V

His face is covered in fur. Teeth run down his centerfold of fur. His eyes glow sweetly in the open sun. In the wind off the holy mesa, he runs his fingers through his fur and gathers himself down on his haunches, watching me.

I am aware of his thighs in the moonlight. They are covered in fur. Fur along the full long length of him, narrow in the starlight. His scent is dark, his scent is fresh meat cooked over a fire of winter piñon.

In the dawn he circles my adobe. In the antechamber between sun and moon his claws light, then heavy along the tiles. My door opens on its own. My door swings open for him. He circles the house outside and he wonders about possessing what is inside the house. I can hear the rhythms of his heartbeart, deliberate and enigmatic. He knows where I am. The muscle of his heart empties and fills with the knowledge of who and where I am.

These are his paws on the stairsteps. These are his claws in my hair. He has found me between the sheets of yesterday and tomorrow.

In the morning, his prints have made arcane patterns around my adobe. I follow them, and sink my fangs into his poison mark.

Weaning, a Love Story

Elizabeth Rosner

O n the first night, the worst night, my two-year-old niece's cries were so piercing and desperate that the wall-sharing neighbors called in alarm to report an abandoned infant. They were right, of course. Even though three of us were there to comfort her—father, older sister, aunt—none of us could begin to compensate for what was being denied. Her lament was a stream of words and agonized sobbing.

where is mommy where is mommy where is she daddy
where is she I want mommy I want to go home
I want mommy where is mommy
I want milk where is mommy I want to go there
why daddy why daddy why why why

We distracted her, we held and stroked her, we played calming music and murmured words of love. And yet we couldn't begin to explain, especially not in the midst of her despair, why she couldn't have the only person she wanted, needed, and had never before been kept away from.

If you think this is a story about losing a mother, you're right. But not in the way that you might imagine.

Following a tradition established with his first two daughters, my infinitely compassionate and patient—dare I say, heroic?—brother was weaning his youngest daughter by taking her out of town for a few days, leaving Mommy at home in Vermont. According to my brother, who gets to be considered an expert, this process works.

In the previous chapters of this family story, weaning took place at our sister's home in nearby Massachusetts. In this third chapter, my brother flew with two of his three daughters to a condominium in Miami Beach, Florida. That's where I flew to meet them, hoping to provide some moral support. I soon realized I was there to bear witness—to an experience so existential and primal, so heartbreaking and unavoidable, that I would never be quite the same.

Let me fill in a few more details here: this particular weekend marked the end of my yearlong treatment for breast cancer, the same disease that had killed our mother nine years earlier. My brother's first daughter, born two months after our mother's death, is named after her grandmother. I have no children by choice, and a few weeks after this trip, I was scheduled for a procedure called a bilateral salpingo-oopharectomy: that is, surgical removal of my ovaries and tubes. This was a prophylactic measure to prevent ovarian cancer, another disease with high-risk factors I inherited from my mother.

As for Miami Beach? The place was vivid with pastels and palm trees, white sand and turquoise water. Postcard-worthy in a vintage way, yet poignant too. We were staying just a few blocks from the last residence of our maternal grandmother, who had died decades earlier from a cancerous lesion in her brain. All these years past that death, her apartment hotel was still standing, but when I wandered past, I saw the place transformed, just like most of South Beach.

A neon sign and a lobby filled with chic furniture proclaimed its trendy new personality. In fact, the entire neighborhood where she had lived among so many retired and—let's face it—dying elders now resembled a gigantic disco, complete with more fla-grantly displayed and surgically enhanced breasts than I have ever seen. Even the mannequins in the windows of the ubiquitous bikini stores were proud owners of double-D cup size. This town was all about mammaries.

Coincidence? Divine plan? Collective remedies for unresolved attachments?

By the second day of the trip, and into the third and fourth, with diversions like sandcastles on the beach and frothy chocolate milkshakes, my niece seemed easier to console, though her ques-tions were unchanging. She clung to my brother like a shipwreck victim, and each night she exhausted herself back into sleep. *Where is mommy, I want mommy, why can't I go there?* My own losses floated around me in the darkness. My mother, now gone. My grandmother, long gone before that. Not to mention the loss of part of my right breast, the imminent loss of my ovaries, all the losses yet to come.

As I helplessly listened to my niece's wails, I kept thinking about the epic nature of this abandonment, the depth and breadth of it. The way it has to be borne as yet another excruciating separa-tion from mother, from the body we belonged to and which has belonged to us. Only death, the last separation—which, if we're lucky, happens long after leaving home to become an independent adult—can be any more final than this.

What a price we pay to be human! To be a daughter, a mother, a father, a sister, a brother. To bond so fully and to let go so perma-nently. To love what we must always inevitably lose.

In the subsequent weeks and months, whenever I imagined I could still hear my niece's grief, I was reminded of how many ways we fail to appreciate what our mothers give, often until it's far too late to thank them. Even now, the images of that Miami unvacation remain with me more vividly and permanently than any photo album might have captured. Have I mentioned my brother's vast empathy? All the days of our trip, he cherished his daughter unrelentingly, and he remained steadfast in her gaze, fully present for every moment of her journey. I was there; I saw and felt it.

And though some residue of my own motherloss dissolved too, I understand that we all carry wounds from the very same breakage. In this beautiful tragedy, we are each alone and also together.

Watchfires

Hilary Plum

<hr>

Did he speak with an accent? She looked up. Between her and the
screen were arrangements of chairs which bodies occupied
nervously. No, the interviewee said, he sounded just like you
and me. Things we'd talk about would be like which rapper was
best.

Onscreen people used the phrase *tight-knit community*. Here in
the waiting room unironically a woman knitted.

In the theater he was unconscious. Is there an *I* to the anesthetized
body? To the still-beating heart or the mechanism, halted, of peri-
stalsis? My belly was opened three times; through the largest incision they removed the large intestine. He would say: I had colon
cancer. He is thirty years old.

Four months ago his father had died of cancer born in the colon.
His father's father had died of cancer at forty-one, his father in turn
at thirty-three. How fortunate we are to live in an age of advanced
detection. In the waiting room she opened her book, which could
be called a masterpiece of the Palestinian catastrophe: the plight
of the refugees, the failures of the resistance.

Four days ago and four hundred miles away two bombs had detonated. How may we describe it? Her brother had lived for years in that city and still she could only drive anywhere there if she started at that yuppie hardware store. Like hundreds of thousands she'd been a student on the city's outskirts. Once a year it was Marathon Monday and for days after the cheering no one on campus could speak. She'd once jumped into the race to help pace a friend and had ducked out just before the finish line. At the finish line two bombs exploded. Thirteen years passed between these moments, though as the race measured time they were close: the difference between nine and nine and a half minutes per mile. There were two bombs, first one, then the other. There were two brothers, one older, one younger.

There were cameras everywhere and later the brothers would appear on every channel: baseball caps and zip-up jackets, dark nylon backpacks, the brothers walking around a corner, or standing facing the race amid the crowd.

By the time she learned the brothers' names the older was dead, a *shootout with the police.* The boy was, what is the phrase, *in the wind?* A manhunt. A lockdown. Do not leave your homes, the governor instructed the people of the city. Onscreen every few minutes a police spokesman approached a microphone. The trains had stopped running, the buses, cars. In certain neighborhoods SWAT teams were checking each room of each residence.

Upon hearing the name of one neighborhood she stepped outside to call a friend. Her friend said: The SWAT team came through at 6 A.M. We ran out of wine at 9.

The novel she read was in English, though it had been written in no language she knew. Such transformations are possible. The cancer was caused by a genetic mutation; no, the mutation was linked to a high incidence of cancer, a statistical likelihood. If someone knew precisely how this mutation caused tumors, or allowed tumors, or fostered—it wasn't she; she didn't have even a verb. His father had

had the mutation and so, one might assume, did his father, and his. To think that when in that last winter they had helped the father into and out of bed, his legs swollen beyond what she could have imagined, his hiccups, which jolted exactly the site of the tumor, a continual torment, to think that even then in the belly of the son the offspring of the father's tumor was growing, feeding on the nourishment meant for every good cell, every other cell.

Is it a coincidence, the word *cell?* A terrorist cell? the newscasters wondered all morning, the long hours authorities hunted the boy. A sleeper cell? Did they act alone?

That day in the waiting room she had occasion to consider coincidences. Her first novel had just been published, a novel she had written a few years before, during the height of the Iraq War. In the novel a group of Americans undertake (this the verb she'd used in the obligatory descriptions) a series of bombings to protest the war. The brother of one of the activists served in Iraq and upon returning home commits suicide. One of the activists will die as a result of one of his own bombs.

Since the marathon bombing friends had been writing her. Was there something prescient to the novel? So far the only radical ideas the brothers, authors of the bombing, had been known to espouse was an opposition to the U.S. wars in Iraq and Afghanistan. That and the facts, widely noted, that they were Muslim and immigrants: their father was Chechen and after a life as refugees in Kyrgyzstan and Russia they had come to the U.S. in 2002. Chechnya, a land known for its sufferings, its terrorism or resistance, let's use both words for now, the news ceaseless and the operation taking hours, long enough to imagine every disaster. She imagines his death; together the screen and the book in her lap testify to almost every possible horror, but in this moment she fears only his death. Now someone has located the father of the bombers, who had returned to Russia a few years ago, he was sick and wished to be sick among family in a city of refugees and not in America. The father believed nothing said of his boys, and such love might hearten were it not terrifying, that a father could out of love deny any and all evidence, evidence his sons offered in word and deed.

Not prescience, but coincidence—not chance, but simultaneity. She was American *born and bred,* but she too had felt a current of rage move through her. She had remained within the borders of the novel, an imagined territory. She had not bought a pressure cooker, packed it with ball bearings, set the backpack down among cheering families, restaurant managers, for instance, international students, eight-year-olds. Copley Square, the Boston Public Library, the anniversary of the shot heard round the world. The novel she had written had nothing to do with the boy whose face appeared always so young on the screen. But could emotion be a current into which strangers swim, their limbs brush one another's, their limbs tangle? There are words for emotions felt in common: patriotism; or the anxiety of this waiting room; or the standby *Zeitgeist.* In the waiting room she spoke to no one, other than one elderly man volunteer, who twice offered her tea just as she was lifting a mug of coffee to her lips.

In a moment of reflection a pundit observed that the brothers' opposition to the war in Iraq was evidence of nothing, since a majority of Americans held this same view.

The logic of two consecutive bombs: the second targets those who have rushed to help the victims of the first. So common is this strategy that it shadows the very words *first responder.*

In college, in a course on love, she had been taught that even the great pacifists believed in self-defense. Nonviolence was right for social movements, for any cause, any nation or would-be nation, but if they come to your lawn, your home, your body: defend yourself. She agreed. The problem arose in how one defined the self.

She wanted to present herself to the surgeons and say: he is mine. Any error you make, the loss will be mine. Surely they understood this; this was their work. She liked that their scrubs were undignified, allied them not with the workaday world but with their patients: gowned, bare-assed and slackjawed, every kind of fluid pumped in and out or leaking. Surgeons never wear gloves, his mother observed days later, meaning not for surgery but the exams: a surgeon had been by his room and examined the incision barehanded.

They might think of the incision as theirs, since they had made it, since their hands had spent hours in this torso, and this line of staples, bruised and crusting darkly, was the trace left of their action. Now their fingers prospecting freely a wound in this room, the next, the next. To protect ourselves against ourselves; to protect what is ours from ourselves, and vice versa.

For twelve years she'd had a *chronic illness* and for the last five she had not been *financially independent.* If not for her husband's good middle-class job she'd have applied for federal disability. Disabled as citizen: member of a nation, unable. *Martyr* would be a more dignified label, but not appropriate; no intention could offer her suffering to a cause.

Twelve years had passed since the April she had first collapsed. She was running and went down midstride. Looking like, a friend said, one of those cheap toys: press the base of the platform and the creature on top slumps over. The illness was neurological and these past three years had been worsening. It came on in what she called *episodes,* between which she was fine. Lately there had been little time between; lately it had been a sort of siege, but in place of the drama that word might suggest, an ungovernable dullness. When sick she couldn't read or write or work and could barely walk, passed her days on the couch or in bed watching television or skimming a mystery novel or a book meant for children. Days, weeks, months thus confined. Since she saw few people when she was ill, most people knew only, she came to believe, one version of her: the one who was out in the world and seemed, we might say, *normal*. She could speak of the other life she lived, confined all those days, but it felt like a story, something people would nod to but then ask the wrong question, and since her illness had yet to be definitively diagnosed she didn't have even a name to offer. It had come to feel as though her normal self was a lie, a fiction others welcomed and in which she too believed for hours at a time but which would inevitably dissolve. To others, she thought, it seemed as if she were one of them, when in fact, a jet-setting Persephone, she belonged day by day to a distant kingdom.

And so like everyone she lived two lives, public and private. But for her the division between was exceptionally violent. A claim that may also describe, for instance, the life of a refugee, displaced and living in a foreign country. Not that she and the refugee had an experience in common; but perhaps in the fact of this inexpressible schism—the public cleaved from the private—they might more easily imagine one another.

The spring the cancer took root in his gut she got better.

Soon cries will commence to try the boy, a citizen, one of us, as an *enemy combatant*. Most who now bear that label are imprisoned, without trial, offshore in that prison not legal enough for American soil. This spring one hundred prisoners are on hunger strike; to feed them twice a day navy medics force a tube down the noses and into the stomachs of the recalcitrant.

Soon she will be buying cough drops for her husband, his throat raw from just such a tube, his nose bleeding.

Every competent patient, the code of doctors states, *has the right to refuse medical intervention, including life-sustaining interventions.*

What happened to the boy? What changed him? These were the questions the news pored over, in ceaseless stylized pronouncements from talking heads, whose highlights and shoulder pads and soft-bellied suits streamed all day over the television's surface. The metaphor was of a poison lurking among us, within us, in the body of our nation. Living like our neighbor, accepting our welfare checks, attending our schools, speaking our language, and then, without warning, attacking. A cancer. You might say.

Of the 171 men still imprisoned that spring in Guantanamo Bay, 89 have been cleared for release. But what should be done with them, where will they go? It seems more than a decade has been required to answer these questions, though many answers would do. They remain imprisoned, no end in sight.

Two months into the hunger strike, forty more military medics were shipped to the camp to help keep its prisoners alive, a task that now requires the use of force.

A few years ago forty prisoners were released to be resettled in sixteen countries. These are called *third countries:* the first being their home; the second, it seems, the United States. The U.S. imprisoned them; but they were never there.

Some prisoners say the present strike was sparked by a shakedown in which guards mishandled prisoners' Qur'ans. Authorities deny this.

They feel like they're living in graves, one lawyer noted on a recent visit.

They won't let us live in peace, and they won't let us die in peace.

The brothers might have learned strategy close to home. In Afghanistan and Pakistan the U.S. has deployed drones to strike those who'd gathered to aid the victims of the strike before.

It's not that each explanation requires metaphor; it's that each explanation is only metaphor. Metaphorically speaking, are we now in the age of autoimmune disease? Now the enemy is ourselves: we can no longer tell friend from foe; we mistake self for other. Helpless we mount full-force attacks against ourselves. (If the body could speak—could defend itself—would it name this a *pre-emptive strike?*)

Her husband will spend ten days in the hospital and she will be there every day. She'll read three novels, suck on hard candies, and walk through the field surrounding the hospital complex. Each morning she'll bathe him: he'll stand in the bathroom hunched with pain and attached to an IV pole, and she'll fill a basin with sudsy water and with a washcloth clean the bruised skin of his back and torso, the bruise that extends from his incision in every direction. In his morphined bluntness he corrects her technique. Her intimacy with his body seems less than useful; the skill lies not in tending to one's husband but in tending to any vulnerable body.

Right before he's released a surgeon comes by and, displeased with the discharge of a hematoma, plucks out seven or eight of the couple dozen stitches that bind the incision. You'll just have to pack these sites with gauze, he says, pointing to the holes he has created, bright red gashes.

At home the next morning they realize the nature of their task: to stuff a thumb's worth of gauze right into these chasms in the belly. She watches her husband's fingers disappear into his own torso and understands why people faint at such sights. What should be invisible made suddenly visible. Rupture, violation.

Photographs from the finish line show a man, bearded and wearing a cowboy hat, disappearing into the smoke. Later the man, still with cowboy hat, is seen bent over a man in a wheelchair, pinching closed an artery in the man's bloodied leg. The man in the cowboy hat was there to cheer for a group of military servicemen who were marching the course in honor of fallen soldiers, including the man in the cowboy hat's son, killed in Najaf in 2004. The servicemen marched in full uniform and bore forty-pound rucks, their efforts dedicated not only to those who had died in combat but those lost to suicide upon their return.

When in 2004 three marines came to tell the man in the cowboy hat of his son's death, he could not believe them, and in his grief he doused the marines' van in gasoline, from within set it on fire, set himself on fire. Later he traveled around the country to protest the war and the military's recruitment practices, which he believed had been intended to deceive his son. *As long as there are marines fighting and dying in Iraq, I'm going to share my mourning with the American people*, he told a reporter, interviewed beside a coffin he had transformed into traveling memorial.

P.S. Please send some info. about Afghanistan, Saudi Arabia, Iran, Iraq. We get very little amounts of info. down here. . . . But I have heard some little things here and there about Conflicts, War, Deployments, etc., his son wrote from boot camp in 2002.

In 2011 the soldier's brother—the man in the cowboy hat's younger son—committed suicide. He had suffered from depression, his family said, since his brother's death.

The injured man in the photograph, pale and ash-smeared in the wheelchair, would lose both legs but survive.

The military servicemen may be seen in photographs, wrenching a fence clear of the blast scene, trying to get to those injured within.

Please don't let them be Muslim, commentators wrote in the short days between bombing and manhunt. She sympathized, but the wishfulness annoyed. Why shouldn't they be Muslim, given the violence the U.S. had perpetrated for decades across the Muslim world?

The U.S. army psychiatrist who in 2009 killed thirteen and wounded thirty at Fort Hood in a *shooting rampage* was Muslim. He was about to be deployed to one of America's two war zones; the soldiers he attacked were in a processing center to be vaccinated before being sent overseas. A first responder shot the psychiatrist four times; he survived, paralyzed from the chest down.

At his trial, set to begin this summer, he will represent himself. He argues that his actions were a *defense of others:* in his assault he acted to defend the leaders of the Taliban from American forces. The judge will not allow this defense.

After the marathon bombing, after this or that mass shooting, a chorus arises: why do we mourn those innocents felled in Boston but not those in Baghdad, in Homs? This cry for justice itself becomes spectacle, predictable stage of the civic immune response: to condemn the limits of others' perceptions, find others guilty. To affirm oneself as one who possesses the right sentiment. Hit refresh; repeat.

The dead in Homs, the dead in Boston, were not sacrificed that we might prove our compassion. Yet this is one use to which they may be put. In this sense a foreign body possesses more value. In this sense.

If the one who detonates the bomb is a soldier, our compassion extends to him. If the one who detonates the bomb is a Muslim, an Arab, or the boy, we may require his sacrifice. Our compassion may manifest in his death; if we have named him *terrorist,* he may fulfill this name with his death. If he lives we will not see him; we will see him only by the light of his orange jumpsuit. If he insists on living, or dying, to spite us. If he insists on living in the grave.

One expert describes cancer as a *microscopic rebellion:*

As a body lives and grows, its cells are constantly dividing, copying their DNA . . . and bequeathing it to the daughter cells. They in turn pass it to their own progeny: copies of copies of copies. Along the way, errors inevitably occur. . . .

Over the eons, cells have developed complex mechanisms that identify and correct many of the glitches. But the process is not perfect, nor can it ever be. . . . Every so often a certain combination will give an individual cell too much power. It begins to evolve independently of the rest of the body. Like a new species thriving in an ecosystem, it grows into a cancerous tumor. For that there can be no easy fix.

A later investigation will assert that the brothers' motivation for the bombing was not political but personal. Not that of global jihad, but *rooted in the turbulent collapse of their family and their escalating personal and collective failures.* One doctor suspects the older brother of schizophrenia; for years he had told his mother he heard an angry voice within him, *inside his head, someone who wanted to control him, to make him do something.* It felt like *two people inside of me.*

If, the article muses, the bombing was born of *private motives,* that would make the brothers *homegrown murderers,* like the other young men—young white men—whose deeds we know well, whose deeds we unwillingly recognize.

Photographs from the battlefield at Gettysburg were, notoriously, falsified. Falsified not by a curator's hand, but the photographers themselves. The dead in one photograph named Confederate, in the next Union: nearly a century later it would be proved these were the same dead; only the position of the camera has changed. Another photograph famously captures a sniper dead in the *sharpshooter's den.* But his weapon is not a sniper's, and this same man may be seen fallen elsewhere on the slopes. It seems that the photographers lifted this corpse into a more picturesque location, arranged his limbs, his gun. These facts alter our sympathies not for the corpses so much as for the photographers, who have framed falsehood in the guise of truth.

War feels to me an oblique place, Emily Dickinson wrote to Colonel Thomas Wentworth Higginson in 1862.

In the same letter the line before reads: *I should have liked to see you before you became improbable.* Transplanted this seems better elegy than most for the boy who now sits in a prison west of

Boston, a few restrictions recently lifted, his trial yet to begin; after long delay it's announced that he will face the death penalty.

What are we to do with the gift of survival?
    Daily into the wound we thrust a pinchful of gauze.
    Legend claims that the first man to run a marathon died at its end. He ran from the battle where the Persians had been defeated to the heart of Athens. *We won!* he cried out and fell dead.

April–August 2013

Sources: Jeremy Lazarus, president of the American Medical Association, writing to Secretary of Defense Chuck Hagel, April 25, 2013; "Hunger Strikes at Guantanamo Nearly Double," *Al-Jazeera*, March 19, 2013; Paul Harris, Tracy McVeigh, and Mark Townsend, "How Guantánamo's Horror Forced Inmates to Hunger Strike," *Guardian*, May 4, 2013; David A. Fahrenthold, "Boston Marathon Bystander Says He Acted Instinctively," *Washington Post*, April 16, 2013; Tasneem Raja, "These Soldiers Did the Boston Marathon Wearing 40-Pound Packs," *Mother Jones*, April 16, 2013; "Peace Activist Carlos Arredondo Hailed as Hero for Aid to Boston Marathon Bombing Victims," *Democracy Now*, April 16, 2013; Trymaine Lee, "A Father with a Coffin, Telling of War's Grim Toll," *New York Times*, February 1, 2007; Elise Forbes Tripp, *Surviving Iraq: Soldiers' Stories* (Northampton, MA: Olive Branch Press, 2007), chap. 29; George Johnson, "Why Everyone Seems to Have Cancer," *New York Times*, January 6, 2014; Sally Jacobs, David Filipov, and Patricia Wen, "The Fall of the House of Tsarnaev," *Boston Globe*, December 15, 2013; Jim Hicks, "Observers: The Real War and the Books," in *Lessons from Sarajevo: A War Stories Primer* (Amherst: University of Massachusetts Press, 2013).

Breaking Down

Donna Ford

The tow truck driver and I have a strange intimacy that makes the long silence between us bearable. The cab of his truck smells of sweat and Juicy Fruit gum. When I had been heading south on Route 287, the rattle I thought was coming from the truck behind me was actually coming from my car.

One day, long before, while lying in the safe nest of our bed, I had told my husband one of my biggest fears was to be stranded on a road. I had no idea that my words would find purchase in a series of aging Subarus that left me on dark roads often lacking cell coverage, on major interstates where my tow service was forbidden to go. The universe seemed to conspire to show me such terror was unfounded, yet on the day when my car literally screamed in pain, I had been on my way to New Jersey to see my mother.

Her breast cancer had returned; complications from chemotherapy had landed her again in the hospital. It had not been a year since my father had died suddenly of pancreatic cancer. When I learned of my mother's cancer diagnosis, I blamed her immense and often terrifying grief after his death. Her sadness had teeth and claws and could shred anyone within reach, meaning that my siblings and I had to offer up our own grieving to feed that monster. During my visits to her house, the only place her grief could not reach me was the shower.

In the tow truck, no longer en route to see my mother in the hospital, my main wish is to give in to crying. All those weeks after my father's death, my car's solitude had served as such a useful sanctuary: each time, all the way home from her house, I could cry. Guilty over my escape and eager for all to be as it once had been: dad alive, mother untroubled, and still getting to be that adult child unheeding of loss. And despite the tow truck driver's apparent comfort with our silence, I doubt if he could tolerate even quiet tears.

As if on cue, we pass the hospital where my father died. Tearing me from the quiet truck cab, memory has me walking across the parking lot with my family on that day, my siblings a phalanx around my mother. Both grateful and terrified, I veer away from them, glad for a few moments alone, cutting across the lawn to seek my car on the street. That day, staring up at the older part of the hospital, an older memory hits me: was it not here that at age five I stood with my father among blooming rhododendrons and looked up at a third-floor window where my mother held my new baby brother, waving down to us?

Past this heaping up of memory, through narrow Trenton streets, the tow truck driver navigates his enormous rig. Like my father, he has a graceful, confident air about him while he drives. The garage where I will leave my car is a low square building without a sign; and as the robotic beep signals the backward motion of the truck, he says nothing, just parks and begins the process of unburdening his truck, while I walk into the small dirty office stinking of grease and ashtrays. A mechanic fills in my name, address, and the make of my car on a form, and hands me the greasy pen he has just used so I can sign my name. "Be in touch," he says. I want to ask him how old he is but I walk outside, grateful for sunlight and air. As if he has just read my mind, the tow truck driver speaks: "He's a good guy. Good mechanic."

"Oh." This is all I say.

"Somebody picking you up?"

This is the question toward which all has been narrowing. Now I could truly cry and it will not be until later when I collapse, exhausted, that I realize how much strength it took for me to hold back the sobs, the tears clawing at the back of my throat. If I speak I know that everything will come spilling out, a deluge wild with terror, despair, and loneliness. My siblings are at work and my point of coming down was to relieve them of caring for my mother so they could return to their jobs and family. My mind quickly tries to access how much I have left on my credit card, in my bank account—would a cab break me? Nothing is clear. I shake my head.

"Come on. Where are you going?"

For what I think is the first time, I take a look at the tow truck driver. He is a compact man, almost cartoonish in his squareness, his face natural, passive, and illegible, neither smiling nor frowning. With a rusty voice I tell him where I am going, but on this ride, out of Trenton, I speak with the relief of one not stranded: of my mother's cancer, my father's death, and now the cab smells not of chewing gum but of something like old coffee—the stench of my words.

As we approach the hospital, the tow truck driver lets out a long whistle, the kind men make in old movies when they spot a beautiful woman, since, down to the circular driveway and the hideous fountain in the entryway, the place looks like a luxury hotel, down to the valet in red jacket and jaunty cap.

Despite my suspicion that the repairs to my car will clean out my checking account, in the gift shop I buy my mother an overpriced scarf, creating a turban out of it to cover her bald head. In the world's most uncomfortable cot, I spend the night just so I can tell the nurses not to put the blood pressure cuff on my mother's bad arm, to make sure she is checked for fever every hour. Together my mother and I eat terribly rich food from the lobby restaurant, watching a new Tyler Perry movie. She keeps telling me I didn't have to come right up until the point when her doctor comes in and tells her that she can go home soon. "You are the Energizer bunny," he tells her, but a nurse corrects him. "No. More like what they said about Timex watches. Takes a licking and keeps on ticking." Then something my father once said returns: "You keep getting up until one day you don't"—words that brighten me far more. What the doctor and nurses speak of is immunity from danger; I know better.

Outside, the tow truck driver picks me up, reminding me again I can call if I need a ride, yet this time, during our quiet ride to the garage, our prior intimacy feels soiled, somewhat shameful.

I stare out of my window. He looks straight ahead. When we get to the garage he walks ahead to find the mechanic in the bay under a car afloat over his head. The tow truck driver is strangely animated when he speaks to him. After I pay the bill, after the mechanic hands me my keys, I follow the driver out into the sunlight and air. He asks a simple question that comes out as a kind of benediction. "You're going to be all right?" And for the first time that year, I believed.

(Rifle, Morphine)

Carolyn Cooke

The hog sniffs at cornhusks while the father touches the muzzle of his 30-30 to its forehead. The father hopes to shoot once, as perfectly as he can. Two hogs on the other side of the pen kick dust, their curled tails twitching. Karnell stands in the path between sunflowers and cosmos whetting his knife. The scratch of his blade against the stone makes a *tisk, tisk* sound, which the hogs can probably hear.

Chester stands near the tractor and calls out advice: *Watch out for ricochet—it's a big gun.*

The gun that tamed the West! says Karnell. Chester and Karnell are cousins, sixteen or seventeen years of age. Since they were kids they've helped with the hogs.

The father fires and the first hog is down in the dust. Chester jumps in the tractor and drives close. Karnell approaches the hog with his knife, holds the head, and slits the throat. Chester and Karnell haul the animal out of the pen by its legs. *Watch out, he's still kicking,* says Chester, and it's true. The fibrillating heart pumps blood down the legs to the hooves. The hog kicks the whole way to the tractor, though it's already dead.

The two other hogs root in the stained dirt, their socket noses covered with blood. Long white eyelashes almost cover their eyes; rust-colored lice and liver spots show through the white hog hair.

Karnell fits a grappling hook behind the dead hog's heel. He uses a winch to raise the hog until its head clears the ground. The father and Chester hose down the hide; then the father scrubs it with a stiff brush. The hog weighs 230 to 250 pounds; once they've removed the hide, head, hooves, and disemboweled it, they expect 180 pounds of hams, chops, bacon, and ribs. This family doesn't use every part of the hog, but almost.

He's kind of buggy, says Chester, pointing out lice beneath the hair.

They could scald the hog in a bathtub of boiling water. Leaving the hide on would tenderize the pork, and it's the old-fashioned way. Before cold lockers, people usually preserved the meat in brine. But they won't need brine if they hang their pork to age in Vic Soldani's cold locker. Vic will butcher, too; he charges thirty cents a pound.

Karnell and Chester use Buck knives to peel back the hide toward the head. Chester gains leverage by wedging the heel of his boot between a foreleg and the belly. Without its hide the hog is a shiny zeppelin of lard; its midsection glows red with organs. Later, their mothers will render the lard and preserve it in jars to use for their piecrusts. The hogs don't have names. The process of killing and gutting an animal so thoroughly and with such attention to the future is intimate, but it's not personal.

Chester holds the forelegs and Karnell saws off the head. He uses a regular triangular saw. The secret to decapitating a hog is to cut between a set of vertebrae through cartilage, not bone. The process is bloodless. The heart pumped out the blood while it was still a pump. A sudden popping, as if someone has opened a magnum of champagne, is followed by the sound of the head falling onto the ground. Green flies with oily whorls of color on their backs explode onto the scene.

The father cuts open the belly. The lungs are pink and full of air, the kidneys hard. The liver looks like any corn-fed liver—rich and silky. The stomach, distended with corn, gleams white; the heart is a red rock. Chester plans to take the lungs to his physiology class, so he hoses them off. They leave the viscera in the dirt.

They saw the hog in half lengthwise. Already it looks more like food than an animal; those are hams that were his legs; the chops and ribs lie in their corners in the ribcage. The loin's the tender, fancy part, and the belly's bacon. The saw cut leaves intact for a minute the pink rope of the spinal cord and the tiny jellyfish between the vertebrae. Karnell cuts off the two front hooves and tosses them down the hill. They fall with a dense, dead sound; dust sprays over the raspberries on the vines.

Chester and Karnell cover the hog halves with a bedsheet.

The father showers the remaining two hogs with popcorn, which they snuffle with lively grunts of appreciation while he reloads.

He shoots the second hog behind the ear. The third hog lifts its head toward the sun, detached as Buddha.

I left the hog notes on my desk—not really my kind of story—and rushed to Oakland Airport while my ninety-eight-year-old nana, Eleanor, wheezed and waited in Boston.

Every day she learned that she could not eat; a nurse poured Ensure into a hose. She wasn't allowed in the dining room: no wheelchairs. It was like the top deck of the *Titanic* in there: old Yankees with their martinis, mothy tweeds, Episcopal politics, and strong characters ignoring the cries of the second-class passengers as the ice water played around the deck chairs. Eventually Nana developed pneumonia. She wasn't expected to live, but the timing was, because of drugs, malleable. She called to ask whether my coming East would be too much trouble.

For two days, then, we held hands at the pajama party of death.

My grandfather took the elevator from his apartment upstairs and met us in her room. He had only his own idea of what to do to comfort the dying: for hours at a time he read aloud from Fielding's *Tom Jones*—I recall a scene of young Tom being spanked by a man called Thwackett. He paused once in his reading so Nana could speak by telephone to my children—her great-grandchildren—in California. She couldn't talk easily; she was already drowning. *Never. Give. Up,* she rasped, her parting shot. She put down the receiver.

I left her once, for an hour. While the nurse poured the can of Ensure into her hose, her last meal, my grandfather treated me to two martinis and a cod in the formal dining room in which his wife of thirty-five years was no longer allowed. I enjoyed the moment of artifice and illusion, my grandfather's dry wit tinged with important sorrow, the glasses of clear, abstracting gin, the quiet knives and good china. After his ice cream my grandfather went to bed. I returned to Nana's room. She was sitting up with her knees under her chin.

Hurry up! She beckoned to no one.

Who is it, Nana? I asked. She pointed with her bent finger to the doorway.

The staff understood that she was beyond small assistance and avoided us. Eight o'clock came and went; so did midnight. An atmosphere of buzzers, cries, moans, apparitions in white nightgowns. I may have imagined the floating, screaming specters in every doorway. But I do not exaggerate them. Nana had come home from the hospital to die in a polite and dignified atmosphere. Why was the atmosphere not more dignified and polite? I complained to the nurse, who gave me a Dixie cup filled with blue morphine. And a dropper. *You can give it to her sublingually,* the nurse said. *As much as she needs.* Or something like that.

I filled the dropper and released liquid under her tongue. She hadn't drunk anything by mouth in nearly two years and seemed to revel in tasting. We held hands. Her breathing sounded like a plumbing drain. I dipped the mouth of the dropper into the paper cup, sucked up the morphine, and shot it under her tongue. Her eyes turned bluer and more distant, her hand squeezed mine, and her bulldog energy flowed between us. Her eyes remained open.

At two o'clock in the morning my grandfather answered his telephone, and I said, *Nana's gone.*

Gone? he said. *You mean dead? We won't see Eleanor anymore?*

Death redeemed us; the nurse came in, took the platinum rings from Nana's fingers, and put them in my hands. I called the number I'd kept in my wallet for months. Two men in bright suits came and carried her away. She would be bone and ash in a pale blue box. We had talked before, inconclusively, about where she might like her ashes to be scattered. Boston was her town, but as she said, *Town is not what it was,* meaning that she didn't understand it anymore. It was illegal, too, to scatter ashes in the river or the harbor, and Nana would not want to be dispersed unlawfully. Years later her son-in-law would open the box and scatter her ash on the Benjamin River in Maine.

I don't regret squeezing morphine into Nana's mouth, but do feel the weight of the act. That's why, a few years after these events took place, I made the presumptuous leap into what is now "this story"—in which human sympathy is expanded by brutality—and killed them all again.

Afternoon and After

Debra Jo Immergut

I know this town down to the buckles in the pavement along the shortcuts through the back blocks. I know the cats crouched on its porches and the graffiti scribbled beneath its bridges and the hollows of its aging trees.

But why should I know it, this New England place, too far north for the likes of me and mine? The question unearths the afternoon.

We're inundated with memories of the morning, but no one seems to recall the quiet hours later on. The city went mute, where I was, in midtown, four or five hours after the fall.

Walking west on 57th Street, at maybe 1:30 P.M., I was one of only a few people around. The afternoon was soaked in sun and sky, quite hot actually. Vacant acres of sidewalk reflected the glare. If people passed me, they kept their heads down. The silence scorched more than the sun did.

Somewhere near Lexington, I stopped into a deserted Duane Reade drugstore to buy athletic socks. I had only been in my job for two days; I was the new boss, and thus I'd chosen nice shoes, no socks. At checkout, the cashiers avoided eye contact—to be expected in any Duane Reade, but this afternoon's anomie had a special thickness. Fear?

Socks on, destroying any trace of the managerial look I'd aimed for that morning, I headed west again. At this point, the subways had been halted for hours. The office towers had emptied out; the walkers had walked on toward the city's exits, toward the stations. Who knew how they'd left, but they were gone.

The streets were mostly carless, the few vehicles creeping along with a guilty reticence, and I thought, This city is over. It's done. And then came a fuzzed roar, which gradually, painfully collected itself into something sharp and deafening. In the blank blue sky, sliced up over midtown, a grid of fighter jets shot into view, low, shockingly low, then vanished. I walked on, trembling. I don't generally tremble.

When I hit the western avenues, 6th, 7th, 8th, I could see the far-off charred smudge to the south. What I didn't know: This empty street had already become the still point of my turning world. Turning toward the life of now.

Finally I met John outside his office building, near 11th Avenue. We paused together, not saying much that I recall, and we began to walk all the way back across. We had a two-year-old, after all, way out in Brooklyn, needed to get to him, and we'd heard trains were running in the outer boroughs.

At the 57th Street bridge, we discovered a crowd walking to Queens, and joined them. At the highest point of the crossing, the whole plume claimed the sky to the south, an extravagance of blackness, impossible to ignore. Everyone looked, no one spoke.

If you were around, in Brooklyn, downwind from downtown, you recall the days that followed. First, the ash, then the acridity. How it lingered.

Then, as the city awoke from its stupor, lurched back into movement and noise, we all shared the sense that this was just the beginning, that the nightmare would recur.

In the weeks after, the subway felt like a death trap. John and I began to drive to work, the two of us falling into a hush on the approaches to tunnels and bridges. Soldiers peered into our back seat. Every lousy action movie montaged in my mind, the car tumbling from a broken span, a fire cloud billowing toward us from far off down the tunnel. We prepared to die every morning, every crossing. We kissed our son goodbye at his daycare around the corner from our house, with the knowledge that he might be orphaned by day's end.

Four years passed and the next disaster never arrived. But that sense of peril and entrapment never left. So we did. I can't say that we ever fit the profile for what you might call "diehard New Yorkers." But we owned a house, all our work was there, friends, some family.

Now it's more than fifteen years after the afternoon. Now I'm embedded deep in a crowded life in a small Massachusetts town, a place that I barely knew existed until I the first time I descended the ramp at exit 18 off Interstate 91.

If I accept that this life was always waiting, a dappled and tangled garden thriving, untended by my awareness, behind the wall of distance and time, then what got me here was a void. The stillness of that afternoon. The void that grew and swallowed our New York future. The jobs we might have had, the days in the park and the nights in our little backyard, over which the old tenements loomed.

I remember wanting to live in New York because, at twenty-two, I relished the anonymity. Wear pajamas, pee in the street, no one blinked.

Now I can't make a run for a quart of milk without seeing four people I know. If I appear distracted as I walk down the street, a friend will roll up, lower her passenger-side window, and ask me what's on my mind. I know who grows azaleas on Elm and the precise shade of magenta they'll bloom. I notice a new Honda in someone's driveway and whose children are slipping into the woods behind the school.

I landed on the head of a pin.

And how is it possible that this life-sized miniverse—the bristling oak we planted, the red screen door that slams all summer, the teenagers in the kitchen and the dog that sleeps in the corner, the grass and the gravel, the corner markets and garages, Barton and Jan, Margot and Pablo, and Tamara and Ms. Bitgood—would be locked away from me, unknown or nonexistent or extant in some alternate plane of reality, certainly inaccessible, beyond my consciousness, happening elsewhere or not at all, if not for the dread-filled silent moment at the heart of that cruel day?

This line of questioning defeats me. I am overmatched.

The event was an accelerator. So much matter crashed, vaporized. In any attempt at reckoning, my course shift isn't worth notice.

I continue to puzzle over it, though, because it's all I know. I welcome any information that might clarify. Not much comes my way. I'm left to hoard the occasional hints supplied by the bark of the screen door, the whine of the dog, the tremor of arrivals on the porch steps, and the soft violent collisions between my fingertips and these keys.

Contributors

Rebecca Bell-Gurwitz is a therapist and writer of many genres currently based out of Portland, Oregon, though formerly and in her heart a proud East Coast native. Her writing has previously been featured in publications such as the *Dead Beats,* the *Citron Review,* and *Thrice Magazine.* She is a fan of agender characters and surrealist works of fiction, stories about mothers and daughters in kitchens, and finding language to reclaim trauma narratives. Her bangs are slowly turning silver.

Kris Brandenburger owned an electrical repair workshop in West Berkeley, California, for many years before becoming an accidental academic. She has more than twenty years of experience working with adult learners in academic programs. She has also worked in academic administration as a program chair, associate dean, dean, accreditation liaison officer, and chief academic officer at three different institutions. Her personal interests include bicycling, opera, and the arts in all forms. She is deeply engaged in cultures of inquiry and learning.

Laynie Browne's most recent books include a poetry collection (*You Envelop Me*), a novel (*Periodic Companions*), and a collection of short fiction (*The Book of Moments*). Her honors include the National Poetry Series Award, the Contemporary Poetry Series Award, and a Pew Fellowship. She teaches at the University of Pennsylvania and Swarthmore College.

Ana Castillo is a celebrated and distinguished poet, novelist, short story writer, essayist, editor, playwright, translator, and independent scholar. Among her award-winning, best-selling titles are the novels *So Far from God, The Guardians,* and *Peel My Love Like an Onion,* and her poetry collections include *I Ask the Impossible.* Her honors include an American Book Award from the Before Columbus Foundation, a Carl Sandburg Award, a Mountains and Plains Booksellers Award, and fellowships from the National Endowment for the Arts in fiction and poetry. Her memoir *Black Dove: Mamá, Mi'jo, and Me* was released to critical acclaim and received a 2016 International Latino Book Award for autobiography and the 2017 Lambda Award for best bisexual nonfiction, and her novel *Give It to Me* won the 2015 Lambda Literary Award for best bisexual fiction. Ana is editor of *La Tolteca,* an arts and literary 'zine dedicated to the advancement of a world without borders and censorship.

Carolyn Cooke is the author of the novel *Daughters of the Revolution* and two collections of short fiction: *Amor and Psycho* and *The Bostons,* winner of the PEN/Robert Bingham Award. Her fiction and essays have been featured in *AGNI, The Best American Short Stories, The O. Henry Prize Stories,* the *Paris Review, New California Writing,* and the *Nation.* She teaches in the interdisciplinary MFA programs at California Institute of Integral Studies in San Francisco.

Rachel Cole Dalamangas grew up between Denver, Colorado, and the Smoky Mountains of Tennessee. She earned an MFA in literary arts from Brown University in 2011. Her writing has appeared in *Bookslut, zingmagazine, N/A Literary Journal,* and *BOMB,* among other publications. She currently lives in Brooklyn.

Debbie DeFord-Minerva is a longtime copyeditor at Penguin Random House. She has an MFA in creative writing from Emerson College and a dual BA in English and psychology from the University of Michigan. She was named a Robin Hood Foundation Hero in 2015 for mentoring teens. Debbie lives with her family and pets in New York City, where she in-line skates daily and volunteers often. This is her first publication.

Emmalie Dropkin holds an MFA in fiction from the University of Massachusetts Amherst, where she taught undergraduate composition and creative writing. Her work has appeared in *McSweeney's Internet Tendency, Electric Literature,* and *Kaaterskill Basin Literary Journal,* and her fiction has been nominated for the PEN/Robert J. Dau Short Story Prize for Emerging Writers.

Rikki Ducornet is the author of nine novels, three collections of short fiction, and two books of essays, and she has received numerous awards, including the Bard College Arts and Letters Award, the Lannan Literary Award for Fiction, and an Academy Award in Literature. Her work is widely published abroad.

Sonia Feigelson is an MFA candidate in fiction at New York University and the fiction editor of the *Washington Square Review.* Her work appears or is forthcoming in the *Los Angeles Review, Passages North, Hobart,* and *Puerto del Sol,* among other journals. She has won awards from *Glimmer Train* and the Random House Creative Writing Competition.

Donna Ford has a PhD in English from the Graduate School and University Center at the City University of New York. She teaches literature and American studies at Bard College and is a founding faculty member of the Bard Prison Initiative. Donna is a compulsive gardener and knitter and is currently at work on a novel and a short story collection.

Thaisa Frank's sixth book of fiction, *Enchantment,* was named one of the best books of 2012 by the *San Francisco Chronicle.* Her novel *Heidegger's Glasses* was published in 2010 and foreign rights have been sold to ten countries. Her recent work has been anthologized in *New Microfictions* and *Creative Short Fiction.* Thaisa lives in California and is a member of the San Francisco Writers' Grotto.

Bonnie Friedman is the author of the bestseller *Writing Past Dark: Envy, Fear, Distraction, and Other Dilemmas in the Writer's Life* as well as *The Thief of Happiness,* and, most recently, *Surrendering Oz: A Life in Essays,* which was longlisted for the PEN/Diamonstein-Spielvogel Art of the

Essay Award. Her work has appeared in *The Best American Movie Writing*, *The Best Writing on Writing*, and *The Best Buddhist Writing*.

Indira Ganesan has written three novels: *The Journey, Inheritance,* and *As Sweet as Honey.* She has held fellowships from the Paden Institute for Writers of Color, the Mary Ingraham Bunting Institute at Radcliffe College, and the Fine Arts Work Center in Provincetown, and she received the W. K. Rose Fellowship from Vassar College. Indira teaches at Emerson College and reviews books for Phi Beta Kappa's *Key Reporter.*

Judy Grahn is internationally known as a poet, a writer, and a cultural theorist. Her writings helped to globally fuel second-wave feminist, gay, and lesbian activism as well as women's and queer spirituality. She is the author of fourteen books; currently in print are *The Judy Grahn Reader* and a memoir, *A Simple Revolution,* as well as two poetry collections. The essay in this anthology will be part of a collection on consciousness, *Touching Creatures, Touching Spirit.*

Sharon Guskin is the author of the novel *The Forgetting Time,* which has been published in more than twenty countries and was an international bestseller. She holds degrees from Yale College and Columbia University and lives in New York, where she sometimes teaches Buddhist meditation.

Noy Holland is the 2018 recipient of the Katherine Anne Porter Prize from the American Academy of Arts and Letters. She is the author of the novel *Bird* and four collections of short fiction: *The Spectacle of the Body, What Begins with Bird, Swim for the Little One First,* and *I Was Trying to Describe What It Feels Like: New and Selected Stories.*

Debra Jo Immergut is the author of a novel, *The Captives* (with a second one forthcoming in 2019), and a short story collection, *Private Property.* She holds an MFA from the Iowa Writers' Workshop and is a both a Michener and a MacDowell fellow. Her literary work has appeared in *American Short Fiction* and *Narrative,* her journalism in the *Wall Street Journal* and *New York Magazine,* among other places. She lives in Northampton, Massachusetts.

Sheila Kohler is the author of ten novels, three volumes of short fiction, a memoir, and many essays. Her most recent novel is *Dreaming for Freud* and is based on the Dora case. Her memoir *Once We Were Sisters* was released in 2017. She has won numerous prizes including the O. Henry twice, and been included in *The Best American Short Stories*, most recently in 2013. Her work has been published in thirteen countries. She has taught at Columbia University, Sarah Lawrence College, Bennington College, and has been at Princeton University since 2007. Her novel *Cracks* was made into a film directed by Jordan and Ridley Scott. You can find her blog at the *Psychology Today* website.

Dale Kushner is the author of the acclaimed debut novel, *The Conditions of Love*. She writes a monthly blog for the *Psychology Today* website that reflects her investigation into Buddhism and Jungian psychology. Kushner lives in Madison, Wisconsin, with her husband and is completing her second novel, *The Lie of Forgetting*. Her new book of poetry on desire and loss is forthcoming from 3: A Taos Press in 2019.

R. O. Kwon's first novel, *The Incendiaries*, was released in 2018. She is a National Endowment for the Arts literature fellow. Her writing has appeared in the *Guardian, Vice, BuzzFeed, Noon, Time, Electric Literature, Playboy,* the *San Francisco Chronicle,* and elsewhere. She has received awards and fellowships from Yaddo, MacDowell, the Bread Loaf Writers' Conference, the Sewanee Writers' Conference, Omi International, and the Norman Mailer Writers' Colony.

Clarinda Mac Low started out working in dance and molecular biology and now creates participatory installations and events that investigate social constructs and corporeal experience. She is the executive director of Culture Push, an experimental organization that links artistic practice and civic engagement, and is a medical journalist specializing in HIV/AIDS.

Sarah Ladipo Manyika was raised in Nigeria and has lived in Kenya, France, and England. She holds a PhD from the University of California, Berkeley, and has taught literature at San Francisco State University. Sarah currently serves on the boards of Hedgebrook and the Museum of the African Diaspora in San Francisco. She is a novelist, essayist, a San Francisco Library laureate, and the founding books editor at ozy.com.

Edie Meidav is the author of three novels, most recently *Lola, California* and *Crawl Space,* as well as *Kingdom of the Young,* a collection of short fiction with a nonfiction coda. Her work has been awarded support from the Howard, Lannan, and Whiting foundations, the Bard and Kafka fiction prizes, the Fulbright Scholar Program, MacDowell, and Art/OMI, among other entities. She is a permanent member of the MFA faculty at the University of Massachusetts Amherst.

Melinda Misuraca is drawn to naps under trees, conversations in parked cars, flip sides, overlaps, disappearances. Her work has appeared in *Alternet, Salon, Natural Bridge,* the *Portland Review, The Best Travel Writing,* and elsewhere. The essay in this volume is excerpted from a memoir-in-progress. She lives in northern California.

Danica Novgorodoff is an artist, writer, graphic novelist, and horse wrangler from Kentucky who currently lives in Brooklyn. Her graphic novels include *The Undertaking of Lily Chen, Refresh Refresh, Slow Storm,* and *A Late Freeze.* She was awarded a 2015 New York Foundation for the Arts fellowship in literature, and was named Sarabande Books' 2016 writer in residence.

Hilary Plum is the author of the novel *Strawberry Fields,* winner of the 2018 Fence Modern Prize for prose. She has also published a work of nonfiction, *Watchfires,* and the novel *They Dragged Them Through the Streets.* With Zach Savich she edits Rescue Press's Open Prose Series. Hilary teaches at Cleveland State University and is associate director of the CSU Poetry Center.

Jenni Quilter teaches writing at New York University. She is the author of *Neon in Daylight: New York School Collaborations and Connections.*

Elizabeth Rosner's newest book, *Survivor Café: The Legacy of Trauma and the Labyrinth of Memory,* published in 2017, was a finalist for a National Jewish Book Award. National Public Radio named Elizabeth's third novel,

Electric City, one of the best books of 2014; and her previous novels, *Blue Nude* and *The Speed of Light*, were acclaimed bestsellers and have been translated into multiple languages. *The Speed of Light* was shortlisted for the Prix Femina in 2002. Along with writing poetry and essays, she is a frequent book reviewer for the *San Francisco Chronicle*. She lives in Berkeley.

Liesl Schillinger is a literary critic, writer and translator, and teaches journalism and criticism at the New School in New York City. Her articles, reviews, and essays have appeared in the *New York Times, Foreign Policy*, the *New York Review of Books, Vogue*, the *Daily Beast, O*, the *New Yorker*, the *New Republic*, the *Washington Post*, and other publications; and her short stories and literary translations have appeared in *Playboy, Tin House*, and *Words without Borders*. She has translated novels from the French and the German for Penguin Classics, Viking, and New York Review Books, and currently is writing a memoir and translating a French debut novel. She is the author of *Wordbirds: An Irreverent Lexicon for the 21st Century*. In 2017 she was named a Chevalier of the Ordre des Arts et des Lettres of France.

Andrea Scrima is the author of the novel *A Lesser Day*, which has also been published in German. She received a writer's fellowship from the Berlin Senate for Cultural Affairs and is currently completing a second novel, which won second prize in the Glimmer Train Fall Fiction Open. Andrea writes literary criticism for the *Brooklyn Rail, Music & Literature, Schreibheft, Manuskripte*, the *Quarterly Conversation*, and other publications. The work published here is excerpted from a piece that appeared on her blog (https://andreascrima.wordpress.com).

Sejal Shah is a 2018 New York Foundation for the Arts fellow in fiction. Her essays and stories have appeared in *Brevity, Conjunctions, Denver Quarterly*, the *Kenyon Review*, the *Massachusetts Review*, the *Rumpus*, and elsewhere, as well as in several anthologies. She has received fellowships and residencies from the Anderson Center, the Blue Mountain Center, Kundiman, the Millay Colony, and the Ragdale Foundation. Sejal lives in Rochester, New York, and teaches at Writers & Books, a community-based literary center, as well as privately.

Heather Sheehan, a MacDowell Colony fellow, thrives on a visual arts practice that informs her written works. Through her sculptures, performances, and photography, she reaches audiences within and beyond her adopted homeland in central Europe, where her works appear in several museums of contemporary art. When not in her atelier manifesting experience into form, Heather inspires others with her boundless curiosity and belief in the healing powers of human nature.

Terese Svoboda, the recipient of a Guggenheim fellowship for fiction and the Graywolf Nonfiction Prize, is the author of six books of fiction, seven books of poetry, a memoir, a book of translation from the Nuer, and a biography of the radical poet Lola Ridge. New stories are forthcoming in *Granta, AGNI, Epiphany, Story Quarterly* and the *Bennington Review;* and her collection *Great American Desert* is forthcoming soon.

Pamela Thompson is the author of the novel *Every Past Thing* and directs Bard College's Clemente Course in the Humanities in Holyoke, Massachusetts. She teaches at Smith College.

Quintan Ana Wikswo is a transdisciplinary artist whose conceptually based hybrid works integrate fiction, nonfiction, memoir, poetry, and essays with original photographs, performance, and video. Widely anthologized, she is the author of a collection of stories and photographs, *The Hope of Floating Has Carried Us This Far;* and a novel with photographs, *A Long Curving Scar Where the Heart Should Be.* Her work appears in *Tin House, Guernica,* the Berlin Jewish Museum, the Brooklyn Museum of Art, *Conjunctions,* St. Mark's Church in the Bowery, the Smithsonian Museum, and F.A.C.T./UK and is supported by fellowships from Creative Capital, the Pollock Krasner Foundation, the National Endowment for the Arts, Yaddo, and others.

Rebecca Wolff is the author of four books of poems: *Manderley, Figment, The King,* and *One Morning—.* She is also the author of a novel, *The Beginners.* A founding editor of the literary journal *Fence,* Fence Books, and the *Constant Critic,* she is also a doula and housing activist, and lives in Hudson, New York. She is at work on a novel titled *A Cinch* and a memoir titled *Show Me How You Got Lost,* of which this essay is one chapter.

Permissions